Big TEN BASKETBALL

Peter C. Bjarkman

MP
MASTERS PRESS

A Division of Howard W. Sams & Co.

Masters Press (A Division of Howard W. Sams & Co.)
2647 Waterfront Parkway, East Drive, Suite 300
Indianapolis, IN 46214

Library of Congress Cataloging-in-Publication Data

Big Ten Basketball /
Peter C. Bjarkman
      p. cm.
      ISBN: 1-57028-003-7: $12.95
      1. Big Ten Conference – United States – History.
      2. Big Ten Conference – United States – Statistics.
      3. Big Ten Conference – United States – Middle West – History. I. Title

GV958.5.B54B53 1995
796.323'63'0977 – dc20
                                      95-45142
                                           CIP

10 9 8 7 6 5 4 3 2

Credits:
Cover design by Lynne Annette Clark
Cover photos: Richard Mumford (front), Paul E. Isley (back)
Edited by Kim Heusel
Editorial assistance by Holly Kondras and Heather Seal
Text layout by Kim Heusel
Photo reproduction by Terry Varvel

About the Author

Peter C. Bjarkman, author of 32 sports books, is a senior ranking historian of both basketball and baseball. His other recent basketball titles include *The Encyclopedia of Pro Basketball Team Histories* (1994), *Slam Dunk Superstars* (1994), *Shaq: The Making of a Legend* (1994) and *The History of the NBA* (1992). He lives in Lafayette, Indiana.

Dedication

For Mike OrRico, one of the Big Ten's greatest fans.

Acknowledgments

A special debt is owed by the author to Mark Montieth, one of the finest writers on Big Ten basketball, for giving the idea of this book its genesis; also to my editors, Holly Kondras and Kim Heusel, for their patience, support and expertise; and the following Big Ten basketball sports information directors and assistants for their cooperation and aid in supplying photographs: Dick Barnes (University of Illinois), Gregg Elkin (Indiana University), Phil Haddy (University of Iowa), B.J. Sohn (University of Michigan), John Farina (Michigan State University), Marc Ryan (University of Minnesota), Greg Shea (Northwestern University), Bob Goldring (Ohio State University), Jeff Brewer (Penn State University), Mark Adams (Purdue University), and John Estes (University of Wisconsin).

Table of Contents

IV
BIG TEN RECORDS AND STATISTICAL SUMMARY

INTRODUCTION

Big Ten Basketball:
An Unmatched Tradition

Baseball's past seems secure, no matter how much the spoiled millionaire players and tunnel-vision franchise owners monkey with its present: the national pastime is all about memory and nostalgia and legendary heroes of yesteryear. By the same token, basketball's future seems equally certain of unbounded success. The one truly North American game — invented by Canadian James Naismith a little more than a century ago, but not wildly popular until the middle of this century — basketball is indisputably America's favored participant and spectator game of the 1990s and beyond.

Baseball may still be the acknowledged national pastime and football remains a reigning national passion for millions, but basketball now lays undisputed claim to the title of the true American national game. Many more people watch basketball at all levels — high school, college, professional, world amateur and Olympic competition — than all the other major team sports combined. And when it comes to recreational play, basketball — from organized school and pro leagues to one-on-one barnyard and schoolground pickup games — is in an unrivaled league of its own.

While the professional version of the American national game has reached prominence with Magic, Larry Bird and Air Jordan over the past decade, the college game has long been true king of the hill - East Coast to West and from heartland to inner-city ghetto. It all started with the fierce regional rivalries (Fordham, St. John's, City College of New York, Manhattan, Columbia and New York University in the Mecca of New York City, for example) that already flourished during the first quarter of the century. A true boom era for the sport came with a series of popular intersectional rivalries staged in hoopdom's first great showplace, New York's Madison Square Garden. During the late-1930s, these MSG contests (often doubleheaders and even tripleheaders) drew huge throngs of spectators and contributed to the game's growing legends.

The next stage came with the sudden postwar popularity in the same Madison Square Garden venue of a brand new phenomenon — postseason championship tournaments. The National Invitation Tournament, launched to close the 1937-38 season, was the original postseason kingpin through the 1940s and featured titanic battles like that between DePaul's George

Mikan and Bowling Green's Don Otten in 1945, or Utah's stunning upset of Adolph Rupp's Kentucky "Fabulous Five" in 1947. But the rival NCAA postseason classic also grew in stature and fandom after it's own debut with the March 1939 Oregon-Ohio State matchup in Evanston, Illinois.

If the '90s are the true heyday of the NBA, college basketball continues to run neck-and-neck with its glamorous cousin in the ongoing battle for fan allegiance. Today's NCAA Final Four weekend rivals the World Series, Super Bowl, Kentucky Derby and New Year's bowl games as the year's most heralded spectator event. And when it comes to the modern-day version of college basketball, nowhere is competition more heated, or tradition more rich, or fandom more frenzied than in the storied Big Ten Conference.

Big Ten glamour and prestige has rich historical overtones. The league's primacy on the college basketball scene has as much to do with chronological precedent as it does with contemporary rooting passion. Formal league rivalry between neighboring schools actually began on the nation's collegiate scene in 1905 with formation of the Western Conference — granddaddy of the Big Ten and today the nation's oldest remaining uninterrupted college sports confederation. The original seven-school circuit which commenced play in January, 1906, with teams from Minnesota, Wisconsin, Indiana, Illinois, Chicago, Purdue and Iowa has remained a remarkable model of stability as it evolved across the century into today's renamed Big Ten Conference. The league lost but one original member (Chicago dropped out in 1946 after five straight winless seasons) and gradually added five (Northwestern in 1906, Ohio State in 1912, Michigan in 1917, Michigan State in 1950, Penn State in 1990). And while often noted as primarily a "football conference" — based largely on its Rose Bowl connections and legendary Michigan and Ohio State pigskin juggernauts — the Big Ten has also remained the nation's showcase basketball venue.

One measure of Big Ten preeminence is the NCAA tourney itself, where the conference rates first or second in each of the measures of league postseason strength: most Final Fours (33, 1st), most title-game appearances (18, 1st), most championships (9, 2nd to Pacific-10), most total game victories (210, 2nd to ACC), best winning percentage (.644, 2nd to ACC), most appearances (121, 1st). Big Ten basketball has always been the most competitive and talent-laden in the land, from the pioneering days of Piggy Lambert and Doc Meanwell, through the fabulous '60s era of Jerry Lucas, Terry Dischinger and Cazzie Russell, on down to the glamorous present-day era of Bobby Knight's Hurrying Hoosiers, Glenn Robinson and Calbert Cheaney. When talk turns to savoring college basketball, the Big Ten has never been far from the main bill of fare.

Recent decades are filled with bright individual stars, memorable powerhouse teams and unforgettable coaching legends. The league has especially been known for its colorful and sometimes controversial coaches. Perhaps only Adolph "Baron" Rupp at Kentucky still outstrips Indiana's General, Bob Knight, as the largest nonprofessional sports coaching legend (football's Joe Paterno and Bear Bryant don't come close). And in Knight's shadow stands Branch McCracken of Indiana, Meanwell and Foster of Wisconsin, Lambert and Keady at Purdue, O'Connor in Iowa, and Fred Taylor of Ohio State.

If Magic Johnson ushered in a new era of Big Ten respectability with Michigan State's storied Big Ten run at the NCAA collegiate title in 1979, Johnson was indeed only building on

Penn State's John Amaechi soars above the rim to block a shot in a Big Ten game against Iowa. (Penn State University photo)

a tradition already rich and varied. The first Big Ten teams on the national scene were the powerhouse outfits of Lambert at Purdue and Meanwell at Wisconsin. When NIT and NCAA postseason action heated up in the '40s, the Big Ten was in the forefront from the earliest seasons of competition. Ohio State was one of the combatants in the very first NCAA championship contest. Indiana and Wisconsin next took their turns with early national titles in the second and third NCAA postseason years. And the Whiz Kids wonder team out of Illinois stood poised in 1943 for perhaps yet another national title when the disruption of the war years rudely intervened.

Each subsequent decade has witnessed at least one Big Ten Conference team placed smack in the NCAA championship spotlight. First Indiana and then Iowa rose to the top in the early 1950s. McCracken led the Hoosiers to a title with one of the most balanced Indiana outfits ever. On that perfectly constructed 1953 IU championship team, Bob Leonard offered emotional leadership and a trigger for the fast break, Dick Farley was the defensive stalwart, Charles Kraak rebounded without peer and Burke Scott provided stellar ball-handling; all four complemented Don Schlundt who was the instant offense. The original "Fabulous Five" of Iowa then failed in their own bid for a national trophy by losing in the 1956 Finals to Bill Russell and the San Francisco Dons, but Bucky O'Connor's memorable team brought home their own fair share of glory and extended the reputation of the nation's oldest conference. Ohio State and Michigan would rule the turbulent '60s and the OSU team of Lucas, Havlicek and company may have indeed been the slickest in conference history. Michigan's duo of Cazzie Russell and Bill Buntin was doomed to the background by Ohio State under Fred Taylor. But Dave Strack's Michigan outfit was also one of the best collegiate teams ever assembled in any conference and in any decade.

The 1970s brought the undefeated Indiana juggernaut of 1976 and with it the birth of the lasting legend of Bobby Knight. Things didn't slow at all for the Big Ten by the end of the decade as Magic Johnson and the Michigan State Spartans had their long-awaited turn in the spotlight against Larry Bird and the Indiana State Cinderella Sycamores. Knight would be back to rule the '80s with two more title teams. The 1981 outfit will always be remembered for the Final Four play of sophomore Isiah Thomas and in 1987 an unheralded Indiana ballclub benefited from the miracle shot of instant legend Keith Smart and won it all in perhaps one of the biggest surprises of conference history.

Finally it was Michigan's turn to emerge from the shadows, first with a 1989 underdog champion that even outdid the '87 Hoosiers when it came to postseason surprises. And there has been no bigger collegiate basketball story so far in the 1990s than the promise and the failures of Michigan's second generation "Fab Five" team that boasted Chris Webber, Juwan Howard, Jimmy King, Ray Jackson and Jalen Rose. This latest contingent was certainly not the best team of Big Ten annals, but it rated at the top of the pile when it came to generating endless media headlines.

As historian Neil Isaacs has eloquently suggested in his seminal history of college basketball (*All the Moves,* 1978), there is indeed a special mystique surrounding Big Ten basketball. And it is a mystique which stretches back to a time when the coaches were named Meanwell, Lambert, McCracken and O'Connor — not Knight and Keady and Heathcote and Randy Ayres. It extends back well into the primitive era of college hoops, long before World War II and even before the First Great War at the end of the century's second decade. Part of this early mystique came directly from the strength of the Big Ten as a football conference. Football was, for one thing, a source of huge early revenues which aided in the building of substantial field houses as venues for the indoor sport of basketball. It was also a tool well exploited by Big Ten coaches and officials in recruiting prominent athletes for the other major and minor sports — especially basketball. And in a more primitive and less "specialized" era many superb athletes around the league starred simultaneously in both sports. George Halas tossed baskets for the league champion 1916-17 Illini before demonstrating further versatility as a major-league outfielder, NFL footballer, and eventual Hall of Fame coaching legend for decades with the Chicago Bears. Otto Graham also prefaced NFL stardom with collegiate basketball prowess for Northwestern, just as Lamar Lundy did for Purdue, Pat Richter for Wisconsin, and Ron Kramer for Michigan.

A football-inspired reputation for rough and tumble play throughout the conference has, regrettably, not always been quite so glorious, however. There have been a few forgettable incidents — one that was indeed truly regrettable. Ohio State (coached by Fred Taylor) and Minnesota (coached by Bill Musselman) wrote a black page in college sports history with an infamous 1972 brawl that Issacs has described as having "the ugly overtones of a racial rumble on top of the schoolyard fracas." But the Big Ten survived even this momentary embarrassment and moved on to greater and greater heights of hoop respectability.

The highest nationwide reputation for conference excellence perhaps lies on the shoulders of the OSU Buckeyes of 1960-62 and the Michigan Wolverines of four seasons later. The Wolverines of 1964-1965 with the "Dynamic Duo" of Cazzie Russell and Bill Buntin were one of the most colorful teams of college basketball annals. But it was the Ohio State gang of Lucas, Havlicek, Siegfried, Joe Roberts and Mel Nowell that garners most votes for the best conference team of all time. And also one of the most unlucky. But for a single upset (1961 NCAA Finals) and a single injury (Lucas in the 1962 NCAA semifinals) and the three-year OSU club might have rated dead-even with the Lew Alcindor- or Bill Walton-led UCLA Bruins as the greatest collegiate team ever. And the national prominence brought by this collection of great '60s teams carrying the Big Ten banner was continually sustained in the '70s and '80s by Knight's three-time NCAA champion Hoosiers, Jud Heathcote's "miracle-year" 1979 MSU Spartans, Gene Keady's always competitive Purdue Boilermakers, and numerous editions of Lou Henson's underachieving yet always-exciting Fighting Illini.

Through the years, the Big Ten has been perhaps best known for its variety in styles of play. The conference as a whole has long maintained a popular and largely positive reputation for aggressive and physical basketball. Yet there have also been more than a handful of great stars for whom finesse rather than brute strength is the very name of the game. When it comes to grace and artistry, the Big Ten stage has always been crammed with college basketball's most skillful showmen — Rick Mount's sensational guided missiles, Terry Dischinger's uncanny eye for the bucket, Earvin Johnson's unerring passes, Slick Leonard's inspired playmaking, Robin Freeman's or Calbert Cheaney's complete offensive game.

The past several seasons have reassured fans that the Big Ten's reputation for colorful and talented teams has not slackened at all. First there was a heralded Michigan powerhouse with a borrowed name of "Fab Five" made famous by an earlier-generation Iowa team. This

Michigan's Rudy Tomjanovich launches a jump shot against Ohio State in a 1970 game. (University of Michigan photo)

All-American Cazzie Russell, left, formed the foundation of Coach Dave Strack's great Michigan teams of 1964-66. (University of Michigan photo)

Steve Fisher-coached team had been saddled with the most impossible set of expectations ever placed on a group of teenage athletes at any time and any place. The '90s Fab Five was expected by fans and press everywhere to win it all — perhaps even more than once — and "near greatness" could thus only be interpreted as dismal failure. But even while they "disappointed" — with two sloppy performances against Duke and North Carolina in back-to-back NCAA championship games — the Michigan team of Webber, Rose, Howard, Jackson and King added another bright page to the already glorious Big Ten basketball legend.

And beyond the Michigan team of the early '90s there was yet another edition of powerhouse Hoosiers. Calbert Cheaney paced IU to Coach Knight's fourth 30-win season in 1993, amassing enough points to overtake Michigan's Glen Rice as the greatest net rippler in conference history. Keady's Purdue squads continued to make noise as well, this time with superstar Glenn Robinson. Cheaney's national player of the year accolades in '93 were followed by Robinson's in '94 as the self-styled "Big Dog" copped a national scoring title, the first by a Big Ten shooter since Purdue's Dave Schellhase back in 1966. Even perennial tailender Minnesota added a feather to the league bonnet with a hard-fought NIT championship in 1993, the first mark of distinction for the Golden Gophers since a rare conference crown a full decade earlier. Minnesota's NIT title was the fifth to be credited to the Big Ten ledger.

The continued open pipeline of great individual players has not abated, either. Cheaney may have been the finest all-around Big Ten player next to Jerry Lucas and Cazzie Russell. The

Northwestern's Cedric Neloms takes a long-range bomb shot against Wisconsin. (North-western University photo)

Buckeyes' Jim Jackson (two-time All-American and a No. 4 NBA draft pick of the Dallas Mavericks) was perhaps only a shade behind Cheaney when it came to raw talent and tons of NBA potential. Glenn Robinson scored at a phenomenal rate his second season at Purdue (30.3, 1,030 points) and dominated the collegiate basketball headlines, even if his early departure for the lure of NBA dollars left his name off many of the pages of the conference record books and the extent of his true Big Ten greatness very much an open question. Most recently, flashy forward/guard Michael Finley carries the Big Ten banner into the present season as Wisconsin's first legitimate All-America candidate in a handful of decades. And Michigan State backcourt ace Shawn Respert enters his senior season in 1995 — after bypassing NBA early entry — with a chance to overtake Cheaney as the Big Ten's all-time leading scorer.

The following pages celebrate the venerable tradition of the Big Ten as the nation's premier and most historic collegiate basketball conference. The story of each school's deep-rooted hoop traditions is succinctly told — the memorable stars and moments, the hard-earned league championships, NCAA triumphs and failures, postseason adventures and misadventures, and colorful coaching legends. Indeed, all the greatest legends on the playing floor (from Schlundt to Mount to Calbert Cheaney) and on the coach's bench (from Meanwell and Lambert to Knight and Keady) have been here conjured up once again for reliving and reassessment. Each school history includes an all-time team selection, nominations for the best-ever season and greatest individual player in team annals, and year-by-year summaries as well as career, season and single-game school records. Also provided in the book's final sections is a statistical record of conference history that is both detailed and yet usable for quick and easy reference, as well as an entertaining collection of challenging trivia questions that will tax the memory of even the most ardent Big Ten follower.

The story that unfolds here is neither an exhaustive formal history nor an entirely balanced and objective record of past league play. It is meant — with words, pictures, and an ample scattering of statistics — to entertain and to inform, to spark discussion, and even to stir a heated friendly debate or two. Above all else, this book aims to celebrate the greatest game ever invented. It is a fan's book, produced by a fan. And like the game itself, it is meant to be picked up time and again for brief interludes of fast-breaking action. In celebrating past seasons, this version of the Big Ten basketball saga has no greater motive than to enliven future ones.

Big Ten All-Time Basketball Records (Teams Ranked by Total Victories)*

School	Overall Wins-Losses	Percentage
Indiana	1,350-720	.652
Purdue	1,287-724	.640
Illinois	1,261-701	.643
Ohio State	1,230-824	.599
Iowa	1,180-808	.594
Minnesota	1,177-871	.575
Michigan	1,107-711	.610
Penn State	1,097-777	.585
Michigan State	1,094-851	.562
Wisconsin	1,050-942	.527
Northwestern	751-1,089	.408

*All games, conference and non-conference, are included

Big Ten All-Time Basketball Records (Ranked by Winning Percentage)

School	Overall Wins-Losses	Percentage
Indiana	1,350-720	.652
Illinois	1,261-701	.643
Purdue	1,287-724	.640
Michigan	1,107-711	.610
Ohio State	1,230-824	.599
Iowa	1,180-808	.594
Penn State	1,097-777	.585
Minnesota	1,177-871	.575
Michigan State	1,094-851	.562
Wisconsin	1,050-942	.527
Northwestern	751-1,089	.408

I

The Universities —
Championships, Traditions and Memorable Seasons

Chapter 1

ILLINOIS *Fighting Illini*

Playing in the Shadows of the Fabulous "Whiz Kids"

===

All-Time Record: 1,261-701, .643; **Conference Record:** 705-523, .574

Big Ten Championships — 12: (1915, 1917*, 1924*, 1935*, 1937*, 1942, 1943, 1949, 1951, 1952, 1963*, 1984*) * = Co-Champion

National Championships: None

Greatest Player: Andy Phillip (1942-1943, 1947)

Career Scoring Leader: Deon Thomas (2,130 Points, 1990-94)

Most Successful Coach: Harry Combes (1948-67), 316-150, .678 Pct.

All-Time Team: John "Red" Kerr (C, 1952-54), Eddie Johnson (F, 1977-81), Andy Phillip (F, 1942-43, 1947), Bruce Douglas (G, 1982-86), Derek Harper (G, 1981-83)

Best Season: 1942-43 (17-1), Big Ten Champions (Coach: Douglas Mills)

===

University Profile

Location: Champaign-Urbana, Illinois (pop. 110,000); **Founded:** 1867; **Campus Enrollment:** 35,000 (1994); **Started Basketball:** 1905-06. Among its distinguished alumni the University can now count nine Nobel Peace Prize winners and 16 Pulitzer Prize winners among distinguished leaders in all fields of science, industry, education, health service and public service. The Krannert Center for the Performing Arts is a campus showcase where more than 300 performances are held each year. The Krannert Museum of Art is second only to the Art Institute of Chicago among Illinois public art museums.

Team Nickname, Colors and Arena

Nickname: Fighting Illini (since 1930); **Colors:** Orange and Blue; **Arena:** Assembly Hall (16,321 capacity, opened 1963). A rich tradition commenced on November 8, 1930, in New York's Yankee Stadium when student Webber Borchers made his first appearance dressed in the costume of Chief Illiniwek during a football showdown with the powerhouse Army team. One story, oft repeated, is that former football coach Robert Zuppke had first suggested calling the university symbol by the name of Chief Illiniwek (pronounced "ill-EYE-nih-wek"), a name originating with the loose confederation of Algonquin tribes once inhabiting the region that is now Illinois. The state name itself evolves from a French pronounciation, substituting the French "ois" for the final syllable of the difficult Indian name. Illiniwek supposedly means "they are men" and thus was once deemed a fitting description for school athletic teams that were largely, if not exclusively, male. Present-day attitudes toward gender diversification in intercollegiate athletics — as well as toward cultural sensitivity to native American peoples and their traditions — may eventually doom this once proud University of Illinois tradition.

Fighting Illini Basketball History

Illinois basketball started out as a matter of clearcut and sometimes troubling extremes. When the university sent representatives to a meeting of six other midwest schools (Purdue, Iowa, Chicago, Minnesota, Indiana and Wisconsin) on December 2, 1905, basketball and football competition was simultaneously born for both the University of Illinois and the newly founded Western Intercollegiate Conference. (It would be 1917 before Michigan joined Northwestern and Ohio State as add-ons and the press could begin dubbing the circuit "The Big Ten" conference.) And while the formal confederation would survive to become the true grandaddy of the nation's college sports leagues, the tradition-rich Illini basketball program would itself soon become one of the proudest and at the same time one of the most fortune-bit programs in the history of the Big Ten basketball wars.

On the "up" side of things the Illini through the years have stood alongside Indiana and Purdue as the winningest outfit in the Big Ten conference. The three powerhouse programs remain in a virtual dead-heat in the all-time "in-conference" standings. And in overall play, the Illini also remain third (1,261) in total wins and second (.643) in total winning percentage. But at the same time, despite many a near miss, the Illini have remained on the outside when it comes to the sport's biggest doorprize. Only Minnesota and Northwestern (along with newcomer Penn State) join the Illini as Big Ten members who have not yet played in an NCAA title game. Twice the Illinois team has suffered heart-rending two-point losses in the national semifinals and then settled for an NCAA third-place slot. And perhaps the best Illini team ever — the fabled 1943 "Whiz Kids" squad — disappointingly passed up the tourney they were heavily favored to win in a move of war-time austerity.

Thus the record for all its successes remains disheartening. Only Purdue among league members has won more basketball games than Illinois (and then by only one single game in a stretch of nine decades); only Purdue and Indiana boast better overall winning percentages. But there have been no national championship banners flown in Champaign-Urbana and no NIT crowns worn either; there have only been two Big Ten titles to celebrate since the early '50s and no outright crown since 1952. Current Illini coach Lou Henson boasts one of the

High-flying Kendall Gill soared to ninth on the all-time Fighting Illini scoring list. (Illinois photo)

finest overall records in Big Ten history (his 197 conference victories trail only Indiana's Bob Knight and Branch McCracken, and Purdue's Ward Lambert) and his present tenure is surpassed only by Knight's in the longevity department. In the two decades they have shared, however, Knight has won 11 conference banners and three NCAA crowns; Henson, by rude contrast, has managed only a single tie for the league title (1984) and has taken a team to the prestigious Final Four only once, that coming in 1989 when the No. 3 Illini suffered a bitter two-point loss to Michigan in the semifinals after twice beating the Wolverines by double-digit margins during the regular season.

When it comes to individual stars the cupboard in Champaign-Urbana has been nearly as barren — no Illini player of the distant or recent past ranks in the prestigious list of the league's all-time dozen top scorers; there have been no consensus All-Americans on the Illinois campus since the 1952 selection of Rod Fletcher. For all the feast, Illini boosters have had their fair share of famine as well.

And there were also other extremes which highlighted especially the earliest years of basketball play in the twin towns of Champaign-Urbana. When the first-ever Illini game was played it was a 71-4 romp over the outmanned boys from neighboring Champaign High School. That game came before a coach had yet been named and the team was still led by playing captain Roy Riley. But more legitimate college competition from a first year of conference rivals proved a more difficult nut to crack. Thus the inaugural Illinois team under coach Elwood Brown (who took over a few days after the opening one-sided victory) could do no better than three wins and six losses against conference foes during the first winter of Western Conference competition. Victories came at home by close scores over Indiana (27-24), Purdue (25-19) and Chicago (24-21). The first season's overall record was 6-8 and also included an embarrassing one-sided pasting (51-15) at the hands of an Evanston YMCA club team.

Such extremes of performance continued as standard fare even after the initial season of the new game in Urbana. The season which followed under coach F.L. Pinckney turned out to be the worst in school history. More than 100 candidates reported for team tryouts but the beleaguered coach evidently found little usable talent as the 1907 squad was embarrassed with a 1-10 record and with no conference wins in eight tries. It would be the only year in which an Illini squad would not win a single conference game, the low point being a 42-3 shellacking at the hands of first-place Minnesota.

To establish that such extremes were apparently not to be easily avoided in Urbana, a third season under yet a third one-year mentor soon brought the biggest overnight turn-around in the school's basketball history. The 1907-08 team would finish with an excellent 20-6 ledger, though a 4-4 conference mark would be good enough for only third place. Coach Fletcher Lane also would leave the program after one season, but he would do so owning a school record for coaching victory percentage (.769) that would likely never again be equalled.

The period from 1913 through 1920 brought the first era of stability to the Illinois basketball scene, as well as the first long-term successful coach. Ralph Jones (arriving from Purdue and also coaching baseball and freshman football) would know only one losing season over that eight-year stretch and would finish up his tenure with a sterling 85-34 record. In the midst of this highly successful building era Jones also produced what was assuredly one of the best Illinois teams ever. The 1915 squad posted the only perfect record in school annals as it waltzed through an unblemished 16-game schedule. This powerful team also scored more than twice as many points as its outmanned opponents. And in the process it won the school's first conference title by a safe three-game margin over runnerup Chicago.

The powerhouse 1915 team also launched a three-year stretch that has rarely been equalled in Illini hoop annals. This was a period graced by the school's first three individual cage stars. Brothers Ray Woods, a guard, and Ralf Woods, a forward, paced the team in both 1916 (13-3, 9-3) and 1917 (13-3, 10-2). Ralf Woods would lead the squad and the entire league in scoring and simultaneously build a lasting reputation as a stellar free-throw shooter. The prowess of Woods in this latter department is still recognized today by the award eventually named in his honor and presented at the conclusion of each season to the Illini player holding the best record at the charity stripe. The 1917 team would also feature in its lineup football legend George Halas, founder and longtime owner of the Chicago Bears professional gridiron club and a short-term major-league baseballer as well. The 1916 team would tie Northwestern for second place behind Wisconsin and would also play the school's first overtime game. That landmark overtime tussle was a 23-21 home loss to Northwestern, one of two defeats at the hands of the Wildcats that year. A veteran Ralf Woods-led 1917 team would again be strong enough to capture a conference title, the second and last for Jones in the league which was now being popularly called the "Big Nine" for the final season before Michigan's entry the following winter.

After three successful seasons under coach Craig Ruby in the early 1920s, the Illini program suddenly fell once again on hard times. After a tie for the conference title in 1924 (11-6, 8-4), Illinois teams would not finish within the top three in the conference standings again until 1935. The low point of this era came in 1927-28 when the Ruby-coached Illini squad finished only 5-12 overall and registered but two Big Ten victories, poor enough for a last-place deadlock with equally lackluster Minnesota.

But the mid-30s fortunately brought an upswing in on-court fortunes at the very end of Ruby's 14-year tenure. Optimism surrounded the program when the new Huff Gymnasium was inaugurated during the 1934 season. Then a 1935 squad inspired by a flashy sophomore guard named Harry Combes tied Purdue and Wisconsin for the conference title by rallying down the stretch to capture the final four games of the season. But Ruby was finally done after 1936, leaving his post with the school's eventual fourth-best career coaching record and remaining one of only four Illinois coaches to boast 100 or more career victories at the Urbana campus. Ruby had put Illinois basketball once more on sound footing, yet his immediate successor would soon be enjoying an even greater level of success. Douglas Mills would now launch a career with the Fighting Illini that would make him the first mentor in school history to win as many as three conference titles.

Mills debuted in 1937 in truly spectacular fashion as mentor of his first championship team. Illinois recorded a 14-6 ledger during this debut year under Mills and 10 conference victories were enough to tie Minnesota for the first-place spot. Firepower for this showcase club was provided by returning starters Robert Riegel, Joe Vopicka and future coach Harry Combes. This same trio had scored more than half the team's total points a year earlier during the swan song season under Craig Ruby. But the key role was now played by a newcomer in the backcourt named Lou Boudreau. The future major-league baseball star and Hall of Fame manager would lead the 1937 championship team in scoring with a then-credible 8.7 points per game average. Boudreau also was named team captain for 1938 and tabbed for national recognition as well as a Madison Square Garden first-team All-American selection.

The stage was set by Mills' early successes for his greatest team which would arrive in the early 1940s. It was not only Mills' best squad, but indisputably the greatest in school history as well. This team known to future generations as the Illinois "Whiz Kids" was indeed one of the half-dozen truly legendary squads in Big Ten history. In 1941 Art Mathisen had arrived on the scene as the team's leading pointmaker (8.9 ppg). The following season he would be joined by Jack Smiley, Andy Phillip, Gene Vance and Ken Menke. This group would quickly capture the imagination of the nation as the touted Whiz Kids of Coach Doug Mills. They won back-to-back Big Ten titles with league records of 13-2 and 12-0, the latter being the league's first undefeated record since 1930 when Purdue turned the trick. The 1942 team seemed well on the way to an NCAA title when it was upset by Kentucky 46-44 in the opening round of the Eastern Regional. The 1943 returning edition picked up where it had left off and ran to a 17-1 record. The only loss was one that Coach Mills seemingly gave away for the good of the team by playing a largely substitute lineup. In a game against Camp Grant with no conference record at stake Coach Mills decided it would be better to lose one match and thus remove the pressures of an undefeated record.

Illinois' 1943 Whiz Kids were by consensus and performance the best team in the nation during that chaotic war-interrupted season. But they never did enter the NCAA tournament and play for a national title they most likely could have won with unsurpassed ease. Instead, the team was temporarily broken up when all five starters went on active military duty on March 1, 1943. They would return as a unit several seasons later but would never again know the same successes in league play. Four of the five Whiz Kids stars (Mathisen was the exception) later played professionally; Andy Phillip was soon to be a pro star with several teams including the Fort Wayne Pistons and Russell-Cousy-era Boston Celtics. Phillip would, in fact, become the only Illini player ever to make it into the Naismith Memorial Basketball Hall of Fame.

Mills' former star player, Harry Combes, would inherit the coaching reins shortly after the war years, moving across town from his position as head coach at Champaign High School where he captured a state schoolboy title in 1946. Combes more than carried on the winning tradition recently built by Mills and Ruby. His career won-lost ledger would eventually boast more than 300 victories, including an amazing 164-44 overall mark and 94-30 conference ledger during his first 10 seasons on the job. And during this stretch he would win three conference crowns as well. The 20-year tenure by Harry Combes has also remained the longest in school history and will fall only if Lou Henson remains in his current post through the 1996 campaign.

Under the guidance of Combes in the late '40s and early '50s came several of the best Illini teams in history. In one incredible run the 1949, 1951 and 1952 Combes teams would finish third in the NCAA tournament, already by the early '50s the most prestigious year-end venue in the land. Twice the Illinois teams would miss by only the narrowest of margins in their effort to advance into the title game and a shot at a possible national championship. The 1949 club would be blown out 71-47 by two-time champion Kentucky with its super trio of Alex

John "Red" Kerr was an All-Big Ten center in 1954 and later an NBA "Iron Man". (University of Illinois photo)

Groza, Ralph Beard and Wah Wah Jones during the national semifinal matchup. But in 1951 a rematch brought a heart-breaking two-point defeat (76-74) by the same Wildcats, now sporting 7-footer Bill Spivey and future NBA greats Frank Ramsey and Cliff Hagan. A year later there would be another nip-and-tuck two-point semifinal loss (61-59) to eastern power St. John's of New York. The 1949 Illinois team would be the first to win 20 games since way back in 1908. Both the '51 and '52 teams behind All-American guard Rod Fletcher and high-scoring center Red Kerr would post 22 victories, at the time a school record.

Perhaps the best of these great Illinois teams of the early '50s was the veteran '52 outfit, anchored by juniors Irv Bemoras and Jim Bredar, and senior Rod Fletcher who led the school to its third trip to the Final Four in four seasons. This squad was paced, by a newcomer, however — future pro star and NBA iron man John "Red" Kerr, only a sophomore at the time but already the club's leading scorer (with a sophomore-record 357 points) and top rebounder. As a professional with the Syracuse Nats and Philadelphia 76ers, Kerr would enjoy a lengthy career that featured a long-standing record for consecutive games played. As a Big Ten star, the lanky center from Tilden Tech in Chicago replaced Don Sunderlage as the greatest scorer in Illinois history. In his 1954 senior season Kerr would shatter the single-season record for points (556) that Sunderlage had posted three years earlier.

The 1963 season would feature Harry Combes' fourth and final Big Ten championship team. This squad was another 20-game winner at 20-6 (11-3 in the conference). And a season's highlight was the single-game scoring explosion of Dave Downey, who erupted for 53 points in a road loss to Indiana. At the time, the effort also was a Big Ten landmark for both points and field goals in a single contest. The close of that 1963 season eventually provided some of the most exciting days in the school's hoops annals. The spanking new Assembly Hall opened its doors for the first time on March 4th with the Illini a game out of first place and only two league contests remaining. First Illinois defeated Northwestern in a frenzied nail-biter which inaugurated the hall before a crowd of 16,137 wild patrons. Then a victory over Iowa and an overtime loss by Ohio State to Indiana the same night combined to give Illinois an 11th-hour share of the conference crown.

One of the biggest upsets in modern collegiate hoops history came when the inspired Illini upended defending national champion UCLA by a crushing 110-83 count in Assembly Hall at

1989 All-Big Ten pick Nick Anderson slams one against Minnesota's Willie Burton. (University of Illinois photo)

the outset of the 1964-65 season. This was the edition of John Wooden's Bruins which featured a starting lineup of Gail Goodrich, Keith Erickson, Edgar Lacey and Kenny Washington and would soon capture the second in UCLA's long string of '60s-era NCAA crowns. Combes would later call the game "one of the best an Illinois team has ever played."

Combes' long-anticipated retirement ushered in one of the bleakest periods of Illinois basketball history during the early 1970s. Harv Schmidt, another former player, enjoyed little success in molding a consistent winner during his seven years at the helm. One of the few highlights of this largely forgettable era was outstanding offensive play by All-American candidate Nick Weatherspoon, a 20 points per game scorer in 1972 and again in 1973.

A true landmark year for Illinois cage fortunes would arrive in 1976 with the hiring of former New Mexico State coach Lou Henson to direct and resurrect the languid Illini program. Henson would start his long tenure modestly enough in the late '70s with records of 14-13 (1976), 16-14 (1977) and 13-14 (1978). But throughout the '80s the "lucky 13th" coach in school history would prove to be the biggest and most consistent winner of them all. Henson today stands among the top seven Big Ten coaches in all-time winning. He also owns the second highest number of total victories ever by a conference coach and stands fourth all-time in Big Ten victories as well. Before the end of the upcoming 1995 season Henson will join Knight, Lambert and McCracken as the only mentors ever to win 200 or more Big Ten games.

The 1980s under Henson would provide only one Big Ten title, a share of the crown alongside Purdue in 1984. Although the '84 team — probably Henson's finest — boasted the best overall Big Ten mark at 26-5, the Illini never got out of the NCAA third round, falling 54-51 to Kentucky in a regional title game. But the '80s would nonetheless be a period that featured a number of exciting and highly successful teams, especially the 1985 squad which captured 26 games for a second straight season and the 1989 club with a school-record 31 victories. And the decade that stretched from the early '80s to early '90s also showcased a long string of star players headed for solid NBA careers. This list would include Derek Harper (veteran playmaking guard for the 1994 New York Knicks NBA finalists), Nick Anderson (career scoring leader for the expansion Orlando Magic), Kendall Gill (likely a future NBA all-star), Eddie Johnson (for a decade the all-time leading Illini scorer who has also posted three 20 points per game pro seasons with the Kansas City Kings and Phoenix Suns), and Bruce Douglas (one of the NCAA leaders in assists). Deon Thomas, who overtook Eddie Johnson in 1994 as the top career scorer at Illinois, also has been added to the long list of stars.

Records and Summaries
Year-by-Year Illinois Records
(Championship Years in Boldface)

Season	All Games	Conference	Coach(es)	Top Scorer (Points)
1905-06	6-8	3-6	Elwood Brown	No Record
1906-07	1-10	0-8	F.L. Pinckney	Edward Ryan (94)*
1907-08	20-6	4-5	Fletcher Lane	Henry Popperfuss (401)*
1908-09	7-6	5-6	Herb Juul	Carl Watson (142)*
1909-10	5-4	5-4	Herb Juul	Albert Hall (66)*
1910-11	6-6	6-5	T.E. Thompson	Emmett Poston (90)*
1911-12	8-8	4-8	T.E. Thompson	Albert Hall (113)*
1912-13	10-8	7-6	Ralph Jones	Homer Dahringer (169)•
1913-14	9-4	7-3	Ralph Jones	Edward Williford (130)*
1914-15	**16-0**	**12-0 (1st)**	**Ralph Jones**	**Edward Williford (116)**
1915-16	13-3	9-3	Ralph Jones	Ralf Woods (122)
1916-17	**13-3**	**10-2 (1st-T)**	**Ralph Jones**	**Ralf Woods (164)•**
1917-18	9-6	6-6	Ralph Jones	Earl Anderson (201)•
1918-19	6-8	5-7	Ralph Jones	Ken Wilson (118)*
1919-20	9-4	8-4	Ralph Jones	Charles Carney (215)•
1920-21	11-7	7-5	Frank Winters	Charles Vail (108)
1921-22	14-5	7-5	Frank Winters	Charles Carney (249)•
1922-23	9-6	7-5	J. Craig Ruby	Walter Roettger (129)
1923-24	**11-6**	**8-4 (1st-T)**	**J. Craig Ruby**	**Leland Stilwell (129)**
1924-25	11-6	8-4	J. Craig Ruby	Russell Daugherity (111)
1925-26	9-8	6-6	J. Craig Ruby	Russell Daugherity (99)
1926-27	10-7	7-5	J. Craig Ruby	Russell Daugherity (135)
1927-28	5-17	2-10	J. Craig Ruby	John How (125)
1928-29	10-7	6-6	J. Craig Ruby	John How (102)
1929-30	8-8	7-5	J. Craig Ruby	Charles Harper (76)
1930-31	12-5	7-5	J. Craig Ruby	Charles Harper (124)
1931-32	11-6	7-5	J. Craig Ruby	Caslon Bennett (106)
1932-33	11-7	6-6	J. Craig Ruby	Frank Froschauer (140)
1933-34	13-6	7-5	J. Craig Ruby	Frank Froschauer (170)
1934-35	**15-5**	**9-3 (1st-T)**	**J. Craig Ruby**	**Frank Froschauer (147)**
1935-36	13-6	7-5	J. Craig Ruby	Harry Combes (154)
1936-37	**14-4**	**10-2 (1st-T)**	**Douglas Mills**	**Lou Boudreau (157)**
1937-38	9-9	4-8	Douglas Mills	Louis Dehner (223)

1938-39	14-5	8-4	Douglas Mills	Louis Dehner (239)
1939-40	14-6	7-5	Douglas Mills	William Hapac (244)•
1940-41	13-7	7-5	Douglas Mills	Art Mathisen (178)
1941-42	**18-5**	**13-2 (1st)**	**Douglas Mills**	**Andy Phillip (232)**
1942-43	**17-1**	**12-0 (1st)**	**Douglas Mills**	**Andy Phillip (305)•**
1943-44	11-9	5-7	Douglas Mills	Stan Patrick (240)
1944-45	13-7	7-5	Douglas Mills	Walt Kirk (212)
1945-46	14-7	7-5	Douglas Mills	Bob Doster (273)
1946-47	14-6	8-4	Douglas Mills	Andy Phillip (192)
1947-48	15-5	7-5	Harry Combes	Dwight Eddleman (277)
1948-49	**21-4**	**10-2 (1st)**	**Harry Combes**	**Dwight Eddleman (329)**
1949-50	14-8	7-5	Harry Combes	Wally Osterkorn (333)
1950-51	**22-5**	**13-1 (1st)**	**Harry Combes**	**Don Sunderlage (471)**
1951-52	**22-4**	**12-2 (1st)**	**Harry Combes**	**John Kerr (357)**
1952-53	18-4	14-4	Harry Combes	John Kerr (386)
1953-54	17-5	10-4	Harry Combes	John Kerr (556)
1954-55	17-5	10-4	Harry Combes	Paul Judson (363)
1955-56	18-4	11-3	Harry Combes	George Bon Salle (321)
1956-57	14-8	7-7	Harry Combes	Harv Schmidt (414)
1957-58	11-11	5-9	Harry Combes	Don Ohl (431)
1958-59	12-10	7-7	Harry Combes	Roger Taylor (376)
1959-60	16-7	8-6	Harry Combes	Govoner Vaughn (411)
1960-61	9-15	5-9	Harry Combes	Dave Downey (402)
1961-62	15-8	7-7	Harry Combes	Dave Downey (445)
1962-63	**20-6**	**11-3 (1st-T)**	**Harry Combes**	**Dave Downey (513)**
1963-64	13-11	6-8	Harry Combes	Skip Thoren (488)
1964-65	18-6	10-4	Harry Combes	Skip Thoren (533)
1965-66	12-12	8-6	Harry Combes	Don Freeman (668)
1966-67	12-12	6-8	Harry Combes	Jim Dawson (521)
1967-68	11-13	6-8	Harv Schmidt	Dave Scholz (529)
1968-69	19-5	9-5	Harv Schmidt	Dave Scholz (459)
1969-70	15-9	8-6	Harv Schmidt	Greg Jackson (409)
1970-71	11-12	5-9	Harv Schmidt	Rick Howat (474)
1971-72	14-10	5-9	Harv Schmidt	Nick Weatherspoon (500)
1972-73	14-10	8-6	Harv Schmidt	Nick Weatherspoon (600)
1973-74	5-18	2-12	Harv Schmidt	Rick Schmidt (493)
1974-75	8-18	4-14	Gene Bartow	Rick Schmidt (524)
1975-76	14-13	7-11	Lou Henson	Rich Adams (429)
1976-77	16-14	8-10	Lou Henson	Audie Matthews (479)
1977-78	13-14	7-11	Lou Henson	Audie Matthews (327)
1978-79	19-11	7-11	Lou Henson	Mark Smith (404)
1979-80	22-13	8-10	Lou Henson	Eddie Johnson (610)
1980-81	21-8	12-6	Lou Henson	Eddie Johnson (500)
1981-82	18-11	10-8	Lou Henson	Craig Tucker (450)
1982-83	21-11	11-7	Lou Henson	Derek Harper (492)

1983-84	**26-5**	**15-3 (1st-T)**	**Lou Henson**	**Efrem Winters (456)**
1984-85	26-9	12-6	Lou Henson	Anthony Welch (415)
1985-86	22-10	11-7	Lou Henson	Ken Norman (525)
1986-87	23-8	13-5	Lou Henson	Ken Norman (641)
1987-88	23-10	12-6	Lou Henson	Nick Anderson (525)
1988-89	31-5	14-4	Lou Henson	Nick Anderson (647)
1989-90	21-8	11-7	Lou Henson	Kendall Gill (581)•
1990-91	21-10	11-7	Lou Henson	Andy Kauffmann (660)
1991-92	13-15	7-11	Lou Henson	Deon Thomas (542)
1992-93	19-13	11-7	Lou Henson	Deon Thomas (587)
1993-94	17-11	10-8	Lou Henson	Deon Thomas (548)

• = League Individual Scoring Champion; * = Incomplete Scoring Records

All-Time Illinois Individual Career Records

Points Scored ....Deon Thomas (2,130, 1990-94)
Scoring Average .... Nick Weatherspoon (20.9, 1970-73)
Field Goals .... Eddie Johnson (753, 1977-81)
Field-Goal Percentage .... Ken Norman (.609, 1984-87)
Free Throws Made .... Mark Smith (437, 1977-81)
Free-Throw Percentage .... Rob Judson (.875, 1976-80)
3-Point Field Goals .... Tom Michael (119, 1990-94)
Rebounds .... Efrem Winters (853, 1982-86)
Assists ....Bruce Douglas (765, 1982-86)
Steals ....Bruce Douglas (324, 1982-86)
Blocked Shots .... Derek Holcomb (174, 1978-81)

All-Time Illinois Individual Season Records

Points Scored .... Don Freeman (668, 1965-66)
Scoring Average ....John "Red" Kerr (25.3, 1953-54)
Minutes Played .... Eddie Johnson (1215, 1979-80)
Field Goals .... Eddie Johnson (266, 1979-80)
Field-Goal Percentage .... Ken Norman (.641, 1985-86)
Free Throws Made .... Don Sunderlage (171, 1950-51)
Free-Throw Percentage .... Govoner Vaughn (.865, 1959-60)
3-Point Field Goals... Doug Altenberger (76, 1986-87)
Rebounds .... Skip Thoren (349, 1964-65)
Assists ....Bruce Douglas (200, 1984-85)
Steals .... Kenny Battle (89, 1988-89)
Blocked Shots .... Derek Holcomb (86, 1978-79)

All-Time Illinois Individual Single-Game Records

Points Scored .... Dave Downey (53 vs. Indiana, 2-16-63)
Field Goals .... Dave Downey (22 vs. Indiana, 2-16-63)
Free Throws Made .... Jeff Dawson (15 vs. Michigan State, 1-14-74)
                                         Don Freeman (15 vs. West Virginia, 12-11-65)
                                         Otho Tucker (15 vs. Northwestern, 1-11-75)
3-Point Field Goals .... Andy Kaufmann (7 vs. Missouri, 12-9-90)
Rebounds ....Skip Thoren (24 vs. UCLA, 12-28-63)
Assists .... Tony Wysinger (16 vs. Pittsburgh, 12-6-86)
Steals .... Bruce Douglas (8 vs. Purdue, 2-25-84)
Blocked Shots .... Derek Holcomb (11 vs. South Carolina, 12-8-78)

All-Time Illinois Coaching Records

Coach	Overall Record	Conference Record	Seasons
Lou Henson (1976-Present)	386-199 (.660)	197-145 (.576)	19
Harry Combes (1948-67)	316-150 (.678)	174-104 (.626)	20
Douglas Mills (1937-47)	151-66 (.696)	88-47 (.652)	11
J. Craig Ruby (1923-36)	148-97 (.604)	94-74 (.560)	14
Harv Schmidt (1968-74)	89-77 (.536)	43-55 (.439)	7
Ralph Jones (1913-20)	85-34 (.714)	64-31 (.674)	8
Frank Winters (1921-22)	25-12 (.676)	14-10 (.583)	2
Fletcher Lane (1908)	20-6 (.769)	4-5 (.444)	1
T.E. Thompson (1911-12)	14-14 (.500)	10-13 (.435)	2
Herb Juul (1909-10)	12-10 (.545)	10-10 (.500)	2
Gene Bartow (1975)	8-18 (.308)	4-14 (.222)	1
Elwood Brown (1906)	6-8 (.429)	3-6 (.333)	1
F.L. Pinckney (1907)	1-10 (.091)	0-8 (.000)	1

Illinois All-Americans and All-Big Ten Selections

Consensus All-Americans
Bill Hapac, Forward, 1940
Andy Phillip, Forward, 1942-1943
Walton Kirk, Guard, 1945
Rod Fletcher, Guard, 1952

All-Big Ten Selections (since 1948)
Dwight Eddleman, Forward, 1948-1949
Don Sunderlage, Guard, 1951
Rod Fletcher, Guard, 1952
Irv Bemoras, Guard, 1953
John "Red" Kerr, Center, 1954
Paul Judson, Guard, 1955-1956
George Bon Salle, Center, 1956
Bill Ridley, Guard, 1956

Don Ohl, Guard, 1957-1958
Dave Downey, Forward, 1963
Skip Thoren, Center, 1965
Tal Brody, Guard, 1965
Don Freeman, Forward, 1966
Jim Dawson, Guard, 1967
Dave Scholz, Center, 1968-1969
Nick Weatherspoon, Forward, 1973
Eddie Johnson, Forward, 1981
Derek Harper, Guard, 1983
Bruce Douglas, Guard, 1984
Ken Norman, Forward, 1986-1987
Nick Anderson, Forward, 1989
Kendall Gill, Guard, 1990
Deon Thomas, Forward, 1994

Chapter 2

INDIANA *Hoosiers*

Hoosier Hysteria in the Land of Coaching Legends

===

All-Time Record: 1,350-720, .652; **Conference Record:** 704-479, .595

Big Ten Championships — 19: (1926*, 1928*, 1936*, 1953, 1954, 1957*, 1958, 1967*, 1973, 1974*, 1975, 1976, 1980, 1981, 1983, 1987*, 1989, 1991*, 1993) * = Co-Champion

National (NCAA) Championships — 5: (1940, 1953, 1976, 1981, 1987)

National Invitation Tournament (NIT) Championships — 1: (1979)

Greatest Player: Calbert Cheaney (1990-93)

Career Scoring Leader: Calbert Cheaney (2,613 Points, 1990-93)

Most Successful Coach: Bob Knight (1972-Present), 640-223, .742 Pct.

All-Time Team: Kent Benson (C, 1974-77), Don Schlundt (C-F, 1952-55), Scott May (F, 1974-76), Calbert Cheaney (F-G, 1990-93) Steve Alford (G, 1984-87)

Best Season: 1975-76 (32-0), NCAA Champion (Coach: Bob Knight)

===

University Profile

Location: Bloomington, Indiana (pop. 60,000); **Founded:** 1820; **Campus Enrollment:** 35,000 (1994); **Started Basketball:** 1900-01. Indiana University claims the title of "oldest state university west of the Alleghenies" and may boast of being one of America's most distinguished schools as well. With Indiana limestone buildings and Collegiate Gothic designs on 1,861 rolling wooded acres, IU offers one of the most picturesque campus settings anywhere. Among the school's famous living alumni are sportscaster Dick Enberg, actor Kevin Klein, TV newswoman Jane Pauley and Academy Award-winning screen writer Steve Tesich. Another source of pride is the school's reputation as a research center. Nationally noted graduate and undergraduate programs attract students from all states and over 140 countries to one of the 10 largest and finest single-campus institutions in the country.

Team Nickname, Colors and Arena

Nickname: Hoosiers; **Colors:** Cream and Crimson; **Arena:** Assembly Hall (17,357 capacity, opened 1971). No one is quite certain what a "Hoosier" is. The popular folk designation for natives of Indiana has generated as many folk etymologies as any term in the American lexicon. What is certain is that a term once meant to characterize all state residents has become almost exclusively synonymous with Indiana University basketball. The cherished nickname is only one of IU's special monuments to heartland hoops tradition. Another is spacious Assembly Hall, a facility where basketball attendance has never ranked below 10th in the nation after 20 consecutive sold-out seasons.

Hoosier Basketball History

America's heartland of Indiana is a place where basketball is undisputed king of the sports hill. And owning the highest ranking spot in the heartland royal pecking order are the Hoosiers of Indiana University. Indiana University cage tradition is as rich and glorious as it comes. It is the Hoosiers who own the most overall titles (19) and the most outright championships (11) in the nation's oldest and most honored basketball conference. When it comes to national titles, only UCLA and its marvelous Wooden-Alcindor-Walton dynasty claim more than the Hoosiers. (Kentucky has also won five.) But even the Bruins and the Wildcats can't boast of one proud postseason distinction owned exclusively by the Hoosiers: NCAA tournament titles in four different decades (1940, 1953, 1976, 1981, 1987).

Much of the rampant success of Indiana University basketball over the past quarter century is tied up with the personal oncourt successes, as well as the larger-than-life notoriety, of Hoosier coach Bob Knight. Knight has been entrenched at Indiana for nearly 25 years and has built a coaching legacy many contend stands with those of John Wooden and Adolph Rupp to form the ultimate triumvirate of the game's greatest coaching legends. The numbers alone speak for Knight's lasting impact and the cache of distinctions and trophies he has now amassed is perhaps already all but unapproachable: eight Big Ten championships, three co-championships, a 293-109 Big Ten regular-season record (the next best over the same 23-year span is Purdue's at 255-147), a dozen final rankings in the top 10, 18 NCAA tournament appearances, three NCAA titles and an overall 40-15 NCAA record, three NIT appearances with one NIT title, an overall 51-17 postseason tourney record, nine Big Ten MVPs, 29 All-Big Ten first-team selections, 12 first-team consensus All-Americans, 22 Academic All-Big Ten choices, 10 Academic All-American first-team members, and 12 first- and 13 second-round NBA draft picks.

Knight has dominated the IU program with his overbearing personality and a personal resume of achievement that makes his name almost synonymous with coaching greatness and relentless winning. One fallout of the ubiquitous Knight image has been a noticeable absence of giant-proportioned individual stars in the Hoosier camp down through the seasons. One might easily expect such a batch of year-in and year-out winning to produce an equal batch of super stars. But the Hoosiers have always been better known (at least under Knight) for their cohesive five-man units than for one-man gangs a la Oscar Robertson, Jerry Lucas or Pete Maravich. And a patented Indiana phenomenon of balanced teams and shared glory is also an ingrained tradition that extends far back before Knight's 1972 arrival in Bloomington.

There have been a fair share of Hoosier cage heroes, 10 Big Ten MVPs (Don Schlundt, Archie Dees, Steve Downing, Kent Benson, Scott May, Mike Woodson, Ray Tolbert, Randy Wittman, Steve Alford, Calbert Cheaney), for example, all but the first two coached by Knight. Schlundt, for one, was a formidable 6-foot-9 tower of inside scoring and rebounding strength from the early modern era of the '50s. He was a clutch player who left his lasting mark on both the Big Ten and NCAA tournament competition. But Schlundt is hardly a living legend in Indiana and only a mere footnote to college basketball history outside of the Hoosier state. Walt Bellamy also enjoyed a memorable career in Bloomington and seemed to be headed nonstop for unblockable NBA fame. But "Bells" never owned the apparent inner drive necessary to become either a collegiate game-breaker or a lasting pro superstar despite considerable NBA rookie honors, his eventual Naismith Hall of Fame selection and his career Big Ten rebounding record of 1,088 boards which still stands.

When it comes to Knight's pupils, the great Hoosier ballclubs of 1975 and 1976 were textbook cases of perfect team chemistry rather than staging grounds for individual showcase performers. Although Scott May, Bobby Wilkerson and Kent

George McGinnis was a league scoring champ as a sophomore but left school early to pursue careers first in the ABA and later NBA. (Indiana University photo)

Benson all played in the NBA, each (especially Benson, an overall No. 1 pick) was a disappointment upon arrival in the NBA. Other Hoosiers like the VanArsdale twins, Mike Woodson, Steve Alford, Quinn Buckner, and even early-50s backcourt ace Bob "Slick" Leonard, have all authored reasonably credible pro careers. But even these players never matched their collegiate contributions or their projected pro-circuit stock values. Only George McGinnis (1971) and Isiah Thomas (1981) have gone on to bigger and better things after "graduating" from Indiana's team-oriented training. And both left the Hoosier program early (after sophomore seasons). Some cynics have even linked this fact directly to their NBA successes.

Knight arrived with a smashingly successful 1972 club. The first Knight-mentored outfit finished 17-8, 9-5 in the Big Ten, a record good enough for a third-place tie with Michigan and a valued invitation to the postseason NIT. Knight's maiden campaign ended on a down note with a 68-60 opening-round loss at the hands of the Princeton Tigers in Madison Square Garden. But it was a heady debut and a very early sign of the truly big things soon to come. The charmed coach next rattled off four straight Big Ten titles. Bob Knight had arrived in Bloomington and had arrived with a true vengeance.

The best club under Knight was the 1976 undefeated team that claimed the Hoosier coach's first national championship. This was indeed one of the two best teams ever seen in Big Ten play, falling perhaps slightly short of the 1960-62 Ohio State teams for overall and single-year achievements. That Ohio State team, ironically, had been the one on which Knight himself played a key role. Taking up where the nearly undefeated 1975 squad left off, IU's '75-'76 edition ran off a second straight perfect 18-0 conference slate. The two-year unblemished string, still unmatched in league annals, gave the Hoosiers a record 37 conference wins in a row stretching back into the late 1974 campaign. No other school has ever surpassed even 19 straight conference victories leaving the Hoosiers with perhaps one of the most unapproachable records anywhere in Big Ten archives.

The Hoosiers ran through the 1976 NCAA tournament just as they had run roughshod over Big Ten opposition all winter long. It was one of those Big Ten rivals which they ultimately overcame for the cherished NCAA title. The all-conference final was one of the great moments of Big Ten history, but first there would be victories over St. John's, Alabama and Marquette to reach the Final Four in Philadelphia. In the national semifinal matchup, UCLA provided little challenge. The reign of the Bruins (10 NCAA titles in the past 12 years) was clearly over as the Hoosiers rode the balanced scoring of Tom Abernethy (14), May (14), Benson (16) and Buckner (12) to bury Gene Bartow's team, 65-51. In the championship shootout with Michigan, the Hoosiers trailed by six at halftime and suffered a severe blow when starting guard Bobby Wilkerson was felled in the first half with a slight concussion. But May and Benson triggered a second-half onslaught which turned the game into a rout. The Hoosiers outshot the Wolverines 60 percent to 36 percent after intermission and the perfect 32-game season remained intact. On the All-Tournament team, Abernethy, May and Benson filled three of the slots along with Michigan's Rickey Green and UCLA's Marques Johnson. The total domination of Knight's 1976 "dream team" is perhaps best capsulized by the single fact that there has not been another undefeated national champion in the 18 seasons since.

Knight's first NCAA championship team was one that had relied on flawless cohesiveness rather than flashy individualism. But awesome individual talent dotted the lineup as well. Two of IU's 10 conference MVP winners played side-by-side on this exceptional 1976 team. Scott May would become one of a select handful of repeat league MVP honorees when he duplicated his junior-year MVP performance (16.3 points per game and .510 field-goal accuracy) with a senior season encore (23.5 points per game). Benson would also wear a Big Ten MVP badge when he brought the honor back to Bloomington for a third straight season in 1977. Bobby Wilkerson (IU's fourth leading rebounder in '76) and Quinn Buckner (the floor general who directed the offense) would both contribute heavily in scoring and all-around play and then move on to solid NBA careers. Tom Abernethy, a 6-7 senior forward, was something of an unsung hero of the 1976 championship outfit, averaging double figures and supplementing May and Benson in the rebounding department.

Knight's 1975 club which took the floor a year earlier falls only a shade short of the 1976 outfit as perhaps the greatest team in Hoosier cage history. In early March, Knight's well-drilled club defeated Michigan State in a cakewalk (94-79) before the largest crowd in the history of Assembly Hall (17,912) to conclude a Big Ten title chase that had already been wrapped up several weeks earlier. It was a third consecutive league crown for the Hoosiers and meant a perfect 29-0 season as well. IU also breezed through two games of tournament play before losing to Kentucky in a mild upset during the regional finals. The last victory of the year, over Oregon State, meant a record 34 straight wins dating back to March 15th of the previous winter. This 12-month victory skein remains the longest streak ever at a Big Ten school. Anticipated individual honors poured in at season's end. May was named Big Ten MVP for the first of two straight seasons, Steve Green was tabbed for All-American honors (also for the second year running), and Knight was selected as national coach-of-the-year in a landslide vote.

The four seasons before Indiana's next national title under Knight would be anything but a disappointing letdown. First came three solid winning campaigns, each with more than 20 victories, with two second- and one first-place Big Ten finish. The 1978-79 and 1979-80 teams featured names like Mike Woodson, Landon Turner, Ray Tolbert, Randy Wittman and Butch Carter and proved that Knight was again close to building his own special type of championship squad. The 1979 club had not fared well enough in league play (10-8, fifth) during the year of Magic Johnson and Larry Bird to earn an NCAA slot; instead Indiana and Purdue (holder of a share of the league title with Magic's Michigan State Spartans and with Iowa, but also left out in the cold by the NCAA) met in an NIT showdown in New York's Madison Square Garden. An 18-foot baseline jumper by Carter in the final seconds would wrest victory from defeat by a narrow 53-52 count. Purdue had led for most of the exciting contest but Carter's last-second heroics in the end assured the Hoosiers of their only NIT crown. Mike Woodson was an All-American selection at season's end and Carter and Tolbert joined Woodson on the NIT All-Tourney team.

The summer of 1979 would witness continued heroics for the Hoosiers as Ray Tolbert and Mike Woodson (along with incoming freshman recruit Isiah Thomas) played for Knight in PanAm Games competition and brought home an expected Gold Medal for their efforts. The summer's activities also paid huge dividends for the heart of the Hoosier lineup as PanAm experience for Woodson, Tolbert and Thomas translated into the first of two straight additional Big Ten crowns (and three in four years) at the outset of the new decade. Woodson, now a senior, paced the 1980 team (19.3 points per game) and emerged as the Big Ten MVP. Knight was selected Big Ten Coach-of-the-Year. The league title was only clinched, however, in a thrilling overtime contest with Ohio State in the season's finale. But this time it would be the rivals from West Lafayette who would have the last laugh as the Joe Barry Carroll-led Boilermakers from Purdue revenged the earlier NIT defeat and dumped the Hoosiers 76-69 in an NCAA regional semifinal at Lexington. With the 1980 Final Four scheduled for Indianapolis, to the embarrassment of Hoosier supporters everywhere it would thus be Purdue and not IU which would enjoy a rare role as hometown favorites in the season's climactic final weekend.

The setback was only temporary, however, and tears of frustration in March 1980 were soon replaced by endless hurrahs in March of 1981. Everything fell quickly into place for the veteran team which now featured Tolbert (the only senior) at the center slot, juniors Ted Kitchel and Landon Turner along the front wall, and Randy Wittman teaming with the flashy sophomore Isiah Thomas in the backcourt. The 1980-81 lineup may not have been as strong on paper as the '75 and '76 squads or as a handful of other Indiana teams of the past, but it was an impressive unit of talented role players nonetheless. Tolbert was the league's MVP,

Indiana's ninth overall and fifth in just seven seasons. Kitchel also earned a permanent spot in the record books with an 18-for-18 free-throw shooting performance against Illinois in January. A 14-4 league mark and a one-sided 69-48 ripping of Michigan State in the season finale earned a Big Ten title, Knight's sixth.

The 1981 NCAA postseason was largely the Isiah Thomas show as the future NBA great closed out his often tumultuous two-year stay with Coach Knight in most spectacular fashion. One-sided victories over Maryland (99-64), Alabama-Birmingham (87-72) and St. Joseph's (78-46 in the regional finals at Bloomington) put Knight's team into the Final Four. Another rout, this time against LSU (67-49), sealed a championship date with Dean Smith's North Carolina Tar Heels. But it was all Thomas in the title tilt as the flashy backcourt ace netted a game-high 23 points and posted four crucial steals in the second half to key a 63-50 Indiana victory before 18,276 patrons in the Philadelphia Spectrum. A fitting Final Four MVP, Thomas had not only paced IU in scoring (16.0 points per game) but also posted school single-season records of 197 assists and 74 steals.

Thomas might well have owned all the Hoosier records for offensive production had he not bypassed his junior and senior seasons. By the time his scheduled senior campaign had rolled around, Isiah was already an established NBA star in Detroit. Even without Thomas, however, the 1983 Hoosier squad was one of Knight's finest teams. Red-shirt fifth-year performer Randy Wittman had emerged as the backcourt star in Thomas's absence and earned still another Big Ten MVP accolade for IU on a team that maintained the Big Ten title and charged home with a 24-6 overall ledger. But postseason disaster would strike in only the second round of NCAA play in the form of a 64-59 upset loss to Kentucky thus tarnishing an otherwise sterling Big Ten campaign.

The 1984 season brought another 20-victory campaign like clockwork and also witnessed the arrival of one of the brightest individual stars in school history. Steve Alford would launch a four-year career that would amass numerous individual offensive records. Foremost in Alford's bulky collection of milestones was a record career point total of 2,438 surpassed only by Calbert Cheaney. There also were career and season marks for free-throw accuracy, as well as a new career record for steals (178) and a single-game mark for three-point field goals. With Alford running the offense, the Hoosiers slowly evolved into another championship team, one that trailed Michigan by only a game in 1986 and then rose back to the top of the league standings a year later in Alford's senior season.

Alford's career was capped in most fitting fashion with the highly successful 1987 team. With Alford earning yet another league MVP trophy, the Hoosiers beat out a fine field (four teams had five losses or less) for an even share of the league title with Purdue. They then fought their way toward an exciting national championship showdown game with Big East powerhouse Syracuse. On the strength of Alford's deadeye long-range shooting, the Hoosiers had led the nation in three-point field-goal accuracy with a .508 mark that still stands as the national standard. It was that deadly accuracy that proved the Hoosier's strongest suit in the championship showdown. Alford would record an NCAA tourney record by canning seven three-point goals against the Syracuse Orangemen. Keith Smart was the ultimate hero of the final moments of championship play, however, connecting on a running jumper from the left side with the final seconds ticking away, whipping a record New Orleans Superdome

Keith Smart (23) was the hero of the 1987 NCAA championship game. His jumper from the left side gave Indiana a 74-73 victory over Syracuse. (Indiana University photo)

crowd of 64,959 into a final frenzy of excitement. Smart's dramatic shot sealed the 74-73 win and another NCAA crown for Knight and his Hoosiers.

The history of Indiana University basketball does not begin and end with Bob Knight. In final retrospect, it may end with Knight but it begins with Everett Dean and Branch McCracken. McCracken became a star for the Hoosiers and became Indiana's third All-American while playing for Dean, who himself won three Big Ten championships during a 14-year coaching legacy.At his retirement in 1938, McCracken would step in and build a legend in Blooming-ton that only Knight has approached and finally overshadowed.

McCracken provided a half dozen seasons of solid teams in the aftermath of World War II. But his first great squads were finally put together in the early 1950s. The 1952-53 team would bring McCracken his first Big Ten title and earn him the one badge that had so far eluded his IU tenure. McCracken had won nearly 75 percent of his games in a dozen seasons at his alma mater. He had known only one losing season and already earned one NCAA title with a 60-42 pasting of Kansas back in a 1940s championship matchup. But the Big Ten title had so far been an elusive plum to pluck and the loss several years earlier of Indiana high school phenom Clyde Lovellette to Kansas seemed to put title hopes on permanent hold. But the 1953 team not only parlayed the 25.5 points per game scoring of sophomore center Schlundt into a league title, but would excel in postseason play and earn a national championship as well. This was a high-scoring outfit, especially for the era, and in February the "Hurryin' Hoosiers" rattled off a 105-70 whipping of Butler which made the squad the first in school history to crack the century mark in scoring. On March 1, 1953, the Hoosiers would defeat Illinois 91-79 in a road match to clinch the school's first outright Big Ten title.

The NCAA championship team was led by Schlundt, one of the finest multidimensional players in school history. And the team would also be directed by two-year forward guard Bob Leonard, two decades later a local coaching legend with the ABA Indiana Pacers. It was Leonard who provided the floor leadership and who proved to be the perfect athlete to trigger the emerging Indiana fast-breaking offense. Schlundt would roar down the stretch in March of 1953, scoring 41 in the Chicago Stadium game against Notre Dame which earned Coach McCracken's club a berth in the NCAA Final Four. Schlundt's record-breaking 41 points in the crucial tournament game set single-game records for Schlundt, Indiana and the Big Ten. The rugged 6-9 postman would eventually up the mark to 47 a year later during his senior season. But it would be fellow junior "Slick" Leonard who would ultimately save the Cinderella season in the tight 69-68 NCAA championship win over Kansas. A pressure-packed free throw by Leonard with 27 seconds left finally iced the national championship. At season's end, the Hoosiers were for the first time honored as the unanimous No. 1 team, earning that ranking from the Associated Press, the United Press and the International News Service polls.

McCracken would win two more league titles in the late '50s. The next would come only a year later when the team that returned both Schlundt and Leonard ran its two-year overall record to 43-7 and Big Ten mark to 29-4. A highlight of this second Big Ten trophy season for McCracken was a January 9 game at Minnesota's Williams Arena played for a throng of 18,872, the largest crowd ever to watch a basketball game within a college-owned gymnasium. McCracken would also continue his tenure with competitive squads down through the mid-60s. If no longer front runners in McCracken's five final seasons, these teams and the ones that immediately preceded them were known for several of the finest individual players in school annals. First was Archie Dees who logged back-to-back Big Ten scoring titles in 1957 (25.4 points per game) and 1958 (25.9) and was voted a conference MVP both years. Next came Walt Bellamy, the towering 6-10 center and Naismith Hall of Famer who would score proficiently (20.6 at IU and 21,000 NBA points) but earn even larger plaudits with his rebounding skills (15.5 per game for Indiana and more than 14,000 in the NBA). Jimmy Rayl was a slick-shooting guard who overlapped one season with Bellamy and was edged out for two league scoring crowns (1962, 1963) by Purdue's Terry Dischinger and OSU's Gary Bradds. Finally there were the dynamite twins, Dick and Tom VanArsdale, whose IU scoring totals (1,252 for Tom, 1,240 for Dick) were nearly as indistinguishable as their physiques and who were perhaps the finest pair of identical siblings found anywhere in all of collegiate and professional basketball history.

Dean was the third great coach whose epoch still looms large in Indiana University basketball history, even though this first memorable Hoosier mentor remains largely overshadowed by the incomparable legends of Knight and McCracken. Dean built powerhouse teams from the mid-20s through the late 1930s after coming back to Bloomington in 1924 on the heels of a brief three-year tenure at tiny Carleton College in Minnesota. As a player, he had been the first Hoosier to earn an All-American selection when honored by the Helms Foundation in 1921. In 14 campaigns as a head coach of the Hoosiers, Dean would lead three IU teams to first-place ties in the Big Ten predecessor Western Conference. His best Hoosier teams were 1928 (15-2) and 1936 (18-2), and his most renowned ballplayer was none other than captain and forward Branch McCracken, the 1930 conference scoring leader, All-American and fellow Naismith Hall of Fame honoree. Dean would leave Indiana for Stanford in 1938, just in time to build a West Coast powerhouse squad which featured future pioneering NBA all-star Jim Pollard and captured an NCAA tournament title in 1942.

But all of the brilliance of the Everett Dean era in the '20s and '30s and the Branch McCracken era in the '40s and '50s now seems clouded, if not totally obscured, by the massive achievements and larger-than-life personality of Robert Montgomery Knight. Perhaps only Adolph Rupp looms larger in the history of college basketball; certainly only Rupp and Wooden are more thoroughly identified with a single school for so long and so brilliant a tenure. Knight's 1991 induction into the Naismith Memorial Basketball Hall of Fame would leave him as the only Big Ten mentor ever to serve within the league while already owning such an indelible symbol of cage immortality. And it is in the arena of postseason tournament play that Knight has left his most special mark on the school and on the league. During 18 NCAA tourney appearances under Knight, Hoosier teams have won a phenomenal 40 of 55 games (.727). In addition to three NCAA trophies and a 1979 NIT title victory over archrival Purdue, Knight's teams barely missed a second NIT crown (falling to UCLA 65-62 in the 1985 Madison Square Garden finals) and posted a 1974 championship victory (85-60 over Southern Cal) in the first-ever Collegiate Commissioner's Association postseason classic.

Recent seasons have often been as noted for Coach Knight's controversial behavior as for his endless winning records. One incident involved Knight's tossing of a folding chair from the IU bench across the court during an angry display of frustration with officiating during a Purdue-IU matchup in Assembly Hall. Another — one of many such public relations gaffs — featured the Hoosier coach pulling his team off the playing floor in protest during a preseason exhibition contest against a visiting Russia national team. There were several much-publicized public displays of uncontrolled sideline anger aimed at his Hoosier players as well, including an apparent kicking of his son Pat Knight in front of the IU bench during the heat of 1994 game action.

But against this backdrop of turmoil have also been some fine ballclubs and several noteworthy stars since the 1987 NCAA title team. The 1989, 1991 and 1993 IU teams would own outright or share Big Ten titles. The 1992 squad would lead the nation in scoring margin, outscoring its opponents by 17.6 points on average, and climb back into the NCAA Final Four in Minneapolis. Despite only a second-place Big Ten finish, Knight's '92 squad was the seventh to represent the Hoosiers in the final NCAA title chase and raced by Eastern Illinois (94-55), LSU (89-79), Florida State (85-74) and UCLA (106-79), only to lose a semifinal tussle (81-78) with eventual champion Duke.

A season later the 1993 Big Ten championship team featuring senior Calbert Cheaney and junior Damon Bailey would stumble against Kansas (83-77) in the Mideast Regional final canceling out a possible sixth visit for Knight (and eighth for the Hoosiers) to the nation's most celebrated final tournament weekend. Stellar play by Cheaney (who set a new single-season scoring mark by surpassing the 752 points of Scott May in 1976) and Bailey (an honorable mention All-Big Ten selection) during these early seasons of the 1990s was also supplemented by considerable contributions from such Hoosier heroes as Eric Anderson (an agile center with 1,715 career points), Greg Graham (a high 1993 NBA draft choice now playing with the Philadelphia 76ers), Alan Henderson (a 6-9 forward who recovered from a career-threatening 1993 knee injury to emerge as an All-Big Ten selection), and Brian Evans (one of the nation's finest pure shooters who led the Big Ten in three-point field goal percentage in 1994 despite being hampered most of the season by a dislocated shoulder).

But the '90s are perhaps so far best remembered in Hoosierland for the solo scoring of one of the finest all-around players and most productive offensive weapons in school history. Calbert Cheaney would eventually parlay his steady scoring onslaughts into a personal legacy as the greatest scorer in Indiana and Big Ten annals. The 1989 Indiana high school "Mr. Basketball" would finish second to Ohio State's Jimmy Jackson in balloting for 1990 Big Ten Freshman of the Year. Cheaney poured in points at a prolific rate, starting with his 17.1 points per game freshman campaign and continuing through 21.6, 17.6 and 22.4 scoring seasons. The southpaw-shooting 6-7 guard/forward would cap his senior season for the 17-1 Big Ten champs with national collegiate Player of the Year accolades from both the Associated Press and *Sports Illustrated*, as well as Naismith and Wooden awards celebrating his rank as the nation's top college player.

Cheaney's outstanding backcourt performances overlapped for three seasons with those of another former Indiana high school hoop immortal, Damon Bailey. Ripping the nets for a 19.6 points per game senior season, Bailey would eventually edge past 1976 hero Kent Benson into fifth slot on the all-time Hoosier career scoring list. But Bailey (1994 second-round draft choice of the Indiana Pacers) and Cheaney (sixth overall pick in the 1993 NBA draft by the Washington Bullets) have only appended another chapter to the already incomparable legacy of the Bob Knight era at Indiana University with much more undoubtedly left to be written.

Records and Summaries
Year-by-Year Indiana Records
(Championship Years in Boldface)

Season	All Games	Conference	Coach(es)	Top Scorer (Points)
1900-01	1-4	None	J.H. Horne	No Record
1901-02	4-4	None	Phelps Darby	No Record
1902-03	8-4	None	Willis Coval	No Record
1903-04	5-4	None	Willis Coval	No Record
1904-05	5-12	None	Zora Clevenger	No Record
1905-06	7-9	2-2	Zora Clevenger	No Record
1906-07	9-5	0-0	James Sheldon	No Record
1907-08	9-6	2-4	Ed Cook	No Record
1908-09	5-9	2-6	Robert Harris	No Record
1909-10	5-8	3-7	John Georgen	No Record
1910-11	11-5	5-5	Oscar Rackle	No Record
1911-12	6-11	1-9	James Kase	No Record
1912-13	5-11	0-10	Arthur Powell	No Record
1913-14	2-12	1-11	Arthur Berndt	No Record
1914-15	4-9	1-9	Arthur Berndt	No Record
1915-16	6-7	3-5	Allen Willisford	No Record
1916-17	13-6	3-5	G.S. Lowman	No Record
1917-18	10-4	3-3	Dana Evans	No Record
1918-19	10-7	4-6	Dana Evans	No Record
1919-20	13-8	6-4	Edward Stiehm	No Record
1920-21	15-6	6-5	George Levis	No Record
1921-22	10-10	3-7	George Levis	No Record
1922-23	8-7	5-7	Leslie Mann	No Record
1923-24	11-6	7-5	Kenneth Alward	No Record
1924-25	12-5	8-4	Everett Dean	No Record
1925-26	**12-5**	**8-4 (1st-T)**	**Everett Dean**	**Arthur Beckner (108)•**
1926-27	13-4	9-3	Everett Dean	No Record
1927-28	**15-2**	**10-2 (1st-T)**	**Everett Dean**	**No Record**
1928-29	7-10	4-8	Everett Dean	No Record
1929-30	8-9	7-5	Everett Dean	Branch McCracken (147)•
1930-31	9-8	5-7	Everett Dean	No Record
1931-32	8-10	4-8	Everett Dean	No Record
1932-33	10-8	6-6	Everett Dean	No Record
1933-34	13-7	6-6	Everett Dean	No Record
1934-35	14-6	8-4	Everett Dean	No Record
1935-36	**18-2**	**11-1 (1st-T)**	**Everett Dean**	**No Record**
1936-37	13-7	6-6	Everett Dean	No Record
1937-38	10-10	4-8	Everett Dean	No Record
1938-39	17-3	9-3	Branch McCracken	No Record
1939-40#	20-3	9-3	Branch McCracken	Paul Armstrong (203)

1940-41	17-3	10-2	Branch McCracken	William Menke (176)
1941-42	15-6	10-5	Branch McCracken	Ed Denton (173)
1942-43	18-2	11-2	Branch McCracken	Ralph Hamilton (249)
1943-44	7-15	2-10	Harry Good	Paul Shields (198)
1944-45	10-11	3-9	Harry Good	Al Kralovansky (193)
1945-46	18-3	9-3	Harry Good	John Wallace (302)
1946-47	12-8	8-4	Branch McCracken	Ralph Hamilton (267)
1947-48	8-12	3-9	Branch McCracken	Don Ritter (275)
1948-49	14-8	6-6	Branch McCracken	Bill Garrett (220)
1949-50	17-5	7-5	Branch McCracken	Bill Garrett (283)
1950-51	19-3	12-2	Branch McCracken	Bill Garrett (289)
1951-52	16-6	9-5	Branch McCracken	Don Schlundt (376)
1952-53#	**23-3**	**17-1 (1st)**	**Branch McCracken**	**Don Schlundt (661)•**
1953-54	**20-4**	**12-2 (1st)**	**Branch McCracken**	**Don Schlundt (583)•**
1954-55	8-14	5-9	Branch McCracken	Don Schlundt (572)•
1955-56	13-9	6-8	Branch McCracken	Wally Choice (463)
1956-57	**14-8**	**10-4 (1st-T)**	**Branch McCracken**	**Archie Dees (550)•**
1957-58	**13-11**	**10-4 (1st)**	**Branch McCracken**	**Archie Dees (613)•**
1958-59	11-11	7-7	Branch McCracken	Walt Bellamy (382)
1959-60	20-4	11-3	Branch McCracken	Walt Bellamy (537)
1960-61	15-9	8-6	Branch McCracken	Walt Bellamy (522)
1961-62	13-11	7-7	Branch McCracken	Jimmy Rayl (714)
1962-63	13-11	9-5	Branch McCracken	Jimmy Rayl (608)
1963-64	9-15	5-9	Branch McCracken	Dick VanArsdale (535)
1964-65	19-5	9-5	Branch McCracken	Tom VanArsdale (441)
1965-66	8-16	4-10	Lou Watson	Max Walker (380)
1966-67	**18-8**	**10-4 (1st-T)**	**Lou Watson**	**Butch Joyner (481)**
1967-68	10-14	4-10	Lou Watson	Vern Payne (354)
1968-69	9-15	4-10	Lou Watson	Joe Cooke (523)
1969-70	7-17	3-11	Jerry Oliver	Jim Harris (434)
1970-71	17-7	9-5	Lou Watson	George McGinnis (719)•
1971-72	17-8	9-5	Bob Knight	Joby Wright (498)
1972-73	**22-6**	**11-3 (1st)**	**Bob Knight**	**Steve Downing (563)**
1973-74	**23-5**	**12-2 (1st-T)**	**Bob Knight**	**Steve Green (467)**
1974-75	**31-1**	**18-0 (1st)**	**Bob Knight**	**Steve Green (516)**
1975-76#	**32-0**	**18-0 (1st)**	**Bob Knight**	**Scott May (752)**
1976-77	16-11	11-7	Bob Knight	Mike Woodson (500)
1977-78	21-8	12-6	Bob Knight	Mike Woodson (577)
1978-79**	22-12	10-8	Bob Knight	Mike Woodson (714)
1979-80	**21-8**	**13-5 (1st)**	**Bob Knight**	**Isiah Thomas (423)**
1980-81#	**26-9**	**14-4 (1st)**	**Bob Knight**	**Isiah Thomas (545)**
1981-82	19-10	12-6	Bob Knight	Ted Kitchel (568)
1982-83	**24-6**	**13-5 (1st)**	**Bob Knight**	**Randy Wittman (569)**
1983-84	22-9	13-5	Bob Knight	Steve Alford (479)
1984-85	19-14	7-11	Bob Knight	Steve Alford (580)
1985-86	21-8	13-5	Bob Knight	Steve Alford (630)

Steve Alford (12) is No. 2 on the all-time scoring list and was one of the finest all-around guards in IU history. (Indiana University photo)

1986-87#	30-4	15-3 (1st-T)	**Bob Knight**	**Steve Alford (749)**
1987-88	19-10	11-7	Bob Knight	Dean Garrett (467)
1988-89	**27-8**	**15-3 (1st)**	**Bob Knight**	**Jay Edwards (680)**
1989-90	18-11	8-10	Bob Knight	Calbert Cheaney (495)
1990-91	**29-5**	**15-3(1st-T)**	**Bob Knight**	**Calbert Cheaney (734)**
1991-92	27-7	14-4	Bob Knight	Calbert Cheaney (599)
1992-93	**31-4**	**17-1 (1st)**	**Bob Knight**	**Calbert Cheaney (785)**
1993-94	21-9	12-6	Bob Knight	Damon Bailey (589)

= National (NCAA) Champions; ** = NIT Champions; • = League Individual Scoring Champion

All-Time Indiana Coaching Records

Coach	Overall Record	Conference Record	Seasons
Bob Knight (1972-Present)	538-173 (.757)	293-109 (.730)	23
Branch McCracken (1939-65)	364-174 (.677)	210-116 (.644)	24
Everett Dean (1925-38)	162-93 (.635)	96-72 (.571)	14
Lou Watson (1966-71)	62-60 (.508)	31-39 (.443)	5
Harry Good (1944-46)	35-29 (.547)	14-22 (.389)	3
George Lewis (1921-22)	25-16 (.610)	9-12 (.429)	2
Dana Evans (1918-19)	20-11 (.645)	7-9 (.438)	2
Leslie Mann (1923-24)	19-13 (.594)	12-12 (.500)	2
G.S. Lowman (1917)	13-6 (.684)	3-5 (.375)	1
Ewald Stehm (1920)	13-8 (.619)	6-4 (.600)	1
Willis Coval (1903-04)	13-8 (.619)	No League	2
Zora Clevenger (1905-06)	12-21 (.364)	2-2 (.500)	2
Oscar Rackle (1911)	11-5 (.688)	5-5 (.500)	1
James Sheldon (1907)	9-5 (.714)	No Participation	1
Ed Cook (1908)	9-6 (.600)	No Participation	1
Jerry Oliver (1970)	7-17 (.292)	3-11 (.215)	1
Allan Willisford (1916)	6-7 (.462)	3-5 (.375)	1
James Kase (1912)	6-11 (.353)	1-9 (.100)	1
Arthur Berndt (1914-15)	6-21 (.222)	2-20 (.091)	2
John Georgen (1910)	5-8 (.285)	3-7 (.300)	1
Robert Harris (1909)	5-9 (.357)	2-6 (.250)	1
Arthur Powell (1913)	5-11 (.312)	0-10 (.000)	1
Phelps Darby (1902)	4-4 (.500)	No League	1
J.H. Horne (1901)	1-4 (.200)	No League	1

All-Time Indiana Individual Career Records

Points Scored	Calbert Cheaney (2,613, 1990-93)
Scoring Average	Don Schlundt (23.3, 1952-55)
Field Goals	Calbert Cheaney (1018, 1990-93)
Field-Goal Percentage	Matt Nover (.571, 1990-93)
Free Throws Made	Don Schlundt (826, 1952-55)
Free-Throw Percentage	Steve Alford (.898, 1984-87)
3-Point Field Goals	Calbert Cheaney (148, 1990-93)
Rebounds	Walt Bellamy (1088, 1959-61)
Assists	Quinn Buckner (542, 1973-76)
Steals	Steve Alford (178, 1984-87)
Blocked Shots	Uwe Blab (204, 1982-85)

All-Time Indiana Individual Season Records

Points Scored .... Calbert Cheaney (785, 1992-93)
Scoring Average .... Jimmy Rayl (29.8, 1961-62)
Field Goals .... Scott May (308, 1975-76)
Field-Goal Percentage .... Matt Nover (.628, 1992-93)
Free Throws Made .... Don Schlundt (249, 1952-53)
Free-Throw Percentage .... Steve Alford (.921, 1984-85)
3-Point Field Goals .... Steve Alford (107, 1986-87)
Rebounds .... Walt Bellamy (428, 1960-61)
Rebound Average .... Walt Bellamy (17.8, 1960-61)
Assists .... Isiah Thomas (197, 1980-81)
Steals .... Isiah Thomas (74, 1981)
Blocked Shots .... Dean Garrett (99, 1988)

All-Time Indiana Individual Single-Game Records

Points Scored .... Jimmy Rayl (56 vs. Michigan State, 1963)
Field Goals .... Jimmy Rayl (23 vs. Michigan State, 1963)
Free Throws Made .... Greg Graham (26 vs. Purdue, 1993)
3-Point Field Goals .... Steve Alford (8 vs. Princeton, 1987)
                                                            Jay Edwards (8 vs. Minnesota, 1988)
Rebounds .... Walt Bellamy (33 vs. Michigan, 1961)
Assists .... Keith Smart (15 vs. Auburn, 1-7-87)
Steals .... Scott May (9 vs. Michigan, 1976)
Blocked Shots .... Dean Garrett (8 vs. Montana State, 1987)
                                                            Dean Garrett (8 vs. Iowa, 1988)

Indiana All-Americans and All-Big Ten Selections

Consensus All-Americans
Branch McCracken, Forward, 1930
Vern Huffman, Guard, 1936
Ernie Andres, Guard, 1939
Ralph Hamilton, Forward, 1947
Don Schlundt, Center, 1954
Scott May, Forward, 1975-1976
Kent Benson, Center, 1976-1977
Isiah Thomas, Guard, 1981
Steve Alford, Guard, 1986-1987
Calbert Cheaney, Guard, 1993

All-Big Ten Selections (since 1948)
Lou Watson, Guard, 1950
Bill Garrett, Center, 1951
Don Schlundt, Center, 1953-1954-1955
Bob ("Slick") Leonard, Guard, 1953-1954
Archie Dees, Center, 1957-1958
Walt Bellamy, Center, 1960-1961
Jimmy Rayl, Guard, 1961-1963
Tom Bolyard, Forward, 1963

Dick VanArsdale, Forward, 1964
Harry Joyner, Forward, 1967
George McGinnis, Forward, 1971
Joby Wright, Forward, 1972
Steve Downing, Center, 1973
Steve Green, Forward, 1974-1975
Quinn Buckner, Guard, 1974-1975
Scott May, Forward, 1975-1976
Kent Benson, Center, 1975-1977
Mike Woodson, Forward, 1979
Isiah Thomas, Guard, 1980-1981
Ted Kitchel, Forward, 1983
Randy Wittman, Guard-Forward, 1983
Steve Alford, Guard, 1984-1986-1987
Uwe Blab, Center, 1985
Dean Garrett, Center, 1988
Jay Edwards, Guard, 1989
Eric Anderson, Forward, 1991
Calbert Cheaney, Forward, 1991-1992-1993
Greg Graham, Guard, 1993

Chapter 3

IOWA *Hawkeyes*

Original "Fab Five" and Sharpshooting "Six Pack"

All-Time Record: 1,180-808, .594; **Conference Record:** 573-562, .505

Big Ten Championships — 8: (1923*, 1926*, 1945, 1955, 1956, 1968*, 1970, 1979*) * = Co-Champion

National Championships: None

Greatest Player: Roy Marble (1986-89)

Career Scoring Leader: Roy Marble (2,116 Points, 1986-89)

Most Successful Coach: Pops Harrison (1944-50), 91-32, .740

All-Time Team: Acie Earl (C, 1990-93), Don Nelson (F, 1960-62), Roy Marble (F, 1986-89), B.J. Armstrong (G, 1986-89), Ronnie Lester (G, 1977-80)

Best Season: 1955-56 (20-6), NCAA Runner-Up (Coach: Bucky O'Connor)

University Profile

Location: Iowa City, Iowa (pop. 50,000); **Founded:** 1847; **Campus Enrollment:** 28,000 (1994); **Started Basketball:** 1901-02. Widely recognized as one of the nation's leading centers for the fine arts and liberal arts, creative writing, space physics, hydraulics, basic health and science research, and communications studies, the University of Iowa is also internationally renowned as home to the largest university-owned teaching hospital in the United States. Iowa's most distinguished alumni include actor Gene Wilder, footballer Alex Karras, Exxon president Randall Meyer, novelists John Irving and W.P. Kinsella, and Pulitzer Prize-winning playwright Tennessee Williams.

Team Nickname, Colors and Arena

Nickname: Hawkeyes; Colors: Old Gold and Black; Arena: Carver-Hawkeye Arena (15,500 capacity, opened 1983). The origin of the "Hawkeye" nickname seems buried somewhere in the dim pre-history of the school's proud sports program. But whatever its origins, the university moniker was never more appropriate than when it was attached to the 1969-70 Iowa basketball squad. That undefeated Big Ten club (20-5 overall) shot the ball with such unerring accuracy that it piled up dozens of school and league scoring standards, many of which still stand a full quarter-century later. It was that 1970 Iowa team which averaged an incredible 102.9 points in conference games and thus earned immortality as the highest scoring outfit in Big Ten hoops history.

Hawkeye Basketball History

They seemingly take their basketball very seriously out in the plains state of Iowa, especially when it comes to the annual fortunes of their beloved if inconsistent Iowa Hawkeyes. At the prep school level, for starters, Iowa women's basketball has long gloried in unrivalled tradition that stretches back across the entire century. Iowa boys' scholastic action also claims a frenzied following rivaling anything found in neighboring Kentuckiana. But when it comes to the Hawkeyes, the boasting points touch a special place of pride. Who, after all, once produced the nation's first recognized NCAA individual scoring champion back in 1948? And which school provided the hoops world with the original "Fab Five" glory team of the mid-50s? And from Don Nelson on down to Brad Lohaus and Acie Earl and to the parquet floor of the spanking new Carver-Hawkeye Arena, what proud collegiate program can offer more intimate connections with the pro game's richest winning tradition — that known as Celtic Mystique?

Sometimes the tradition is admittedly a little difficult to comprehend. There haven't been many Big Ten titles in the land of the Hawkeyes — only eight, none over the past decade and a half — yet that hasn't dimmed much of the enthusiasm. One can start, for example, with the storied career of long-forgotten Murray Wier. Wier receives nary a mention in Neil Isaacs' standard 1975 history of college basketball entitled *All the Moves* and is mostly ignored in other historical accounts of the collegiate game as well. Wier's career at Iowa hardly began with a bang, after all; the 5-foot-9 forward who first wore uniform No. 3 was a starter as a freshman and sophomore but failed to score in double figures either season while playing on teams that finished first and third within the conference. But Murray Wier would save his best for last and do so with remarkable good timing and perhaps a bit of luck spurred by a switch in uniform number. In his senior season, now wearing No. 17 to enhance his luck, the diminutive frontcourt player would rack up a school record (at the time) 21 points per game scoring average. And since 1947-48 happened to be the very year in which the NCAA began recognizing a national scoring leader, it would be Murray Wier of Iowa whom the record books would henceforth display as the first individual collegiate point-making champion.

Murray Wier would be Iowa's first consensus All-America selection as well as its first and only national scoring pacesetter. He would be followed a few short seasons later by Iowa's only other concensus All-American, Charles Darling, a late-blooming center who still holds

Hawkeye Murray Wier, Iowa's first All-American, earned a unique place in Big Ten history as the first recognized NCAA scoring champion. (University of Iowa photo)

school records for rebounds in a season (387, 1951) and rebounds in a single game (30, 1952). But Wier and Darling were not the very first Hawkeyes to draw notice on the national cage scene. Wier's teammates, Dick Ives and Herb Wilkinson, for example, would both draw recognition on several earlier All-American squads, both selected as first-teamers in 1945 (Ives was an *Argosy* magazine choice and Wilkinson a Helms Foundation selection). It was also Ives and Wilkinson and the 1944-45 war-era team (17-1, 11-1) that would earn for Iowa its first outright conference crown by a slim one-game margin over runner-up Ohio State. And this early sensational Iowa duo, playing under coach Pops Harrison, would combine to earn selections to five different All-American squads during their combined seven seasons of play with the Hawkeyes.

But the first Iowa team to make a large splash on the national scene did not arrive until several seasons after Wier, Ives and Wilkinson had first written the name of Iowa squarely on the collegiate basketball map. This memorable Hawkeye contingent would be Bucky O'Connor's

"Fabulous Five" squad which took the floor for both the 1954-55 and 1955-56 campaigns, locking up two Big Ten titles as well as making two serious runs at national honors in March of both years. It all started with the 1955 club, a 19-7 team with but three league losses and a slim final conference lead over both Illinois and Minnesota. Only the Ives-Wilkinson squad a full decade earlier had previously brought a Big Ten crown outright to Iowa City. But this 1955 team would be the school's first to enter post-season NCAA tournament play. And it would be the first as well to average 80 points per game for a full season of play. Center Bill Logan was the scoring star for the new Big Ten powerhouse with a 15.9 average and a team-best 11 rebounds per game to boot. Additional support came from forward Carl Cain (an eventual 1,000-point career scorer), Bill Seaburg (the playmaker and outside shooting threat), Sharm Scheuerman (Seaburg's running mate at guard), and Bill Schoof (a top reserve center who moved into the other starting forward slot before season's end).

With his "Fabulous Five" lineup now in place, Hawkeyes coach O'Connor was ready to launch Iowa onto the national stage in only his third season at the helm. Only 24 teams began the NCAA post-season derby back in the mid-50s and Iowa charged from its 1955 Big Ten launching pad to romp in an opening second-round match over Penn State, 82-53. A hard-fought 86-81 triumph against Marquette would next suddenly thrust the previously unheralded Hawkeyes into the prestigious Final Four event alongside San Francisco (with Bill Russell and K.C. Jones), La Salle (with the country's most sensational player, Tom Gola), and darkhorse Colorado. The semifinal matchup of Eastern teams would pit Iowa and La Salle at Kansas City and Gola would simply prove too much for the inexperienced Hawkeyes. Gola easily dominated the boards and outscored Logan 23-20 in a game which went to the Explorers by a 76-73 count. There would still be one more 1955 test left, however, for this first edition of the "Fabulous Five" lineup. That would be a consolation-game shootout with Colorado, which would be lost as well, 75-54, thus slamming the door somewhat rudely on an otherwise delightful fourth-place national finish for the surprisingly successful Iowa City team.

But Iowa would not be unheralded for long and even better things were in store a mere season later. Bill Schoof (10.8) was entrenched in the starting lineup from opening day alongside Cain (15.8), Seaberg (13.9), Logan (17.7) and Scheuerman (10.1), thus forming "Edition No. 2" of the high-scoring "Fabulous Five" lineup. Four decades before Michigan would appropriate the same name for its own widely heralded freshman lineup of 1992, Iowa's exciting crew would now etch its place forever in the hearts of dedicated Hawkeye followers everywhere.

Big Ten league play offered little challenge, with only a single January conference-opening loss to Michigan State before 13 straight victories were rattled off in quick succession. Carl Cain was team MVP and a first-team All-American while Bill Logan repeated as Big Ten scoring champion. In post-season play, the team that had smelled victory 12 months earlier now roared back to the Final Four with cakewalks over Morehead State and Kentucky, followed by a semifinal 83-76 triumph against high-scoring guard Hal Lear (the tournament MVP) and his Temple Owls. The NCAA Finals were this time scheduled into a familiar setting, Northwestern's McGraw Hall arena in Evanston, and the "home team" Big Ten club from Iowa would now finally get its deserved crack at the USF Dons and shot-blocking wizard Bill Russell. But that long-awaited opportunity would turn out in the end to be nothing more than a gallant effort made largely in vain. San Francisco — the first true college basketball dynasty team of the modern era — was simply invincible as long as Russell was tending the goal and minding the boards and the Hawkeyes could do no better than a noble 83-71 defeat in their one and only crack at a national championship trophy.

It would be the late '60s before Iowa would next return to the top of the conference heap, this time under the guidance of six-year head coach Ralph Miller. O'Connor had finally retired at the end of the 1958 campaign, owning a .634 (71-41) conference winning percentage that only Miller would eventually surpass. "Fabulous Five" standout Steve Scheuerman had tried his hand at coaching for six undistinguished seasons during the early '60s but had been blessed with only one solid club capable of reaching second place (1961), deep in the shadow of Ohio State with All-Americans Jerry Lucas and John Havlicek. But Miller brought in solid winners in 1968 (tied for first with Ohio State) and again in 1970 (20-5 and undefeated in conference play). The 1969-70 squad would indeed be the only one in Iowa history to pass through an entire Big Ten season entirely unblemished. This high scoring unit was affectionately known as the "Six Pack" and established a host of scoring records

John Johnson's 27.9 points per game scoring average in 1970 remains the highest single-season mark in Hawkeye history. (University of Iowa photo)

on its way to only the second 20-victory season in school annals. A 1970 scoring average of 102.9 points per game remains the highest in the Big Ten record books. Four starters (led by John Johnson at 27.9) would average better that 17 points per game that year, and the club topped 100 points a dozen times, including a final NCAA second-round 104-103 loss to Jacksonville and a curtain-call 121-106 thrashing of Notre Dame in a tacked-on NCAA regional consolation contest.

The 1960s also were noted in Iowa for a handful of individual stars destined for proud pro careers a few seasons down the road. John Johnson, for one, paced the high-scoring 1969 and 1970 teams and upped the school single-season point-making record to 699 in 1970 on his way to 1,172 career points. A single notable player during the earlier Scheuerman tenure was center Don Nelson, who averaged more than 23 points per game in both his junior (1961) and senior (1962) seasons. Sam Williams was a Helms All-American in '68 and '69 and also surpassed the 1,000-point career plateau in only two seasons of varsity play. "Downtown" Fred Brown also manned a guard slot for two campaigns and bombed away for a 27.6-point average (second in the conference behind Indiana's sensational sophomore George McGinnis) in the first full season of the 1970s.

Iowa's career scoring leader, Roy Marble, deposits two more during Big Ten action against Michigan State. Marble finished his career, at Iowa with 2,116 points. (University of Iowa photo)

More recent outings of the late '70s and '80s have produced coaching successes first by Lute Olson (1978-83) and later Dr. Tom Davis (1987-present), as well as the thrilling offensive onslaughts of four of the most prolific scorers in Hawkeye history. These four talented sharp-shooters were postman Greg Stokes (1,768 points, 1982-85), forward Roy Marble (2,116, 1986-89), Marble's three-year backcourt teammate B.J. Armstrong (1,705 points), and most recently, center Acie Earl (1,779, 1990-93). Olson's teams posted 20 or more victories six times, five of these heady seasons coming in a row. Davis has also posted four 20-victory seasons and one memorable campaign that even reached the magical 30-win level.

Olson would win only one Big Ten title, a share of the 1979 crown split three ways with Purdue and eventual NCAA champion Michigan State. And if that 1979 team would be rudely and immediately upended by Mid-America Conference champion Toledo in the opening round of the Mideast Regional, it would nonetheless show plenty of future potential with a starting lineup featuring Kevin Boyle, Steve Waite, Vince Brookins, Steve Krafcisin and Ronnie Lester — a unit slated to return intact and presumably improved for the following season.

The touted 1980 outfit — long on experience with a talented sophomore backcourt of Boyle and Arnold with senior leader Ronnie Lester in reserve — would nonetheless be blocked from anticipated possession of the top spot by a rash of injuries that effectively crippled what was universally acknowledged as the most talented team in the conference. All was not lost, however. Olson's charges mended sufficiently at season's end to launch a post-season stretch drive that would take them all the way to a Final Four date in Indianapolis and an eventual third-place consolation loss to conference rival Purdue. For his late-season heroics, Ronnie Lester would garner second-team All-American honors. Kenny Arnold (13.5 ppg) would pace the Hawkeye scoring parade. And for the only time outside of the mid-50s Fab Five era, an Iowa team could now hold its head high as an elite Final Four entrant.

Olson's career in Iowa would wind down by 1983 when he was lured away by an attrac-tive large-dollar offer from Pac-10 powerhouse Arizona. Successor George Raveling lasted but three winters in Iowa City before departing on the heels of two 20-win seasons for greener pastures, also escaping for a Pac-10 home and the dream of reviving a long-suffering Southern Cal program. The debut three seasons under Raveling's replacement, Dr. Tom Davis, were close to spectacular, however. For starters, Davis' rookie year at the helm would witness the only 30-win season in school history. The winningest Iowa ballclub of all time would drop only five ballgames, all by margins of less than 10 points. Yet four of these losses would fall on the conference schedule and a 14-4 Big Ten mark would be good enough for only third place in a loaded conference field stacked with eventual national champion Indiana as well as 25-5 Pur-due. Davis' second and third seasons were almost as strong, resulting in 24 and 23 victories, respectively, and buoyed by third- and fourth-place conference perches.

Davis, despite his fast start, has yet to earn a first Big Ten trophy. But his high-powered winning clubs have continued as recently as 1991 (21-11) and 1993 (23-9). Perhaps the Davis era is most notable, however, for the indivdual exploits of headline-grabbing stars such as Roy Marble and Acie Earl. Both would fall short of All-American recognition, yet Marble would nonetheless conclude his productive Hawkeye career as the school's all-time scoring leader (2,116) and only career 2,000-point scorer. Earl (a 6-11 first-round 1993 draft pick of the Boston Celtics) would carve his own mark as both a prolific scorer (second in school history)

B.J. Armstrong (10) leads the fast break in a 1988 Big Ten game against Northwestern. Armstrong holds the Iowa record for three-point field goals in a career. (University of Iowa photo)

and one of the Big Ten's most intimidating shot blockers and defensive post players of the past several decades.

After a bright start under Davis during its most recent season, Iowa stumbled into something of a skid (11-16, 5-13). This sudden fall was all the more surprising since it came smack on the heals of a prosperous 23-9 year that was one of the best of the post-World War II era. Acie Earl would peak his junior season (1992) as a scorer (19.6), then set new conference standards for shot blocking (71, 3.94 per game) during his senior campaign. Earl also paced the talented 1992-93 club to a distant third-place finish in the conference derby, six full games behind Indiana. But Earl is now departed and already making his tentative mark in the pro ranks with the Celtics. Beyond the individual play of Earl, recent seasons have seen little to cheer loudly about in Iowa City's plush new Carver-Hawkeye Arena since no Iowa club has won as many as a dozen Big Ten games in any of the past half-dozen seasons. There are some tentative signs of rebuilding, however, like rugged 6-7 sophomore Jess Settles who paced the losing 1994 club in points, field-goal accuracy, rebounds and scoring average. And Davis will assuredly become the winningest Iowa coach in school history before the conclusion of the 1994-95 season. Entering 1994-95, Davis needs only a half-dozen more victories to overtake Lute Olson for that honor.

Numerous star players have graced the Iowa basketball program through the decades. Only nine performers from the past, however, have earned special immortality with the ultimate honor of retired uniform numbers. As a unique badge of proud basketball tradition in Iowa City, the Hawkeyes have taken a page normally reserved for professional sports teams and retired from future use nine jersey numbers worn by some of the brightest among the school's past cage stars. The retired numbers include those of Armstrong (10), Lester (12), Stokes (41), Chris Street (40), and the entire "Fab Five" starting lineup of Cain (21), Seaberg (22), Logan (31), Schoof (33) and Scheuerman (46). Stokes remains the current school record holder for field-goal percentage and is third on Iowa's all-time scoring list. Armstrong and Lester were perhaps the greatest all-around backcourt performers in school annals. Chris Street was a special memorial selection after a tragic automobile accident ended his life only 15 games into his 1993 junior season.

A final boasting point of the tradition-laced Iowa basketball program is state-of-the-art Carver-Hawkeye Arena, one of the true showcase venues for Big Ten basketball action. One of the 10 largest university-owned arenas in the land, the plush 16,000-seat oval opened to Big Ten play in January 1983 and has now celebrated a decade of exciting and winning Iowa basketball tradition. The Hawkeyes at one point enjoyed 60 consecutive sellout crowds in the new arena and also hold a winning edge there on every Big Ten opponent. A replacement $60,000 parquet floor was a novel addition to the facility in 1988 and now provides a classy Boston Celtics look for one of the most tradition-bound collegiate basketball programs found anywhere in America's heartland.

Records and Summaries
Year-by-Year Iowa Records
(Championship Years in Boldface)

Season	All Games	Conference	Coach(es)	Top Scorer (Points)
1901-02	10-2	None	Ed Rule	No Record
1902-03	4-3	None	Fred Bailey	No Record
1903-04	6-2	None	Ed Rule	No Record
1904-05	6-8	None	John Chalmers	No Record
1905-06	11-5	None	Ed Rule	No Record
1906-07	5-5	None	John Griffith	No Record
1907-08	10-6	None	Ed Rule	No Record
1908-09	8-7	1-5	John Griffith	No Record
1909-10	11-3	2-2	John Griffith	No Record
1910-11	9-4	2-2	Walter Stewart	No Record
1911-12	6-8	0-4	Walter Stewart	No Record
1912-13	9-13	1-5	Floyd Thomas	No Record
1913-14	9-7	1-5	Maury Kent	No Record
1914-15	9-8	2-6	Maury Kent	No Record
1915-16	11-4	2-4	Maury Kent	No Record
1916-17	7-9	1-8	Maury Kent	No Record
1917-18	6-8	4-6	Maury Kent	No Record
1918-19	8-7	4-7	Edwin Bannick	No Record
1919-20	9-10	6-6	James Ashmore	No Record
1920-21	9-9	6-5	James Ashmore	No Record
1921-22	11-7	5-6	James Ashmore	No Record
1922-23	**13-2**	**11-1 (1st-T)**	**Sam Barry**	**Jack Funk (143)•**
1923-24	7-10	4-8	Sam Barry	No Record
1924-25	6-10	5-7	Sam Barry	No Record
1925-26	**12-5**	**8-4 (1st-T)**	**Sam Barry**	**No Record**
1926-27	9-8	7-5	Sam Barry	No Record
1927-28	6-11	3-9	Sam Barry	No Record
1928-29	9-8	5-7	Sam Barry	No Record
1929-30	4-13	None	Rollie Williams	No Record
1930-31	5-12	2-10	Rollie Williams	No Record
1931-32	5-12	3-9	Rollie Williams	No Record
1932-33	15-5	8-4	Rollie Williams	No Record
1933-34	13-6	6-6	Rollie Williams	No Record
1934-35	10-9	6-6	Rollie Williams	No Record
1935-36	9-10	5-7	Rollie Williams	No Record
1936-37	11-9	3-9	Rollie Williams	No Record
1937-38	11-9	6-6	Rollie Williams	No Record
1938-39	8-11	3-9	Rollie Williams	Ben Stephens (215)
1939-40	9-12	4-8	Rollie Williams	Vic Siegel (189)
1940-41	12-8	4-8	Rollie Williams	Vic Siegel (194)

1941-42	12-8	10-5	Rollie Williams	Tom Chapman (245)
1942-43	7-10	3-9	Rollie Williams	Ben Trickey (229)
1943-44	14-4	9-3	Pops Harrison	Dick Ives (327)•
1944-45	**17-1**	**11-1 (1st)**	**Pops Harrison**	**Dick Ives (217)**
1945-46	14-4	8-4	Pops Harrison	Dick Ives (187)
1946-47	12-7	5-7	Pops Harrison	Murray Wier (227)
1947-48	15-4	8-4	Pops Harrison	Murray Wier (399)•
1948-49	10-10	3-9	Pops Harrison	Charlie Mason (146)
1949-50	15-7	6-6	Pops Harrison/Bucky O'Connor	Frank Calsbeek (333)
1950-51	15-7	9-5	Rollie Williams	Charles Darling (358)
1951-52	19-3	11-3	Bucky O'Connor	Charles Darling (561)•
1952-53	12-10	9-9	Bucky O'Connor	Deacon Davis (327)
1953-54	17-5	11-3	Bucky O'Connor	Bill Logan (315)
1954-55	**19-7**	**11-3 (1st)**	**Bucky O'Connor**	**Bill Logan (413)**
1955-56#	**20-6**	**13-1 (1st)**	**Bucky O'Connor**	**Bill Logan (460)**
1956-57	8-14	4-10	Bucky O'Connor	Dave Gunther (271)
1957-58	13-9	7-7	Bucky O'Connor	Dave Gunther (435)
1958-59	10-12	7-7	Sharm Scheuerman	Dave Gunther (482)
1959-60	14-10	6-8	Sharm Scheuerman	Don Nelson (380)
1960-61	18-6	10-4	Sharm Scheuerman	Don Nelson (570)
1961-62	13-11	7-7	Sharm Scheuerman	Don Nelson (572)
1962-63	9-15	5-9	Sharm Scheuerman	Dave Roach (289)
1963-64	8-15	3-11	Sharm Scheuerman	Dave Roach (367)
1964-65	14-10	8-6	Ralph Miller	Chris Pervall (507)
1965-66	17-7	8-6	Ralph Miller	Chris Pervall (458)
1966-67	16-8	9-5	Ralph Miller	Sam Williams (544)
1967-68	**16-9**	**10-4 (1st-T)**	**Ralph Miller**	**Sam Williams (632)**
1968-69	12-12	5-9	Ralph Miller	John Johnson (473)
1969-70	**20-5**	**14-0 (1st)**	**Ralph Miller**	**John Johnson (699)**
1970-71	9-15	4-10	Dick Schultz	Fred Brown (662)
1971-72	11-13	5-9	Dick Schultz	Rick Williams (469)
1972-73	13-11	6-8	Dick Schultz	Kevin Kunnert (460)
1973-74	8-16	5-9	Dick Schultz	Candy LaPrince (457)
1974-75	10-16	7-11	Lute Olson	Bruce King (298)
1975-76	19-10	9-9	Lute Olson	Scott Thompson (567)
1976-77	20-7	12-6	Lute Olson	Bruce King (524)
1977-78	12-15	5-13	Lute Olson	Ronnie Lester (536)
1978-79	**20-8**	**13-5 (1st-T)**	**Lute Olson**	**Ronnie Lester (524)**
1979-80	23-10	10-8	Lute Olson	Kenny Arnold (444)
1980-81	21-7	13-5	Lute Olson	Vince Brookins (411)
1981-82	21-8	12-6	Lute Olson	Michael Payne (308)
1982-83	22-9	11-7	Lute Olson	Greg Stokes (548)
1983-84	13-15	6-12	George Raveling	Greg Stokes (417)
1984-85	21-11	10-8	George Raveling	Greg Stokes (638)
1985-86	20-12	10-8	George Raveling	Roy Marble (399)
1986-87	30-5	14-4	Tom Davis	Roy Marble (520)

1987-88	24-10	12-6	Tom Davis	B.J. Armstrong (592)
1988-89	23-10	10-8	Tom Davis	Roy Marble (675)
1989-90	12-16	4-14	Tom Davis	Les Jepsen (417)
1990-91	21-11	9-9	Tom Davis	Acie Earl (520)
1991-92	19-11	10-8	Tom Davis	Acie Earl (586)
1992-93	23-9	11-7	Tom Davis	Acie Earl (542)
1993-94	11-16	5-13	Tom Davis	Jess Settles (414)

\# = NCAA Runners-Up; • = League Individual Scoring Champion

All-Time Iowa Coaching Records

Coach	Overall Record	Conference Record	Seasons
Lute Olson (1975-83)	168-90 (.651)	92-70 (.568)	9
Tom Davis (1987-Present)	163-88 (.649)	75-69 (.521)	8
Rollie Williams (1930-43, 1951)	146-141 (.509)	72-101 (.416)	15
Bucky O'Connor (1950, 52-58)	114-59 (.659)	71-41 (.634)	7
Ralph Miller (1965-70)	95-51 (.651)	54-30 (.643)	6
Pops Harrison (1944-50)	91-32 (.740)	45-29 (.608)	7
Sharm Scheuerman (1959-64)	72-69 (.511)	38-46 (.452)	6
Sam Barry (1923-29)	62-54 (.534)	43-41 (.512)	7
George Raveling (1984-86)	54-38 (.587)	26-28 (.481)	3
Maury Kent (1914-18)	42-36 (.538)	10-29 (.256)	5
Dick Schultz (1971-74)	41-55 (.427)	20-36 (.357)	4
Ed Rule (1902-04-06-08)	37-15 (.712)	None	4
James Ashmore (1920-22)	29-26 (.527)	17-17 (.500)	3
John Griffith (1907, 1909-10)	24-15 (.615)	3-7 (.300)	3
Walter Stewart (1911-12)	15-12 (.556)	2-6 (.250)	2
Floyd Thomas (1913)	9-13 (.409)	1-5 (.167)	1
Edwin Bannick (1919)	8-7 (.533)	4-7 (.364)	1
John Chalmers (1905)	6-8 (.429)	None	1
Fred Bailey (1903)	4-3 (.571)	None	1

All-Time Iowa Individual Single-Game Records

Points Scored .... John Johnson (49 vs. Northwestern, 1970)
Field Goals .... John Johnson (20 vs. Northwestern, 1970)
Free Throws Made .... Don Nelson (21 vs. Indiana, 1962)
3-Point Field Goals .... Jeff Moe (7 vs. Oral Roberts, 1988)
Rebounds .... Charles Darling (30 vs. Wisconsin, 1952)
Assists .... Cal Wulfsberg (16 vs. Ohio State, 1976)
Steals .... Acie Earl (9 vs. Texas Southern, 1993)
Blocked Shots .... Acie Earl (9 vs. Wisconsin, 1992)

All-Time Iowa Individual Career Records

Points Scored .... Roy Marble (2,116, 1986-89)
Scoring Average .... Sam Williams (24.0, 1967-68)
Field Goals .... Roy Marble (787, 1986-89)
Field-Goal Attempts .... Roy Marble (1,459, 1986-89)
Free Throws Made .... Roy Marble (516, 1986-89)
Free-Throw Attempts .... Acie Earl (725, 1990-93)
3-Point Field Goals .... B. J. Armstrong (136, 1986-89)
Rebounds .... Kevin Kunnert (914, 1971-73)
Rebound Average .... Kevin Kunnert (12.7, 1971-73)
Assists .... B. J. Armstrong (517, 1986-89)
Steals .... Roy Marble (183, 1986-89)
Blocked Shots .... Acie Earl (365, 1990-93)

All-Time Iowa Individual Season Records

Points Scored .... John Johnson (699, 1969-70)
Scoring Average .... John Johnson (27.9, 1969-70)
Field Goals .... John Johnson (289, 1969-70)
Field-Goal Attempts .... Fred Brown (535, 1970-71)
Free Throws Made .... Sam Williams (194, 1967-68)
Free-Throw Attempts .... Don Nelson (268, 1960-61)
3-Point Field Goals .... Jeff Moe (71, 1987-88)
Rebounds .... Charles Darling (387, 1950-51)
Rebound Average .... Charles Darling (17.6, 1950-51)
Assists .... Cal Wulfsberg (191, 1975-76)
Steals .... Bill Jones (72, 1987-88)
Blocked Shots .... Acie Earl (121, 1991-92)

Iowa All-Americans and All-Big Ten Selections

Consensus All-Americans
Murray Wier, Forward, 1948
Chuck Darling, Center, 1962

All-Big Ten Selections (since 1948)
Murray Wier, Forward, 1948
Chuck Darling, Center, 1952
Bill Logan, Center, 1955-1956
Carl Cain, Forward, 1956
Dave Gunther, Forward, 1959

Don Nelson, Center-Forward, 1961-1962
Sam Williams, Forward, 1967-1968
John Johnson, Forward, 1970
Fred Brown, Guard, 1971
Ronnie Lester, Guard, 1978-1979
Kevin Boyle, Forward, 1981
Greg Stokes, Center, 1985
Ed Horton, Forward, 1989
Acie Earl, Center, 1992

Chapter 4

MICHIGAN *Wolverines*

Sagas of the Dynamic Duo and the New Fab Five

All-Time Record: 1,107-711, .610; **Conference Record:** 583-509, .530

Big Ten Championships —12: (1921*, 1926*, 1927, 1929*, 1948, 1964*, 1965, 1966, 1974*, 1977, 1985, 1986) * = Co-Champion

National (NCAA) Championships — 1: (1989)

National Invitation Tournament (NIT) Championships — 1: (1984)

Greatest Player: Cazzie Russell (1964-66)

Career Scoring Leader: Glen Rice (2,442 Points, 1986-89)

Most Successful Coach: Steve Fisher (1989-Present), 123-45, .730

All-Time Team: Chris Webber (C-F, 1991-93), Rudy Tomjanovich (F, 1968-70), Glen Rice (F, 1986-89), Gary Grant (G, 1985-88), Cazzie Russell (G, 1964-66)

Best Season: 1988-89 (30-7), NCAA Champions (Coaches: Steve Fisher and Bill Frieder)

University Profile

Location: Ann Arbor, Michigan (pop. 115,000); **Founded:** 1817; **Campus Enrollment:** 36,305 (1994); **Started Basketball:** 1917-18. The Big Ten's oldest university was moved to Ann Arbor in 1837, twenty years after the school's founding. As one of the nation's pioneering institutions of higher learning, Michigan boasts a number of impressive firsts: the nation's first university supported completely by public funds, the first university to own and operate a hospital, graduation of the first woman to practice law in the U.S., the nation's first program in aeronautical and nuclear engineering, the first courses in literature and pharmacy, and the first department of dentistry.

Team Nickname, Colors and Arena

Nickname: Wolverines; **Colors:** Maize and Blue; **Arena:** Crisler Arena (13,609 capacity, opened 1967). The small, ferocious, carnivorous mammal native to the Great Lakes region which serves as Michigan's sports mascot is noted for a combative nature and fierce fighting abilities. Thirteen All-American players, 12 Big Ten championship teams and numerous dramatic comeback victories (especially the ones that led to a storied 1989 NCAA championship) attest to the central role of the Wolverine basketball program in building the school's unparalleled athletic traditions.

Wolverines Basketball History

The basketballers at the University of Michigan have spent much of the past four decades imitating a very famous also-ran rental car company, gaining an undue measure of notoriety by capitalizing on the rank of second best. It is the Wolverines, after all, who have stumbled in the NCAA championship game a remarkable four times — 1965 to UCLA, 1976 to conference-rival Indiana, 1992 to Duke, 1993 to North Carolina — staking their claim to college hoopdom's imaginary trophy for tantalizing near misses.

While it is true that no other recent college team has been as excessively hyped and heralded as the Steve Fisher-coached Fab Five, it is equally true that none has been as quickly undone by the glare of overblown expectations or as repeatedly torpedoed by the oppressive weight of endless championship predictions. Not only would the 1990s Michigan Fab Five never reach potential and capture that elusive national title — the one all the ranking pundits predicted could be Michigan's for the mere asking — but they would never muster so much as a Big Ten championship banner, either.

Only when measured against this hopeless specter of damning "potential" is Michigan's latest super team so easily dismissed as an overblown championship bust. The team would remain intact only two seasons, and both years it would vault over all obstacles into the national title game. As freshmen, the 1992 Michigan "wonder five" unit featuring Chris Webber, Ray Jackson, Juwan Howard, Jalen Rose and Jimmy King overcame a third-place conference finish (itself attributable perhaps only to inevitable late-season inexperience) to close out the campaign as national runner-up. While Michigan's frosh were soundly pasted by a mature Duke team (71-51) in their Final Four shootout for the NCAA prize, it was consolation that never before had an all-freshman unit managed such lasting postseason magic. No all-frosh combination had ever made it into the national championship game and expectations for an eventual NCAA title — perhaps more than just one — somewhere during the three upcoming years were soon at fever pitch around Ann Arbor and everywhere else that college hoops is viewed more as a deep religious commitment than a mere recreational spectacle.

As sophomores, Webber and company again finished second-best in the conference race — bridemaids to Indiana's less-heralded Hoosiers — then once again met all the challenges of postseason competition only to fall to a more-experienced and polished ACC team in the NCAA title game. This time it was North Carolina providing the final barrier, and this time victory was nearer at hand only to slip away (77-71) due to costly turnovers in the final seconds.

Minus Webber, who after only two seasons succumbed to the lure of NBA dollars, the junior-year edition of the now somewhat tarnished Fab Five would again close strong in March as conference runners-up (this time trailing Purdue). But again they would fail late in the postseason title chase. When Michigan once more crash-landed (76-68) against eventual champion Arkansas in the Mideast Regional Finals in Dallas, an era of great promise and greater disappointment had abruptly ended. What was left was the mere shell of a once bright championship dream. Howard and Rose would also foresake remaining college eligibility for the mega-salaries of the professional game leaving only Jackson and King for a final crack at an increasingly elusive Big Ten title.

But the story doesn't quite stop here. Michigan's latter-day "Fab Five" can also lay claim to a second less-publicized form of "second-rate" status. For this was not even the original touted "Fab Five" of Big Ten conference history. The genuine Fabulous Five squad — as veteran conference boosters will immediately recall — was a legendary overachieving Iowa Hawkeyes ballclub that gamely battled Bill Russell and San Francisco University in the 1956 NCAA title matchup. (The label was also even earlier attached to Adolf Rupp's back-to-back Kentucky NCAA champions of 1948 and 1949, a scandal-plagued team featuring Alex Groza, Wah Wah Jones and Ralph Beard.) This legendary Iowa "Fab Five" contingent from four decades back played without benefit of today's boom in NCAA basketball and without the "prime-time" media coverage surrounding today's thoroughly pampered athletic teams. Yet the Iowa five matched and perhaps even surpassed on every count the modern-day Michigan version in both regular- (two Big Ten titles) and postseason play.

The Michigan Fab Five seemingly made a whole short-lived career of playing the role of "second-best" team around. Their climb to the championship showdown with Duke in 1992 was a truly unprecedented feat for so raw and inexperienced a ballclub — despite the awesome talent level of players like Webber, Rose and Howard. But the 20-point thrashing by a talented Duke team in the title match demonstrated that the much-publicized Wolves were hardly invincible. With its easy victory, Duke, led by prototype point guard Bobby Hurley and offense-minded forward Christian Laettner, became the first back-to-back NCAA champion since John Wooden's UCLA Bruins.

After a school-record 31 victories a season later, the heralded Fab Five, as expected, returned to the NCAA Finals, this time to meet another veteran ACC powerhouse team, North Carolina. Again, the Michigan youngsters would stumble and this time the defeat would be an even more bitter pill to swallow. Uncharacteristic sloppy offensive play and a huge mental blunder (Webber calling for a last-second time out when the team had none left) marred the closing moments of a tight 77-71 defeat and cancelled a stellar effort by the super group of sophomores. With only Webber missing from the junior-year edition, Fisher's talented unit would again underachieve in a big way. After falling flat in the Big Ten race to NCAA player-of-the-year Glenn Robinson and his Purdue Boilermakers during the final week of the conference campaign, Michigan lost out on a third-straight Final Four appearance by succumbing to eventual champion Arkansas (78-71) in the Midwest Regional championship game.

Michigan's role as a second-place team has more historical roots, however. There were the two straight trips to the NCAA Final Four in the mid-60s when the powerhouse tandem of Cazzie Russell and Bill Buntin, known nationally as "the Dynamic Duo," could bring home no more than a semifinal loss to Duke on their first crack at the title (hardly assuaged by a third-place consolation win over Kansas State) and a defeat in the title game the next year by John Wooden's UCLA Bruins. There were four straight seasons in the first or second slot in the conference derby during the mid-70s as well, which only meant another wasted trip to the final showdown and yet another loss in the NCAA finale. And there have been six finishes in second or third slot in the Big Ten over the past seven seasons without a single championship banner to show for such continuous top-notch efforts.

Even when the Wolverines were blessed with their two finest players and arguably their best top-to-bottom team as well, fate still was stacked against them; fate and some inexorably bad timing. The combo of the flashy Russell at guard and the powerful Buntin at center would post a 47-9 (.839) record during their two years together, good enough for two first-place conference finishes and two Final Four visits. On balance, the two seasons of Russell-Buntin would clearly outstrip the two seasons when the Fab Five played as a unit; the later team stood 56-14 (.800) with no Big Ten titles despite two Final Four visits. The numbers give the edge to Russell and Buntin (with their supporting cast of Jim Myers and John Thompson in the backcourt and Larry Tregoning and Oliver Dardin at the forwards) over the Webber-Rose-Howard-Jackson-King unit. But the 1963-65 Michigan clubs would have the misfortune of playing on the heels of the great Ohio State teams of 1960-62 which featured Jerry Lucas, Larry Siegfried and John Havlicek. And when it comes to nostalgic talk about Big Ten basketball in the 1960s it is almost always the Buckeyes and not the Wolverines who are recalled and revered as the true glory team from one of the most memorable decades in conference history.

Russell and Buntin were indeed among the greatest duos in league history. Only a handful of other combos — Ohio State's Lucas and Havlicek, and perhaps Indiana's Scott May and Kent Benson in 1976 — could match up with them. But neither of the latter pairs posted anything comparable to the combined scoring numbers (48 points per game in 1964, 45.8 a season later). After being robbed of a title showdown with UCLA by a 91-80 semifinal upset by Duke in 1964, Coach Dave Strack's "Dynamic Duo" kept the Wolverines ranked No. 1 throughout the '65 season. Russell (25.7), now a junior, and Buntin (20.1), a senior, were burning the nets for 45.8 points per game. But in the title shootout with Wooden's Bruins, Strack's club would be unable to contain Gail Goodrich (42 points) and would fall by the same 91-80 count as the Duke game a season earlier. With Buntin gone in 1966, Russell's scoring would peak at 30.8 points per game and Michigan would stand atop the conference for a third straight year. But this time Kentucky would end national title dreams during Midwest Regional play.

Russell and Buntin would follow very different career routes after their departures from Ann Arbor. While Russell's memorable pro career was never quite the expected stuff of indisputable Hall of Fame caliber (12,377 points spread over a dozen NBA seasons), the "Jazzie Cazzie" legend continued to expand in new directions. Buntin's pro career by contrast was short-lived and mostly unproductive, consisting of one brief unglamorous season (7.7 points per game) with the Detroit Pistons after becoming Michigan's first player ever picked in the NBA draft. Just a few short years after stardom with the Wolverines, the talented Buntin met a tragic fate. The superb athlete mysteriously died of an unexplained heart ailment, collapsing during a private off-season workout on the basketball court which had been his life's stage.

Although it didn't win a national title, Michigan's 1965 team, which featured Cazzie Russell (33) and Bill Buntin (22) shown in action against Duke, may have been the greatest in school history. (University of Michigan photo)

The Russell-Buntin era featured the inauguration of a new showcase playing venue for the Wolverines. With the Russell-Buntin teams tearing up the conference in the mid-60s and interest in the sport at an all-time high in Ann Arbor, Athletic Director Fritz Crisler commissioned plans for a new facility to replace tiny and outdated Yost Fieldhouse, a dingy building which had been in continuous service since 1927. The new $7.2-million facility — which would appropriately bear Crisler's name but even more appropriately be informally dubbed "The House that Cazzie Russell Built" — would open it doors on Dec. 12, 1967, with a showcase inaugural game against national powerhouse Kentucky. And it would be a memorable debut as sophomore All-American candidate Rudy Tomjanovich established a school record which still stands by corralling 27 rebounds in a losing effort (96-79) against the Wildcats.

The ritual of near misses would continue in almost eerie fashion a full decade after the departure of Russell and company. This time the protagonist would be what may have been Michigan's second-best team ever, a ballclub coached by Johnny Orr and paced by Phil Hubbard in the post and Rickey Green at guard. Behind Green's 19.9 scoring and Hubbard's rebounding prowess the 1975-76 Wolverines sprinted to a 25-7 overall record and a runner-up 14-4 Big Ten mark. Even Strack's best clubs with Russell and Buntin had never reached the 25-game victory plateau. But as good as this Michigan team was, the Indiana Hoosiers of Bob Knight were even better. Indiana owned an 18-0 league tally sheet and boasted an unblemished 27-0 overall record entering NCAA play. Michigan would continue its winning ways in the postseason with victories over Wichita State (74-73), Notre Dame (80-76), Missouri (95-88) and finally Rutgers (86-70) in the national semifinal game. But Knight's club would continue to win as well, setting up an all-Big Ten final for the first time in league and NCAA history.

Clearly fate, history and the multi-talented Hoosiers were heavily stacked against the Maize and Blue and the result was a second NCAA championship-game defeat for Michigan, this time to the tune of a solid 86-68 thrashing that was even more one-sided than the final score might indicate. Scott May, Quinn Buckner and Kent Benson combined for 36 of Indiana's first 38 points of the second half and the rout was immediately on. Michigan's hopes of a title died for good when sensational freshman center Phil Hubbard fouled out of the contest with more than seven minutes to play.

Johnny Orr's contingent of Green and Hubbard rebounded from its 1976 NCAA title defeat to rack up another conference crown in 1977 and establish its own spot near the top of the pecking order of great Michigan teams. The 1977 outfit (with Hubbard and Green averaging 19.6 and 19.5 points per game, respectively) finished 26-4 overall and won the Big Ten by two games over a Purdue squad featuring future NBAers Walter Jordan, Tom Scheffler and Joe Barry Carroll. Again postseason proved to be the bugaboo as an unheralded University of North Carolina-Charlotte team ended the Wolves' title dreams with a 75-68 defeat during an Eastern Regional championship matchup.

Another great Michigan team was the two-year 1985 and 1986 outfits coached by Bill Frieder and led into battle by a starting lineup of Roy Tarpley in the post, Richard Rellford and Butch Wade at the forwards, and Antoine Joubert and Gary Grant at guards. This club would post 26-4 and 28-5 marks and reign as conference titlists both seasons. But when it came down to postseason tests, the record of late-season failures would continue, first with a 1985 defeat at the hands of eventual champion Villanova (59-55) and a 72-69 upset loss in 1986 against Iowa State, both in the second round.

The ultimate achievement of Michigan basketball was of course the storybook team which finally ended the runner-up spell and brought a national championship to Ann Arbor. Magic finally transpired for the Maize and Blue during the unforgettable 1988-89 campaign, a topsy-turvy affair which began with Bill Frieder at the helm and ended with a rookie interim head coach named Steve Fisher taking the Wolverines to a national title before he ever lost his first game or coached a single regular-season contest. The most charmed of all Michigan teams achieved its magical run in the most mysterious of ways.

The 1989 NCAA tournament was a saga of a bona fide "team of destiny" somehow overcoming overwhelming odds to shock the entire collegiate basketball world. First Bill Frieder astounded press and fans at home and around the country by announcing just before the start of tournament play that he had accepted a position at Arizona State for the coming season. Michigan officials had little choice but to dismiss immediately a coach whose loyalties and focus would be no longer placed squarely on the tournament-bound Michigan program. Fisher, a longtime assistant and Frieder's top man for seven seasons, was hastily approved as interim

Rumeal Robinson's two free throws with three seconds left in overtime gave Michigan an unlikely NCAA championship in 1989. He followed that by leading Michigan in scoring the following season. (University of Michigan photo)

replacement only two days before the opening NCAA tipoff. Surprisingly, the unsettled Michigan team kept its feet firmly on the ground and staved off first Xavier (92-87) and then South Alabama (91-82) to advance into regional championship play. Then came a crucial revenge match against North Carolina and veteran coach Dean Smith, a team which had eliminated Michigan from postseason play in both of the previous two years. The third try proved to be the charm for the hot-shooting Wolverines who won by a 92-87 count. A 102-65 slaughter of Virginia opened the door to the Final Four.

In the semifinal shootout, Michigan was matched up with Big Ten rival Illinois which already had beaten the Wolverines twice during league play, including the final regular-season contest which decided second place. But Fisher had his newly inherited club on an emotional roll and the ancient league rivals battled to the wire in a game which saw seven lead changes down the stretch. A buzzer-beating shot by Sean Higgins was enough to dispatch the Illini by a slim 83-81 count. After overhauling Illinois, Michigan faced off with the surprising Seton Hall Pirates in a battle of true Cinderella teams. Michigan opened a 37-32 halftime cushion but improved defense brought the Big East team back to a 71-71 deadlock as time expired. The resulting overtime was the first in an NCAA finale since the 1963 shootout between Loyola and Cincinnati. Two Rumeal Robinson free throws with three seconds left decided the outcome. The 1989 NCAA tourney had certainly not been designed for Michigan fans with weak hearts; three of five dramatic games had been decided with stretch-run heroics and two with last-second shots. With his clutch free throws, Robinson had earned for himself a claim to personal hoops immortality, and for Michigan some overdue national basketball respect.

While the Wolverines have often disappointed their fans when it comes to winning that coveted "big one" during postseason play, there have nonetheless been many fine Wolverine teams across eight decades which have witnessed Michigan's participation in Big Ten play. The very first Western Conference team wearing Michigan maize and blue debuted inauspiciously in 1917-18 with an uninspired 0-10 conference mark. Success soon followed, however, with four conference titles in the 1920s under E.J. Mather (1921, 1926, 1927) and successor George Veenker (1929). Early versatile two-sport hero Bennie Oosterbaan (basketball All-American in '27 and '28 and football All-American three times) soon followed his brilliant undergraduate playing career with an eight-year coaching stint during the World War II era. But Oosterbaan's talents did not extend to the sidelines and this was a painful period of also-ran ballclubs for the Michiganders. Oosterbaan's clubs never finished a Big Ten schedule above the .500 mark. The short two-year stint of Osborne Cowles, which followed Oosterbaan's forgettable tenure, finally brought another league title in 1948 on the eve of the modern era of play. But the decade of the '50s witnessed little that was inspired beyond the all-star play of center Ron Kramer.

Dave Strack coached for two seasons after the departure of Buntin (1965) and Russell (1966). His final two teams would fall below .500 and the only highlight of those transition seasons was the arrival of Rudy Tomjanovich, the greatest rebounder in Michigan basketball annals. Strack's tenure was followed immediately by Orr's 12-year reign. This was destined to be one of the most consistent epochs of Wolverine basketball as Orr slowly built the best conference and non-conference records (measured by total victories) in Wolverine coaching history. Orr's teams would also win two more coveted league titles. The first came in 1974 when the All-American play of forward Campy Russell (23.7 points per game) — one of the most highly touted high school recruits in basketball history — was enough to fashion a first-place deadlock with Bobby Knight's Indiana Hoosiers. The second fell in 1977, following the NCAA championship loss to those same Hoosiers. The "Orr Years" would also showcase Henry Wilmore (two-time All-American forward in 1971 and 1972, 25 points per game scorer his sophomore campaign), Rickey Green (a 1975 junior college transfer who became one of the most tenacious defensive players in school and league history), Phil Hubbard (leading scorer on the 1977 team which paced the Big Ten in scoring as well as victories), and Mike McGee (the first Wolverine since Russell to climb over the 2,000-point plateau). McGee was the least heralded of the lot yet the future Los Angeles Laker would finish his career as Michigan's greatest career scorer (2,439 points) until the onslaught of Glen Rice.

The bridge between Johnny Orr and Steve Fisher was provided by the charismatic Bill Frieder, master of the Michigan coaching slot for nine seasons spanning the 1980s. In addition to the back-to-back Big Ten titles of '85 and '86, the "Frieder Years" produced three 20-win seasons (four counting his "unfinished" campaign of 1989) plus a bonus 1984 NIT championship capped with a resounding 83-63 Madison Square Garden victory over ancient rival Notre Dame. Frieder's 191 overall and 98 Big Ten wins place him second to Orr in both categories on the all-time Michigan list. This period was also memorable for the all-star play of Roy Tarpley (career and single-season leader in blocked shots), Gary Grant (career assists and steals leader, consensus 1988 All-American), Glen Rice (current Wolverine all-time career leader in points scored and games played) and Rumeal Robinson (star of the 1989 NCAA finals, second on the all-time Michigan assists list).

But inexplicably, at the very moment of his impending greatest triumph during the NCAA title run of 1989, Frieder would walk away from all the glory and from the Michigan program he had so carefully nurtured, abandoning the personal glory surrounding a team that he had built from scratch and molded into a solid national championship unit. In hindsight, Frieder's "resignation" on the eve of the NCAA tournament remains perhaps the most misguided personal career decision in NCAA coaching history. On a more positive note for Michigan fans, of course, Frieder's departure also worked to make an instant legend out of Steve Fisher. Never has a long-patient assistant coach been handed a more golden opportunity and never has a coach made more of his unexpected stroke of outlandish good fortune. The Michigan team that Fisher would be handed not only made him the first "interim" coach ever to pilot an NCAA club, but that team also was only the third in history to produce three first-round NBA draft choices off the same college starting five.

Michigan basketball is today poised to enter the post-Fab Five era and thus struggles to emerge from the long shadows cast by a failed championship dream. Anywhere else — and with any other team — two trips to the Final Four would likely result in near euphoria. But this was a Michigan team that was supposed to win it all and do it all more than once. While the Fab Five fell short of lofty — and perhaps outrageous and unreasonable — expectations, Fisher has already built a most impressive coaching legacy. Only two other coaches (ironically both Big Ten members), Illinois' Harry Combes and Ohio State's Fred Taylor, have made three trips to the NCAA Final Four during their first five years on the job. Fisher's NCAA tournament winning percentage (17-3, .850, five appearances and three Final Fours in six seasons) now stands as the unrivaled best in history among coaches who have logged at least 10 tournament games. It is a record that can not be matched by Indiana's Knight, Duke's Krzyzewski, Kentucky's legendary Adolph Rupp, or even UCLA's perennial 1970s champion John Wooden. Given Michigan's history of great recruiting classes and Fisher's postseason track record, another march to the top may not be very far down the road.

Records and Summaries
Year-by-Year Michigan Records
(Championship Years in Boldface)

Season	All Games	Conference	Coach(es)	Top Scorer (Points)
1917-18	6-12	0-10	Elmer Mitchell	No Record
1918-19	18-6	5-5	Elmer Mitchell	No Record
1919-20	10-13	3-9	E.J. Mather	No Record
1920-21	**16-4**	**8-4 (1st-T)**	**E.J. Mather**	**No Record**
1921-22	15-4	8-4	E.J. Mather	No Record
1922-23	11-4	8-4	E.J. Mather	No Record
1923-24	10-7	6-6	E.J. Mather	No Record
1924-25	8-6	6-5	E.J. Mather	No Record
1925-26	**12-5**	**8-4 (1st-T)**	**E.J. Mather**	**No Record**
1926-27	**14-3**	**10-2 (1st)**	**E.J. Mather**	**No Record**
1927-28	10-7	7-5	E.J. Mather	Bennie Oosterbaan (129)•
1928-29	**13-3**	**10-2 (1st-T)**	**George Veenker**	**No Record**
1929-30	9-5	6-4	George Veenker	No Record
1930-31	13-4	8-4	George Veenker	No Record
1931-32	11-6	8-4	Frank Cappon	No Record
1932-33	10-8	8-4	Frank Cappon	No Record
1933-34	6-14	4-8	Frank Cappon	No Record
1934-35	8-12	2-10	Frank Cappon	No Record
1935-36	15-5	7-5	Frank Cappon	No Record
1936-37	16-4	9-3	Frank Cappon	No Record
1937-38	12-8	6-6	Frank Cappon	No Record
1938-39	11-9	4-8	Bennie Oosterbaan	No Record
1939-40	13-7	6-6	Bennie Oosterbaan	No Record
1940-41	9-10	5-7	Bennie Oosterbaan	Mike Sofiak (168)
1941-42	6-14	5-10	Bennie Oosterbaan	Jim Mandler (230)
1942-43	10-8	4-8	Bennie Oosterbaan	Jim Mandler (147)
1943-44	8-10	5-7	Bennie Oosterbaan	No Record
1944-45	12-7	5-7	Bennie Oosterbaan	Walt Kell (111)
1945-46	12-7	6-6	Bennie Oosterbaan	Glenn Selbo (213)
1946-47	12-8	6-6	Osborne Cowles	Mack Suprunowicz (228)
1947-48	**16-6**	**10-2 (1st)**	**Osborne Cowles**	**Mack Suprunowicz (242)**
1948-49	15-6	7-5	Ernest McCoy	Mack Suprunowicz (257)
1949-50	11-11	4-8	Ernest McCoy	Mack Suprunowicz (279)
1950-51	7-15	3-11	Ernest McCoy	Leo Vanderkuy (338)
1951-52	7-15	4-10	Ernest McCoy	Jim Skala (257)
1952-53	6-16	3-15	William Perigo	Paul Groffsky (301)
1953-54	9-13	3-11	William Perigo	Jim Barron (374)

1954-55	11-11	5-9	William Perigo	Ron Kramer (352)
1955-56	9-13	4-10	William Perigo	Ron Kramer (448)
1956-57	13-9	8-6	William Perigo	George Lee (334)
1957-58	11-11	6-8	William Perigo	Pete Tillotson (415)
1958-59	15-7	8-6	William Perigo	M.C. Burton (460)•
1959-60	4-20	1-13	William Perigo	John Tidwell (520)
1960-61	6-18	2-12	Dave Strack	John Tidwell (441)
1961-62	7-17	5-9	Dave Strack	Tom Cole (361)
1962-63	16-8	8-6	Dave Strack	Bill Buntin (534)
1963-64	**23-5**	**11-3 (1st-T)**	**Dave Strack**	**Cazzie Russell (694)**
1964-65	**24-4**	**13-1 (1st)**	**Dave Strack**	**Cazzie Russell (670)**
1965-66	**18-8**	**11-3 (1st)**	**Dave Strack**	**Cazzie Russell (800)•**
1966-67	8-16	2-12	Dave Strack	Craig Dill (471)
1967-68	11-13	6-8	Dave Strack	Rudy Tomjanovich (469)
1968-69	13-11	7-7	Johnny Orr	Rudy Tomjanovich (617)
1969-70	10-14	5-9	Johnny Orr	Rudy Tomjanovich (722)
1970-71	19-7	12-2	Johnny Orr	Henry Wilmore (650)
1971-72	14-10	9-5	Johnny Orr	Henry Wilmore (479)
1972-73	13-11	6-8	Johnny Orr	Henry Wilmore (523)
1973-74	**22-5**	**12-2 (1st-T)**	**Johnny Orr**	**Campy Russell (640)•**
1974-75	19-8	12-6	Johnny Orr	C.J. Kupec (489)
1975-76	25-7	14-4	Johnny Orr	Rickey Green (638)
1976-77	**26-4**	**16-2 (1st)**	**Johnny Orr**	**Phil Hubbard (588)**
1977-78	16-11	11-7	Johnny Orr	Mike McGee (531)
1978-79	15-12	8-10	Johnny Orr	Mike McGee (511)
1979-80	17-13	8-10	Johnny Orr	Mike McGee (665)
1980-81	19-11	8-10	Bill Frieder	Mike McGee (732)
1981-82	8-19	7-11	Bill Frieder	Eric Turner (398)
1982-83	16-12	7-11	Bill Frieder	Eric Turner (519)
1983-84**	24-9	11-9	Bill Frieder	Roy Tarpley (413)
1984-85	**26-4**	**16-2 (1st)**	**Bill Frieder**	**Roy Tarpley (570)**
1985-86	**28-5**	**14-4 (1st)**	**Bill Frieder**	**Roy Tarpley (526)**
1986-87	20-12	10-8	Bill Frieder	Gary Grant (716)
1987-88	26-8	13-5	Bill Frieder	Glen Rice (728)•
1988-89#	30-7	12-6	Bill Frieder/Steve Fisher	Glen Rice (949)•
1989-90	23-8	12-6	Steve Fisher	Rumeal Robinson (575)
1990-91	14-15	7-11	Steve Fisher	Demetrius Calip (594)
1991-92	25-9	11-7	Steve Fisher	Jalen Rose (597)
1992-93	31-5	15-3	Steve Fisher	Chris Webber (690)
1993-94	24-8	13-5	Steve Fisher	Jalen Rose (636)

= National (NCAA) Champions; ** = NIT Champions; • = League Individual Scoring Champion

All-Time Michigan Individual Career Records

Points Scored .... Glen Rice (2,442, 1986-89)
Scoring Average .... Cazzie Russell (27.1, 1964-66)
Games Played.. Glen Rice (134, 1986-89)
Games Started .... Gary Grant (128, 1985-88)
Field Goals .... Mike McGee (1010, 1978-81)
Field-Goal Percentage .... Loy Vaught (.617, 1987-90)
Free Throws Made .... Cazzie Russell (486, 1964-66)
Free-Throw Percentage .... Cazzie Russell (.828, 1964-66)
3-Point Field Goals .... Glen Rice (135, 1986-89)
Rebounds .... Rudy Tomjanovich (1039, 1968-70)
Rebound Average... Rudy Tomjanovich (14.4, 1968-70)
Assists .... Gary Grant (731, 1985-88)
Steals .... Gary Grant (300, 1985-88)
Blocked Shots .... Roy Tarpley (251, 1983-86)

All-Time Michigan Individual Season Records

Points Scored .... Glen Rice (949, 1988-89)
Scoring Average .... Cazzie Russell (30.7, 1965-66)
Field Goals .... Glen Rice (363, 1988-89)
Field Goal Pct. .... Loy Vaught (.661, 1988-89)
Free Throws Made .... Cazzie Russell (184, 1965-66)
Free-Throw Pct. .... Cazzie Russell (.840, 1963-64)
3-Pt. Field Goals .... Glen Rice (99, 1988-89)
Rebounds .... Phil Hubbard (389, 1976-77)
Rebound Average... M.C. Burton (17.2, 1958-59)
Assists .... Gary Grant (234, 1987-88)
Steals .... Gary Grant (86, 1986-87)
Blocked Shots .... Roy Tarpley (97, 1985-86)

All-Time Michigan Individual Single-Game Records

Points Scored .... Cazzie Russell (48 vs. Northwestern, 3-5-66)
                                                     Rudy Tomjanovich (48 vs. Indiana, OT, 1-7-69)
Field Goals .... Rudy Tomjanovich (21 vs. Indiana, OT, 1-7-69)
Free Throws Made .... Tom Cole (17 vs. Indiana, 2-26-92)
3-Pt. Field Goals ....Garde Thompson (9 vs. Navy, 3-12-87)
Rebounds .... Rudy Tomjanovich (30 vs. Loyola, OT, 2-1-69)
Assists .... Gary Grant (14 vs. Western Michigan, 12-7-87)

A 1974 All-American, Campy Russell, above left, was a Big Ten scoring champion while Rudy Tomjanovich, left, current coach of the NBA's Houston Rockets, was a 1970 All-American averaging 30 points and 15 rebounds per game. Above, Gary Grant takes a shot but is Michigan's career and single-season leader in assists and steals. (University of Michigan photos)

All-Time Michigan Coaching Records

Coach	Overall Record	Conference Record	Seasons
Johnny Orr (1968-80)	209-113 (.649)	120-72 (.625)	12
Bill Frieder (1980-89)	191-87 (.687)	98-64 (.604)	9
Dave Strack (1960-68)	113-89 (.559)	58-54 (.518)	8
Steve Fisher (1989-Present)	123-45 (.730)	58-32 (.644)	5
E. J. Mather (1919-28)	106-53 (.667)	64-43 (.598)	9
Bennie Oosterbaan (1938-46)	81-72 (.529)	40-59 (.404)	8
Frank Cappon (1931-38)	78-57 (.578)	44-40 (.524)	7
William Perigo (1952-60)	78-100 (.438)	38-78 (.328)	8
Ernie McCoy (1948-52)	40-47 (.460)	18-34 (.346)	4
George Veenker (1928-31)	35-12 (.745)	24-10 (.706)	3
Osborne Cowles (1946-48)	28-14 (.667)	16-8 (.667)	2
Elmer Mitchell (1917-19)	24-18 (.571)	5-15 (.250)	2

Michigan All-Americans and All-Big Ten Selections

Consensus All-Americans
Cazzie Russell, Guard, 1965-1966
Rudy Tomjanovich, Forward, 1970
Henry Wilmore, Forward, 1971-1972
Campy Russell, Forward, 1974
Rickey Green, Guard, 1977
Gary Grant, Guard, 1988
Chris Webber, Forward, 1993

All-Big Ten Selections (since 1948)
Pete Elliott, Guard, 1948
Bob Harrison, Guard, 1948-1949
M. C. Burton, Forward, 1959
Bill Buntin, Center, 1963-1965
Cazzie Russell, Guard, 1964-1965-1966
Rudy Tomjanovich, Forward, 1969-1970
Henry Wilmore, Forward, 1971-1972
Campy Russell, Forward, 1974
Rickey Green, Guard, 1976-1977
Phil Hubbard, Center, 1977
Mike McGee Forward, 1978-1981
Roy Tarpley, Center, 1985-1986
Gary Grant, Guard, 1987-1988
Glen Rice, Forward, 1988-1989
Rumeal Robinson, Guard, 1990
Chris Webber, Forward, 1993
Juwan Howard, Center, 1994

Chapter 5

MICHIGAN STATE *Spartans*

One "Magic" Season for the New Kids on the Block

All-Time Record: 1,094-851, .562; **Conference Record:** 344-356, .490

Big Ten Championships — 6: (1957*, 1959, 1967*, 1978, 1979*, 1990)
* = Co-Champion

National (NCAA) Championships —1: (1978-79)

Greatest Player: Earvin "Magic" Johnson (1977-79)

Career Scoring Leader: Steve Smith (2,263 Points, 1988-91)

Most Successful Coach: Jud Heathcote (1976-Present), 318-214, .598

All-Time Team: Jay Vincent (C-F, 1978-81), Greg Kelser (F, 1976-79), Steve Smith (G-F, 1988-91), Scott Skiles (G, 1983-86), Earvin "Magic" Johnson (G, 1978-79)

Best Season: 1978-79 (26-6), NCAA Champion (Coach: Jud Heathcote)

University Profile

Location: East Lansing, Michigan (pop. 51,392); **Founded:** 1855; **Campus Enrollment:** 40,047 (1994); **Started Basketball:** 1898-99. Boasting such distinguished alumni as actor James Caan, author Peter Gent, baseballer Kirk Gibson, and 1969 Nobel Prize winner Alfred Hershey (medicine), MSU offers one of the top five medical schools in the nation, as well as the largest university housing system on any U.S. college campus.

Team Nickname, Colors and Arena

Nickname: Spartans (since 1926); **Colors:** Green and White; **Arena:** Jack Breslin Student Events Center (15,138 capacity, opened 1989). Legend has it that Michigan State's "Spartan" nickname originated during the school's first southern baseball spring tour back in 1926. A campus write-in contest had occurred the previous fall to replace an older and no longer appropriate "Aggies" moniker which had been sported back when the school was still officially the Michigan Agricultural College. The winning entry according to school officials had been "The Michigan Staters" but the choice was not at all palatable to George S. Alderton, sports editor of the *Lansing State Journal*. When Alderton substituted his own choice of "Spartans" (which he first spelled as "Spartons" until tipped off about his error by friends) in baseball game accounts that spring, a lasting university tradition was born as such traditions are most often born — more of narrow personal whim than of universal democratic wish.

Spartan Basketball History

Despite a bevy of talented stars and the long tenure of one of the league's most skilled and successful coaches, MSU basketball nonetheless has long managed to remain something of a "poor cousin" in Big Ten play. For starters, only one Spartan team — the Magic Johnson-led 1979 NCAA champion — has grabbed any true measure of national prominence. And despite all the remarkable talent emanating from East Lansing — this was the second school, after Purdue, to boast three different back-to-back league scoring champions — only one MSU player (Johnson) has ever been a consensus first-team All-America selection. In the eyes of fans anywhere other than East Lansing, Michigan State basketball history seemingly peaks with 1979, the NCAA tournament and the saga of Magic Johnson versus Larry Bird. Compared to the Purdues, Indianas, Ohio States, or even the neighboring Wolverines of Michigan, there is little else to crow about concerning MSU's basketball wars.

Indeed, for hoop fans tied by geography or loyalty to the campus at East Lansing, it will always imaginatively be the era of Magic Johnson and Greg "Special K" Kelser — at least in that perfect world of sweet and unfailing memory. For the very first time during that one glorious season a decade and a half ago, the Spartans were the reigning Big Ten titlests for a second year in a row. And for the first time ever Michigan State was competing in the prestigious NCAA postseason classic for a second straight season. The most colorful player in school history (Johnson) was in full control of the playmaking, and one of the best all-around performers in school annals (Kelser) was also on hand and leading the balanced scoring parade. That marvelous winter would be capped, in true storybook fashion, with one of the most dramatic and widely hyped NCAA Finals ever. Magic dueled with Larry Bird during March Madness, and in the end, the Spartans, for the first and so far only time, ruled the basketball world as national champions. It was truly the best and most unforgettable of times.

The short-lived "Magic Johnson Era" actually began a season earlier. The maiden campaign with the talented home-grown freshman in the lineup saw the Spartans capture their first Big Ten title in 11 winters and the first under second-year coach Jud Heathcote. Heathcote himself was newly arrived from a successful five-year tenure at the University of Montana. The 25-5 overall mark compiled that season was a Michigan State record for total victories. No previous Spartan edition had ever topped the 19 wins of Forrest Anderson's 1959 team, also

Guard Scott Skiles scored 850 points in 1986. It still stands as a Michigan State record. (Michigan State photo)

the last MSU ballclub to claim an outright conference crown.

   After a "Magical" Big Ten season, marred only by losses to Indiana, Michigan and Purdue, the Spartans would make their first serious run at the NCAA field since the first tourney entrant had charged all the way to the Final Four back in 1957. With Magic Johnson hobbled by a bruised ankle, the Big Ten champs nonetheless prevailed over Providence College (77-53) in a Mideast Regional opener at Indianapolis. In round two at Dayton, Heathcote's gutsy team coasted over Western Kentucky as Greg Kelser enjoyed a second straight 23-point outing. But the encouraging season finally ground to a sudden halt with a hard-fought 52-49 loss to perennial power Kentucky during the Mideast Regional championship tilt just two days later.

   Momentum was hardly derailed for Heathcote's charges by the season-ending setback to Kentucky, however. With senior Kelser and sophomore Johnson reporting back, and center-forward Jay Vincent growing into a starting role for his sophomore season, the Spartans were indeed more potent than ever. Three quick wins out of the gate signalled a fast getaway before a loss to always tough North Carolina provided something of a momentary reality check. Mid-season saw another win streak which reached six before a pair of exasperating two-point losses to Illinois and Purdue launched the Big Ten portion of the schedule. In what was apparently destined to be a season full of such streaks, the Spartans rebounded to rattle off 10 uninterrupted conference victories before an upset loss to Wisconsin in the final regular-season match. It was good enough for a first-place tie in the Big Ten (with Purdue and Iowa), a new record for team victories (26-6), plus another long-awaited crack at the NCAA title.

   Led by Kelser's scoring and Johnson's aggressive rebounding and stellar playmaking, the Spartans breezed through early-round games with Lamar (95-64) and LSU (87-71). Kelser then spurred a total team effort against neighboring Notre Dame (80-68) that would earn a well-deserved trip back into the Final Four. This time the competition would be Ivy League champ Pennsylvania, independent powerhouse DePaul, and the nation's leading team, undefeated Indiana State and the already legendary Larry Bird. To open college basketball's showcase weekend at the Salt Lake City Special Events Center, the Big Ten team kept its half of a date with destiny by thrashing outmanned Penn 101-67 in one of the most one-sided semifinal get-togethers of recent memory.

   The 1979 NCAA Finals thus came down to a dream matchup between the season's two most glamorous players and two of its true Cinderella teams. Indiana State (33-1) had long played an unglamorous small-college schedule and held no previous claims on basketball fortune and fame. Then came the arrival of an untutored youngster named Larry Bird from a small-town Indiana background. Bird's workmanlike style of play spelled sudden overnight success for the Sycamores. Michigan State (26-6) was an equally unfamiliar visitor to basketball's March Madness mountain top. But the hometown high school star from East Lansing who carried the Big Ten's hopes had in two short seasons pulled Michigan State into its first-ever NCAA title game.

   This was the kind of glamorous one-on-one shootout of two season-long superstars which conjured memories of George Mikan versus Bob Kurland in the 1945 postseason matchup of NCAA and NIT champs, or perhaps of Bill Russell versus Tom Gola in the 1955 NCAA championship slugfest. Bird and Magic would soon become titans of their sport at the pro level and megastars most responsible for the explosion of basketball interest in the early '80s. In retrospect, their first face-to-face meeting was a bona fide historical landmark in the evolution of college basketball. But at the time, it was simply one of the most anticipated and media-hyped Final Four matchups in years. And the title game certainly lived up to all its advanced billing as Magic Johnson (24 points, 7 rebounds, 5 assists) outdueled Larry Bird (19 points, 13 rebounds, 2 assists, but only 33 percent shooting) down the stretch providing Michigan State with its finest basketball hour. Guard Terry Donnelly also provided plenty of fireworks in the Spartans' greatest game ever, hitting 13 of his 15 points down the stretch of the 75-64 MSU victory when a desperate ISU defense collapsed heavily on Kelser and Johnson in the second half and left Donnelly wide open to do the crucial damage.

Only one earlier Spartan edition had ever approached the heroic levels of the 1979 dream team. This was the 1956-57 club which debuted with a talented sophomore phenom named "Jumpin' Johnny" Green. The spindly 6-foot-5 center quickly established himself as one of the most ambitious rebounders in the league and one of its highest-flying jump shooters. It was a team coached by Forrest "Forddy" Anderson and also featured backcourt ace Jack Quiggle as the high scorer (15.4) at shooting guard and slender 6-5 junior Larry Hedden (14.3) at forward. Quiggle would earn honors that year — his junior season — as only the third bona fide All-American in school history. Despite only a 14-8 overall mark, this edition of the green and white managed a solid 10-4 ledger during the conference portion of the schedule to earn a first-ever Big Ten banner. And then came a string of surprising postseason outings recorded during MSU's maiden journey into the NCAA championship playdowns.

Traveling to Lexington, Ken., for Midwest Regional action, the Spartans clung to a narrow lead in the closing moments to edge Notre Dame 85-83 on the strength of Green's 27 rebounds. A bigger surprise came the next evening, however, when the underdog Spartans pulled off one of the biggest tournament shockers in years. MSU mounted a ferocious second-half comeback from a 12-point deficit at intermission and registered an 80-68 triumph over third-ranked Kentucky. The stunning upset marked only the fifth time that Adolph Rupp's Wildcats had been bested in their home quarters in 15 long years.

The NCAA finals of 1957 brought with it the most thrilling single game in school history. For sheer nail-biting drama, the MSU-North Carolina semifinal matchup that year was arguably among the most thrilling contests of NCAA history. The two scrappy clubs battled exhaustingly through three tense overtime periods that witnessed 21 ties and 31 lead changes in all. The top-ranked Tar Heels seemed to have victory at hand in the closing seconds of regulation play until Green snared an all-important rebound and fed Quiggle for an amazing half-court shot which proved to be a buzzer-beater. UNC finally pulled away in the third extra session behind All-American forward Lennie Rosenbluth, but only after Green missed a crucial charity toss that might have sealed victory in overtime period No. 2. This most incredible Final Four weekend was concluded a night later when leg-weary North Carolina somehow survived a second-straight (and much better known) three-overtime tussle with Wilt Chamberlain and the Kansas Jayhawks, while the exhausted Spartans dropped an anticlimactic 67-60 consolation game to San Francisco (sans Bill Russell) and thus had to settle for fourth place.

Johnny Green would follow in Jack Quiggle's footsteps with All-American honors of his own during his 1958-1959 junior and senior seasons, spiced by the school's first Big Ten MVP selection in 1959. During his stellar senior campaign Green, (18.5 points, 16.6 rebounds per game) would once more lead his Spartan teammates back into NCAA tournament play on the strength of the school's second 20-win season (20-4) and second conference title in three years. MSU finished exceptionally strong with 12 wins in the final 13 contests and six straight at season's end to ride a wave of growing confidence into the NCAA opener versus Marquette. Bob Anderegg (the season's high scorer at 19.5) and Horace Walker paced the scoring attack in a 74-69 win, but a day later only Johnny Green's 29 points could crack the talented defense of a taller and more gifted University of Louisville team. Michigan State thus fell quickly from contention with an 88-81 loss to the Cardinals.

The tumultuous 1960s at East Lansing would soon witness the Johnny Green-era being replaced by a four-year dry spell which saw one eighth- and three ninth-place conference finishes. Forddy Anderson's final season at the helm in 1965 was one of the worst campaigns in school history — 5-18 overall, 1-13 in Big Ten play, no memorable individual stars and almost no highlight moments to cheer for, either. A single league triumph over Purdue that season made it the only MSU team to win but one conference game during a season. But a revival loomed directly around the corner under replacement coach John Benington. Benington's initial 1966 campaign witnessed a dramatic rebound to 17-7 and a second-place conference finish. His second year brought a return to full health with a third league title, this time a deadlock with the Indiana Hoosiers. But in the days of a single Big Ten NCAA qualifier there would be no postseason play for the Spartans. Indiana went to the postseason dance instead and was toppled immediately in the second round. It proved to be the last hurrah for Benington whose final two seasons saw another rapid fall into the league's second division.

The 1970s era leading up to the decade-closing triumphs of Magic Johnson and company was an epoch most notable for the exploits of the Spartans' first two Big Ten Conference individual scoring champions. Mike Robinson pulled off the feat in 1972 (27.2 points in conference play) and again in 1973 (26.7). Forward Terry Furlow would duplicate Robinson's efforts in 1975 (21.4) and 1976 (32.7). Only Rick Mount (Purdue), Gary Bradds (Ohio State), Cazzie Russell (Michigan) and Terry Dischinger (Purdue) had posted better in-conference scoring marks than the one Furlow racked up during 1976.

The post-Magic years at MSU would bring four more league scoring champions. At the vanguard of this recent Spartan scoring parade was Johnson-era holdover Jay Vincent who averaged 22.1 points in 1980 and 24.1 in 1981. The muscular center-forward and future NBA standout was not only the school's third individual scoring titlest but also the third to post back-to-back victories in the point-making derby. The three repeat titles in individual scoring by Mike Robinson, Terry Furlow and Jay Vincent, however, were soon to be topped by an even rarer coincidence involving unusual doubles. This came when Jay's younger brother, Sam, paced Big Ten scorers (23.7) several seasons down the road. With Sam Vincent, Michigan State owned the first brother pair to rank as league-leading offensive players.

Guard Sam Vincent had saved his best offensive outburst for his senior season (1985) and was thus not around a year later to defend his scoring title. But the slack was picked up immediately by Vincent's backcourt mate, Scott Skiles, whose stellar 29.1 scoring (1986) assured the Spartans of still another set of back-to-back seasons dominating the league individual scoring category. A final Big Ten scoring title was also later won by future NBAer Steve Smith (23.2) in 1990-91.

Guard Sam Vincent followed in his brother Jay's footsteps to lead the Big Ten in scoring. They became the first brothers to win individual Big Ten scoring titles. (Michigan State photo)

Steve Smith can arguably be seen from today's vantage point as the finest all-around performer in Spartan history. Only Magic Johnson might edge the high-scoring Smith for that honor. Johnson's claim would have to rest on his dependable postseason NCAA play and on his all-around skills as scorer, rebounder and offensive general. There have been eight triple-doubles (double figures in scoring, rebounds and assists) registered in Spartan history and the man known as simply "Magic" still owns them all. Smith's credentials, by contrast, rest with his phenomenal scoring as the MSU career leader in total points (2,263) and with the smooth ballhandling and shooting skills which have already made him a high-profile NBA gate attraction for the NBA Miami Heat.

Indiana native Scott Skiles would also leave behind a considerable legacy as one of the finest performers during the long tenure of coach Jud Heathcote. The feisty Skiles would run the MSU offense in the mid-80s and for awhile own the school career scoring mark (2,145 points) before Smith arrived on the scene. Other school records set by Skiles and still on the books include career standards for field goals, free throw percentage, assists and steals; single-game high-water marks for points scored and field goals made; and a single-game mark for field goals which is shared with 1956 All-American forward Julius McCoy.

Heathcote's own final years in control of the Michigan State program would stretch throughout the entire decade of the '80s and into the mid-90s. Before the end of the 1994 20-12 campaign it had already been announced, however, that the veteran mentor was slated for retirement in the spring of 1995 and that longtime associate head coach Tom Izzo would be inheriting the Spartan program.

Recent seasons have also seen the Spartans move into a plush modern playing venue, the $43 million Jack Breslin Student Events Center, a significant upgrade over quaint but dated Jenison Fieldhouse. The historic inaugural year of play at the Breslin Center would fittingly be topped by a stellar 28-6 record (the best in school history) and a third and final Big Ten crown of the Heathcote reign. There would also be a third 20-win season for the decade in 1992, giving Heathcote an even half-dozen such benchmark campaigns. The Spartans would also return to post-season action in 1983 (lost in the NCAA second round), 1985 (lost in the first round), 1986 (lost the Midwest Regional semifinal), 1989 (lost the NIT semifinal), 1990 (lost the Southeast Regional semifinal), 1991 (lost in the second round), 1992 (again lost in the second round) and 1993 (lost in the first round). It was still business as usual for the always-competitive cage program at Michigan's younger Big Ten entrant.

The best player in Heathcote's final seasons in East Lansing has proven to be agile 6-3 guard Shawn Respert, one of the Big Ten's most potent offensive threats of the '90s (second in scoring in 1993-94 to Glenn Robinson of Purdue) and seemingly destined to follow Steve Smith and Scott Skiles into certain NBA stardom. Respert elevated spirits everywhere on the MSU campus when he bucked popular trends and bypassed an opportunity to leave school early for almost certain 1994 NBA draft lottery selection. With Respert still at the controls of the high-octane Spartan offense and coming off a productive (24.3 ppg) junior season, Heathcote's final tour around the league may yet prove one of the best of his colorful career.

Terry Furlow was the second of three Michigan State repeat Big Ten scoring champions and holds the MSU record for most points in a Big Ten season. (Michigan State photo)

Steve Smith not only was Michigan State's most prolific scorer, he was perhaps the most talented offensive player in school history. (Michigan State photo)

Records and Summaries
Year-by-Year Michigan State Records
(Championship Years in Boldface)

Season	All Games	Conference	Coach(es)	Top Scorer (Points)
1898-99	0-2	Not Member	No Coach	No Record
1899-00	2-2	Not Member	Charles Bemies	No Record
1900-01	3-0	Not Member	Charles Bemies	No Record
1901-02	5-0	Not Member	George Denman	No Record
1902-03	6-0	Not Member	George Denman	No Record
1903-04	5-3	Not Member	Chester Brewer	No Record
1904-05	5-3	Not Member	Chester Brewer	No Record
1905-06	11-2	Not Member	Chester Brewer	No Record
1907-07	14-2	Not Member	Chester Brewer	No Record
1907-08	15-5	Not Member	Chester Brewer	No Record
1908-09	10-5	Not Member	Chester Brewer	No Record
1909-10	10-5	Not Member	Chester Brewer	No Record
1910-11	5-9	Not Member	John Macklin	No Record
1911-12	12-3	Not Member	John Macklin	No Record
1912-13	8-5	Not Member	John Macklin	No Record
1913-14	8-4	Not Member	John Macklin	No Record
1914-15	7-9	Not Member	John Macklin	No Record
1915-16	8-8	Not Member	John Macklin	No Record
1916-17	11-5	Not Member	George Gauthier	No Record
1917-18	6-10	Not Member	George Gauthier	No Record
1918-19	9-9	Not Member	George Gauthier	No Record
1919-20	12-11	Not Member	George Gauthier	No Record
1920-21	13-8	Not Member	Lynn Frimodig	No Record
1921-22	11-13	Not Member	Lynn Frimodig	No Record
1922-23	10-9	Not Member	Fred Walker	No Record
1923-24	10-10	Not Member	Fred Walker	No Record
1924-25	6-13	Not Member	John Kobs	No Record
1925-26	5-13	Not Member	John Kobs	No Record
1926-27	7-11	Not Member	Ben VanAlstyne	Vern Dickeson (162)
1927-28	11-4	Not Member	Ben VanAlstyne	Vern Dickeson (100)
1928-29	11-5	Not Member	Ben VanAlstyne	Arthur Haga (99)
1929-30	12-4	Not Member	Ben VanAlstyne	Roger Grove (91)
1930-31	16-1	Not Member	Ben VanAlstyne	Roger Grove (135)
1931-32	12-5	Not Member	Ben VanAlstyne	Randy Boeskool (80)
1932-33	10-7	Not Member	Ben VanAlstyne	Gerald McCaslin (92)
1933-34	12-5	Not Member	Ben VanAlstyne	Maurice Buysse (126)
1934-35	14-4	Not Member	Ben VanAlstyne	A. Van Faasen (133)
1935-36	8-9	Not Member	Ben VanAlstyne	Ron Garlock (109)
1936-37	5-12	Not Member	Ben VanAlstyne	L. Oesterink (112)
1937-38	9-8	Not Member	Ben VanAlstyne	Geo. Falkowski (173)

1938-39	9-8	Not Member	Ben VanAlstyne	Geo. Falkowski (119)
1939-40	14-6	Not Member	Ben VanAlstyne	Chet Aubuchon (169)
1940-41	11-6	Not Member	Ben VanAlstyne	Max Hindman (144)
1941-42	15-6	Not Member	Ben VanAlstyne	Joe Gerard (239)
1942-43	2-14	Not Member	Ben VanAlstyne	John Cawood (118)
1943-44		*Cancelled (World War II)*		
1944-45	9-7	Not Member	Ben VanAlstyne	Sam Fortino (203)
1945-46	12-9	Not Member	Ben VanAlstyne	Sam Fortino (251)
1946-47	11-10	Not Member	Ben VanAlstyne	Bob Geahan (235)
1947-48	12-10	Not Member	Ben VanAlstyne	Bob Brannum (344)
1948-49	9-12	Not Member	Ben VanAlstyne	Bill Rapchak (211)
1949-50	4-18	Not Member	Alton Kircher	Dan Smith (207)
		Big Ten Conference		
1950-51	10-11	5-9	Pete Newell	Ray Steffen (186)
1951-52	13-9	6-8	Pete Newell	Keith Stackhouse (236)
1952-53	13-9	11-7	Pete Newell	Al Ferrari (351)
1953-54	9-13	4-10	Pete Newell	Julius McCoy (409)
1954-55	13-9	8-6	Forrest Anderson	Al Ferrari (442)
1955-56	13-9	7-7	Forrest Anderson	Julius McCoy (600)
1956-57	**16-10**	**10-4 (1st-T)**	**Forrest Anderson**	**Jack Quiggle (384)**
1957-58	16-6	9-5	Forrest Anderson	Johnny Green (397)
1958-59	**19-4**	**12-2 (1st)**	**Forrest Anderson**	**Bob Anderegg (450)**
1959-60	10-1	5-9	Forrest Anderson	Horace Walker (473)
1960-61	7-17	3-11	Forrest Anderson	Dick Hall (390)
1961-62	8-14	3-11	Forrest Anderson	Pete Gent (311)
1962-63	4-16	3-11	Forrest Anderson	Pete Gent (329)
1963-64	14-10	8-6	Forrest Anderson	Pete Gent (506)
1964-65	5-18	1-13	Forrest Anderson	Stan Washington (490)
1965-66	15-7	10-4	John Benington	Stan Washington (397)
1966-67	**16-7**	**10-4 (1st-T)**	**John Benington**	**Matthew Aitch (376)**
1967-68	12-12	6-8	John Benington	Lee Lafayette (405)
1968-69	11-12	6-8	John Benington	Lee Lafayette (430)
1969-70	9-15	5-9	Gus Ganakas	Ralph Simpson (667)
1970-71	10-14	4-10	Gus Ganakas	Rudy Benjamin (520)
1971-72	13-11	6-8	Gus Ganakas	Mike Robinson (594)•
1972-73	13-11	6-8	Gus Ganakas	Mike Robinson (608)•
1973-74	13-11	8-6	Gus Ganakas	Mike Robinson (515)
1974-75	17-9	10-8	Gus Ganakas	Terry Furlow (509)•
1975-76	14-13	10-8	Gus Ganakas	Terry Furlow (793)•
1976-77	12-15	9-9	Jud Heathcote	Greg Kelser (565)
1977-78	**25-5**	**15-3 (1st)**	**Jud Heathcote**	**Greg Kelser (531)**
1978-79#	**26-6**	**13-5 (1st-T)**	**Jud Heathcote**	**Greg Kelser (602)**
1979-80	12-15	6-12	Jud Heathcote	Jay Vincent (582)•
1980-81	13-14	7-11	Jud Heathcote	Jay Vincent (609)•
1981-82	12-16	7-11	Jud Heathcote	Kevin Smith (436)
1982-83	17-13	9-9	Jud Heathcote	Sam Vincent (498)

1983-84	16-12	9-9	Jud Heathcote	Scott Skiles (405)
1984-85	19-10	10-8	Jud Heathcote	Sam Vincent (666)•
1985-86	23-8	12-6	Jud Heathcote	Scott Skiles (850)•
1986-87	11-17	6-12	Jud Heathcote	Darryl Johnson (618)
1987-88	10-18	5-13	Jud Heathcote	Carlton Valentine (371)
1988-89	18-15	6-12	Jud Heathcote	Steve Smith (585)
1989-90	**28-6**	**15-3 (1st)**	**Jud Heathcote**	**Steve Smith (627)**
1990-91	19-11	11-7	Jud Heathcote	Steve Smith (752)•
1991-92	22-8	11-7	Jud Heathcote	Shawn Respert (474)
1992-93	15-13	7-11	Jud Heathcote	Shawn Respert (563)
1993-94	20-12	10-8	Jud Heathcote	Shawn Respert (778)

= National (NCAA) Champions; • = League Individual Scoring Champion

All-Time Michigan State Individual Career Records

Points Scored .... Steve Smith (2,263, 1987-91)
Scoring Average .... Mike Robinson (24.2, 1971-74)
Games Played .... Mark Montgomery (126, 1988-92)
Field Goals .... Scott Skiles (837, 1982-86)
Field-Goal Percentage .... Ron Charles (.639, 1976-80)
Free Throws Made .... Sam Vincent (476, 1981-85)
Free-Throw Percentage .... Scott Skiles (.850, 1982-86)
3-Point Field Goals .... Kirk Manns (212, 1986-90)
Rebounds .... Greg Kelser (1,092, 1975-79)
Rebound Average ....Johnny Green (16.4, 1956-59)
Assists .... Scott Skiles (645, 1982-86)
Steals .... Scott Skiles (175, 1982-86)
Blocked Shots .... Ken Johnson (96, 1983-85)

All-Time Michigan State Individual Season Records

Points Scored .... Scott Skiles (850, 1985-86)
Scoring Average ....Terry Furlow (29.4, 1975-76)
Field Goals .... Scott Skiles (331, 1985-86)
Field-Goal Percentage .... Ron Charles (.676, 1979-80)
Free Throws Made .... Magic Johnson (202, 1978-79)
Free-Throw Percentage .... Darryl Johnson (.910, 1986-87)
3-Pt. Field Goals .... Kirk Manns (81, 1989-90)
Rebounds ....Johnny Green (392, 1957-58)
Rebound Average ....Johnny Green (17.8, 1957-58)
Assists .... Magic Johnson (269, 1978-79)
Steals .... Magic Johnson (75, 1978-79)
Blocked Shots .... Ken Johnson (72, 1984-85)

All-Time Michigan State Individual Single-Game Records

Points Scored .... Terry Furlow (50 vs. Iowa, 1-5-76)
Field Goals ....Julius McCoy (20 vs. Notre Dame, 12-21-55)
Scott Skiles (20 vs. Minnesota, 1-18-86)
Free Throws Made ....Al Ferrari (21 vs. Indiana, 2-28-55)
3-Point Field Goals .... Shawn Respert (9 vs. Indiana, 1-11-95)
Rebounds .... Horace Walker (28 vs. Iowa, 1-23-60)
Assists ....Magic Johnson (14 vs. Western Kentucky, 3-16-78;
Western Michigan, 12-13-78; Wisconsin, 1-4-79)
Steals .... Greg Kelser (8 vs. Northwestern, 2-2-76)
Darryl Johnson (8 vs. Ohio State, 1-10-87)

All-Time Michigan State Coaching Records

Coach	Overall Record	Conference Record	Seasons
Jud Heathcote (1976-Present)	318-214 (.598)	168-156 (.519)	18
Ben VanAlstyne (1927-49)	232-163 (.589)	None	22
Forrest Anderson (1954-65)	125-124 (.502)	69-85 (.448)	11
Gus Ganakas (1969-76)	89-84 (.514)	49-57 (.462)	7
Chester Brewer (1904-10)	70-25 (.736)	None	7
John Benington (1965-69)	54-38 (.587)	32-24 (.571)	4
John Macklin (1911-16)	48-38 (.558)	None	6
Pete Newell (1950-54)	45-42 (.517)	26-34 (.433)	4
George Gauthier (1917-20)	38-35 (.520)	None	4
Lyman Frimodig (1921-22)	24-21 (.533)	None	2
Fred Walker (1923-24)	20-19 (.513)	None	2
George Denman (1902-03)	11-0 (1.000)	None	2
John Kobs (1925-26)	11-26 (.297)	None	2
Charles Bemies (1900-01)	5-2 (.714)	None	2
Alton Kircher (1949-50)	4-18 (.182)	None	1

Michigan State All-Americans and All-Big Ten Selections

Consensus All-Americans
Earvin "Magic" Johnson, Guard, 1979

All-Big Ten Selections (since 1950)
Julius McCoy, Forward, 1956
Jack Quiggle, Guard, 1959
Johnny Green, Center, 1958-1959
Horace Walker, Forward, 1960
Stan Washington, Forward, 1966
Lee Lafayette, Center, 1969
Ralph Simpson, Forward, 1970

Mike Robinson, Guard, 1972-1973-1974
Lindsay Hairston, Center, 1974-1975
Terry Furlow, Forward, 1975-1976
Earvin "Magic" Johnson, Guard, 1978-1979
Greg Kelser, Forward, 1979
Jay Vincent, Center, 1980-1981
Kevin Smith, Guard, 1982
Sam Vincent, Guard, 1985
Scott Skiles, Guard, 1986
Steve Smith, Guard, 1990-1991
Mike Peplowski, Center, 1992

Chapter 6

MINNESOTA *Golden Gophers*

Gopher Holes and Breeding Grounds for Pro Talent

All-Time Record: 1,177-871, .575; **Conference Record:** 582-637, .480

Big Ten Championships — 8: (1906, 1907*, 1911*, 1917*, 1919, 1937*, 1972, 1982) * = Co-Champion

National Championships: None

National Invitation Tournament (NIT) Championships —1: (1993)

Greatest Player: Mychal Thompson (1975-78)

Career Scoring Leader: Mychal Thompson (1,992 Points, 1974-78)

Most Successful Coach: L.J. Cooke (1897-1924), 238-122, .660

All-Time Team: Mychal Thompson (C, 1974-78), Kevin McHale (F, 1976-80), Jim McIntyre (F, 1946-49), Trent Tucker (G, 1978-82), Willie Burton (G, 1986-90)

Best Season: 1992-93 (22-10), NIT Champion (Coach: Clem Haskins)

University Profile

Location: Minneapolis, Minnesota (pop. 370,000); **Founded:** 1851; **Campus Enrollment:** 39,000 (1994); **Started Basketball:** 1895-96. Founded as a preparatory school in 1851 and reconstituted as a land-grant college in 1862, the University of Minnesota has emerged during the past half-century as an international research institution of unsurpassed reputation for quality education and public service. The Minneapolis campus of the statewide Minnesota university system is also home to the world's leading kidney transplant program as well as to the James Ford Bell Museum of Natural History.

Team Nickname, Colors and Arena

Nickname: Golden Gophers; **Colors:** Maroon and Gold; **Arena:** Williams Arena (14,300 capacity, opened 1928). A long-range and somewhat cynical view of the Minnesota basketball program might prompt any clever wag to suggest that here is a school with an embarrassingly appropriate mascot and moniker. The gopher's propensity for tunneling into the ground might well suggest the burrows that have so regularly taken the Gopher teams of the past into the deepest reaches of the Big Ten standings. But then again, these are the Golden Gophers, which itself might conjure images of so many past Minnesota players who have mined sudden NBA gold (in the form of lucrative pro contracts) out of their brief careers on usually mediocre Gopher ballclubs.

Golden Gopher Basketball History

Bloomington, Indiana, remains one spot where unmatched coaching legends are magically contructed. West Lafayette is home to a noble winning college basketball tradition second to few in the land. Columbus and Ann Arbor have been productive pipelines for a steady stream — even a flood — of incomparable big-time hoops talent. And when it comes to such indelible reputations for college basketball fecundity, the far northern outpost of Minneapolis and the Big Ten campus it houses also has its own special claim to fame.

Admittedly, few championship teams have been produced in Minnesota. And the handful of successful coaches — L.J. Cooke and Dave MacMillan are two Gopher mentors who stand among the 15 winners of at least 100 Big Ten games — can't compare to names like Meanwell, Lambert, McCracken, Taylor, O'Connor, Knight and Keady. Yet when it comes to supplying wholesale NBA talent, the Minnesota Gophers take a backseat to no one. For a program that has won but two conference titles over the four-plus decades since the end of World War II, the Minnesota tradition has kept pro basketball scouts busy with a steady stream of fresh recruits ready to fill the ranks of the professional game.

Martin Manley's revolutionary statistical analysis of the cage sport, found in his touted 1988 book *Basketball Heaven*, offers a set of all-university teams based on outstanding alumni performance in the pro leagues. These teams are based on Manley's own Position Dominance Ratings (over at least a six-year period of NBA or ABA play) for 14 universities with enough players qualifying by such a standard. Five Big Ten schools appear in the rankings, with Ohio State (Jerry Lucas, Neil Johnston, John Havlicek, Arnie Risen, Herb Williams) standing at the top of the list. Indiana is fifth, Minnesota seventh, Illinois ninth and Michigan 13th. Among Big Ten-grown pro lineups, the Minnesota all-time contingent of Lou Hudson, Ray Williams, Kevin McHale, Mychal Thompson and Archie Clark trails only the Buckeye entry, and the Indiana lineup of George McGinnis, Isiah Thomas, Walt Bellamy, and Dick and Tom VanArsdale. The Hoosiers and Buckeyes — both at the very top of the heap (along with Purdue, a surprise absentee when it comes to NBA all-star alumni teams) — might well be expected to appear on Manley's list, but the Gophers from the middle of the Big Ten championship pack seem a most surprising entry indeed.

But if Gopher basketball has done anything, it has fed the NBA coffers. In all, 42 Gophers have had their names called over the years in the NBA collegiate draft; another nine were drafted by ABA clubs between 1968 and 1975. Bud Grant launched the Gopher NBA draft call in 1950. Tom Kondla (1968, Miami) was the first Minnesota ABA selection and Mark Olberding (1975, San Antonio) the last. And the Minnesota-NBA connection has been further extended on the coaching front as well. John Kundla (1959-68), Bill Musselman (1971-75) and Bill Fitch (1968-70) have all manned NBA benches as well as mentoring the Golden Gophers. No other Big Ten school can count as many as three past or future NBA coaches among its list of past or present bench bosses.

The better-known pro talents who have earned their collegiate training in the uniform of the Minnesota Golden Gophers comprise an impressive list of highly visible names extending well beyond Manley's all-star five — Dick Garmaker (the school's first NBA star with the Mikan-era Lakers), Whitey Skoog, Hudson, Clark, Jim Brewer, Ron Behagen, Ray Williams, Corky Taylor, Thompson, McHale (perhaps an NBA Hall-of-Famer), Trent Tucker (one-time holder of the NBA standard for three-pointers in a single game), Randy Breuer, Jim Peterson, Olberding, Tommy Davis, John Shasky and Willie Burton, among others.

And the list includes a few additional surprising names as well. There is Dave Winfield — yes, that Dave Winfield — the future base-

Lou Hudson, 1965 MVP, was one of the earliest in a long line of Gophers to go on to NBA stardom. (University of Minnesota photo)

ball Hall of Famer who was an NBA fifth-round draftee of the Atlanta Hawks in 1973 (as well as a sixth-round choice of the ABA Utah Stars). Winfield was a key performer on the 1972 Gopher team which split two NCAA Mideast Regional tournament games, and again on the 1973 club that lost in the NIT postseason quarterfinal round. And there is Bud Grant — the same Bud Grant of NFL playing and coaching fame who carved his reputation with the Minnesota Vikings. Grant was a worthy performer for the NBA powerhouse Minneapolis Lakers who had picked him in the 1950 pro draft. He also was the first Gopher ever selected by the NBA, taken off the Minnesota campus in the very first season of the newly organized league.

The earliest pipeline between the NBA and the Minnesota campus came with the territorial draft picks of the Lakers in the early 1950s. In addition to Grant, others of note were Meyer "Whitey" Skoog, Ed Kalafat and Dick Garmaker. Skoog played a crucial role in the Lakers' 1952 championship drive. That team was better known for the presence of George Mikan, Jim Pollard and Vern Mikkelsen. And Garmaker would become a solid NBA contributor (four seasons with the Lakers and two more with the New York Knicks) after a stellar Minnesota career which found him the school's first true basketball superstar. Garmaker (1953-55) still holds a flock of Minnesota offensive records four decades after his graduation including career scoring average (22.9 points per game) and single-season free throws (both made and attempted).

Most famous among pro basketball recruits earning their wings with the Gophers are the six top stars from the past three decades. First came Lou Hudson in the 1960s, a six-time NBA all-star. Hudson poured in nearly 18,000 NBA points and maintained a 20 points per game average over a 13-year career with St. Louis, Atlanta and Los Angeles. Jim Brewer, who trails only Thompson and McHale in Minnesota career rebounding, was the second overall choice in the 1973 draft (taken by the Cleveland Cavaliers) and twice earned NBA all-defensive team honors. Thomspon followed in the late 1970s, climbing to the top of the Minnesota career scoring and rebounding lists before piling up 12,500 points in the uniforms of the Portland Trail Blazers, San Antonio Spurs and Los Angeles Lakers. While Hudson and perhaps even Brewer were more productive pro players, Thomspon's four-year career with the Golden Gophers remains the unchallenged best in school history.

Trent Tucker also played alongside Thompson before becoming one of the classiest three-point shooters of NBA history. Tucker, who spent all but the twilight of his pro career with the New York Knicks, still stands fifth on the NBA all-time 3-point field goal accuracy list. Next came rangy and agile 6-foot-10 forward Kevin McHale, the 1978 Big Ten field-goal percentage leader and a member of the league 1,000-point club. McHale would follow immediately after Thomspon and the team on which he played as a senior posted a 21-11 mark, advanced to the finals of the NIT tourney and was one of the best in recent school history. Finally there was Willie Burton during the late 1980s. Burton also left his mark on the school record book (second-highest career and single-season scorer), as well as his reputation for flashy play still freshly etched in the memories of Gopher fans.

But for all its impact on the pro version of the game, the Minnesota basketball tradition actually begins a full half-century before the birth of the modern play-for-pay circuit known as the National Basketball Association. Minnesota was producing solid teams, if not great star players, from the very outset of Western Conference history. The Gophers were one of the original six conference members, alongside Wisconsin, Indiana, Chicago, Illinois and Purdue. When the newly organized league played its first short season of competitive games in the late winter of 1906, it would be the Minnesota Gophers who would come out on top of the heap with a 6-1 record, nudging Wisconsin which had an identical victory total but had played and lost one more conference game. It would thus be Minnesota which would from the start lay claim to a trophy that no other conference school will ever be able to match — the very first Big Ten (nee Western Conference) basketball championship honors.

The winning would not continue for long in Minneapolis, at least not on a championship level. The initial successes of the 1906 team were matched a year later when the squad of longtime coach L.J. Cooke tied for the conference crown, deadlocking this time with Chicago and Wisconsin who also owned 6-2 conference records. Cooke had already been coaching the sport at the Minnesota campus for eight winters by the time the Western Conference was officially formed. His 1902 and 1903 squads posted back-to-back undefeated campaigns and

Kevin McHale (44), who went on to become a star for the Boston Celtics, began his basketball legend in the uniform of the Minnesota Golden Gophers. (University of Minnesota photo)

the 1902 unit was honored as Helms Foundation National Champions. Cooke's tenure would continue through 27 seasons, a "golden era" marked by 18 winning years and 244 victories. His winning percentages within the conference and overall rank among the highest of all time for coaches at Big Ten schools.

Minnesota won three more Big Ten titles under Cooke. The 1911 and 1917 teams tied for the crown, the 1911 team posting an 8-4 mark and deadlocking with Purdue and the 1917 team standing at 10-2 alongside Illinois. Both those seasons would also find Gopher stars pacing the conference in individual scoring. Frank Lawler established a league record with 143 points in 1911 while Harold Gillen tied for the honor with Illinois sharpshooter Ralf Woods during the second title year of the decade. Then in 1919 would come the only undefeated team in the school's Big Ten history, a 13-0 outfit that captured 10 of those victories against the other nine conference opponents. Indiana, Wisconsin, Illinois, Purdue and Iowa were beaten twice while conference games were not scheduled against Chicago, Northwestern, Michigan and Ohio State. But the 1919 squad would unfortunately also be the last great team of Cooke's legendary conference-record 30-year reign.

Only one other coach in Gopher history boasts a storied career that can rival that of L.J. Cooke for both longevity and productivity. Dave MacMillan took over the program four seasons after Cooke's retirement and remained on the job for 18 years, a tenure interrupted only by three brief seasons during World War II. Under MacMillan there would be numerous quality teams and winning seasons. But only once would there be a Big Ten title. That would come in 1937 with a squad that lost only two league games (both on the road by a single point each) and tied with Illinois for top honors.

The modern era of Minnesota basketball history breaks neatly into three epochs, those which correspond to the coaching reigns of John Kundla (1959-1968), Bill Musselman (1971-75) and Jim Dutcher (1975-85). The first of these memorable mentors, Kundla, was a local Minneapolis legend who had already led the hometown Lakers to NBA prominance throughout the late '40s and early '50s, then stayed behind at the collegiate level when the pro franchise moved out to Los Angeles at the end of the decade. Kundla would never match his Lakers successes with the Gophers, but his teams were known for steady play and several individual stars. Kundla's 1964 unit would register a 17-7 record and trail only the two powerhouse teams of Michigan (with Cazzie Russell) and Ohio State (with Gary Bradds) for league honors. The following year's club would improve by two games and post a then school-record 19 wins to creep into the second conference spot. Future NBA all-stars Hudson and Clark would play in this era, and Tom Kondla would earn All-American honors. In the penultimate year of Kundla's tenure the similarly named Tom Kondla would enjoy one of the most productive offensive seasons in school history. The rangy center would post the highest season-long conference scoring mark in Gopher annals, averaging 28.3 points per game and winning Big Ten scoring honors.

The brief career of Bill Musselman in Minneapolis would be marked as much by scandal and controversy as by success in the win-loss columns. The energetic coach would bring the school its first Big Ten title in 35 years and only one of three during the postwar decades. This would come in 1971-72 when the Jim Brewer-led club nudged Ohio State by a single game with a sterling league mark of 11-3 (18-7 overall). Musselman's tenure unfortunately will be

Former NBA star Clem Haskins recently coached the Golden Gophers to their first back-to-back 20-victory seasons. (University of Minnesota photo)

remembered, however, more for what was perhaps the ugliest single incident in conference history. It came in the form of a vicious on-court bench-clearing brawl during the final weeks of that 1972 championship campaign during a heated game between the overly aroused Gophers and powerhouse Ohio State. The incident was all the more infamous and embarrassing because it occurred in a contest beamed out to a wide and astonished audience on national television.

The Minnesota career of Jim Dutcher would bring three sterling teams that would post 20-win seasons, as well as another Big Ten title in 1982. This was the proud era of Mychal Thompson and Kevin McHale, arguably the two best big men in school annals. Thompson would be club MVP three straight seasons (1976-1978) with McHale holding the honor for the next two years (1979-80). And Thompson would enjoy a banner year in 1978 (with his second consecutive individual conference scoring crown) which made him the last Gopher through 1993-94 to hold down consensus All-American honors. Dutcher's reign also had its share of notoriety and embarrassment. The 1977 team would win 24 games, only to forfeit all of them because of ineligible players. By contrast, the 1982 title-winning team was one of the strongest in school annals. Its 23-6 mark still stands as the school's best and its lineup featuring future NBAers Randy Breuer, Mark Hall and Trent Tucker was one of the strongest in school history.

The past eight seasons have seen former NBA player Clem Haskins build a solid program which has put Minnesota on the verge of Big Ten greatness, while still never quite emerging as one of the league's elite. Three teams under Haskins (1990, 1993, 1994) have produced 20-victory seasons. Willie Burton (1986-90), one of the finest players in the school's modern history, climbed into second place behind Thompson in the Minnesota career scoring derby with 1,800 points before departing as a first-round draft selection of the NBA Miami Heat. Voshon Lenard has inherited Burton's role as a Williams Arena crowd-pleaser, posting a 17.1 points per game average as a sophomore and an 18.9 mark (eighth in the league) during his junior season in 1994. Lenard declared for the NBA draft after his junior campaign but reconsidered and opted to stay at Minnesota for his senior season.

The highlight of Haskins' reign to date has been the postseason run of 1993 which brought Minnesota an NIT championship. The season was actually the school's sixth with 20 or more victories. The postseason appearance was the school's 10th overall. There had been NCAA trips in 1972 (lost in first round), 1982 (lost in regional semifinal), 1989 (lost in regional semifinal) and 1990 (lost in regional finals). And Minnesota played in the NIT in 1973 (lost in second round), 1980 (lost in finals), 1981 (lost in third round), 1983 (lost in first round) and 1992 (lost in first round). In 1980 the Gophers battled all the way to the NIT Finals — defeating Bowling Green, Mississippi, Southwest Louisiana and Illinois — only to lose in a squeaker to Virginia and freshman Ralph Sampson by a 58-55 margin.

This time the Golden Gophers would not be headed in the postseason challenge. Renovations at Williams Arena forced the first two NIT games to be moved into the spacious Target Center, home of the NBA Timberwolves. More than 30,000 enthusiastic fans turned out for the two relocated "home" contests. Early-round victories came by comfortable margins over Florida (74-66), Oklahoma (86-72) and USC (76-58). In the semifinal at Madison Square Garden the Gophers edged Providence 76-70. The championship game was a classic one-point struggle (62-61) against John Thompson's team from Georgetown University. Junior guard Arriel McDonald joined Voshon Lenard on the NIT all-tourney team.

Throughout the years one enobling feature of Minnesota basketball has been the legendary building in which the team has played its home games since 1928. *Inside Sports* magazine in 1990, for example, would tab the atmosphere-drenched facility as one of the five best college basketball venues in the nation. Historic Williams Arena debuted in a fitting manner Feb. 4, 1928 with a thrilling double overtime game won by Ohio State, 42-40. That dramatic contest was but a foreshaow of decades of games to come, however. The Arena would host the NCAA tournament finals in 1951, a memorable contest in which the invincible Kentucky squad of Bill Spivey, Cliff Hagan, Frank Ramsey and Lou Tsioropoulos would gun down Kansas State for a third national title in four years. But most important, the venerable Williams Arena would long be known as the "House of Pain" for intimidated visiting Big Ten teams who year-in and year-out have had to challenge the feisty Gophers on their special "sixth-man" home floor.

Records and Summaries
Year-by-Year Minnesota Records
(Championship Years in Boldface)

Season	All Games	Conference	Coach(es)	Gopher MVPs
1895-96	4-7	None	No Coach	Not Awarded
1896-97	3-6	None	No Coach	Not Awarded
1897-98	5-8	None	L.J. Cooke	Not Awarded
1989-99	5-5	None	L.J. Cooke	Not Awarded
1899-00	10-3	None	L.J. Cooke	Not Awarded
1900-01	11-1	None	L.J. Cooke	Not Awarded
1901-02**	15-0	None	L.J. Cooke	Not Awarded
1902-03	13-0	None	L.J. Cooke	Not Awarded
1903-04	10-2	None	L.J. Cooke	Not Awarded
1904-05	7-7	None	L.J. Cooke	Not Awarded
1905-06	**13-2**	**6-1 (1st)**	**L.J. Cooke**	**Not Awarded**
1906-07	**10-2**	**6-2 (1st-T)**	**L.J. Cooke**	**Not Awarded**
1907-08	11-7	2-6	L.J. Cooke	Not Awarded
1908-09	8-6	3-6	L.J. Cooke	Not Awarded
1909-10	10-3	7-3	L.J. Cooke	Not Awarded
1910-11	**9-4**	**8-4 (1st-T)**	**L.J. Cooke**	**Not Awarded**
1911-12	7-6	6-6	L.J. Cooke	Not Awarded
1912-13	2-8	2-8	L.J. Cooke	Not Awarded
1913-14	4-11	4-8	L.J. Cooke	Not Awarded
1914-15	11-6	6-6	L.J. Cooke	Not Awarded
1915-16	10-6	6-6	L.J. Cooke	Not Awarded
1916-17	**17-2**	**10-2 (1st-T)**	**L.J. Cooke**	**Not Awarded**
1917-18	9-3	7-3	L.J. Cooke	Not Awarded
1918-19	**13-0**	**10-0 (1st)**	**L.J. Cooke**	**Not Awarded**
1919-20	8-8	4-8	L.J. Cooke	Not Awarded
1920-21	10-5	7-5	L.J. Cooke	Not Awarded
1921-22	5-8	5-7	L.J. Cooke	Not Awarded
1922-23	2-13	1-11	L.J. Cooke	Not Awarded
1923-24	9-9	5-7	L.J. Cooke	Not Awarded
1924-25	9-7	6-6	Harold Taylor	Not Awarded
1925-26	6-10	5-7	Harold Taylor	Not Awarded
1926-27	3-13	1-11	Harold Taylor	Not Awarded
1927-28	4-12	2-10	Dave MacMillan	Not Awarded
1928-29	4-13	1-11	Dave MacMillan	Not Awarded
1929-30	8-9	3-9	Dave MacMillan	Not Awarded
1930-31	13-4	8-4	Dave MacMillan	Not Awarded

1931-32	15-3	9-3	Dave MacMillan	Not Awarded
1932-33	5-15	1-11	Dave MacMillan	Not Awarded
1933-34	9-11	5-7	Dave MacMillan	Not Awarded
1934-35	11-9	5-7	Dave MacMillan	Not Awarded
1935-36	7-17	3-9	Dave MacMillan	Not Awarded
1936-37	**14-6**	**10-2 (1st-T)**	**Dave MacMillan**	**Not Awarded**
1937-38	16-4	9-3	Dave MacMillan	Not Awarded
1938-39	14-6	7-5	Dave MacMillan	Not Awarded
1939-40	13-8	5-7	Dave MacMillan	Not Awarded
1940-41	11-9	7-5	Dave MacMillan	Not Awarded
1941-42	15-7	9-6	Dave MacMillan	Not Awarded
1942-43	10-9	5-7	Carl Nordly	Not Awarded
1943-44	7-14	2-10	Carl Nordly	Not Awarded
1944-45	8-13	4-8	Weston Mitchell	Not Awarded
1945-46	14-7	7-5	Dave MacMillan	Tony Jaros
1946-47	14-7	7-5	Dave MacMillan	Jim McIntyre
1947-48	10-10	5-7	Dave MacMillan	Harry "Bud" Grant
1948-49	18-3	9-3	Osborne Cowles	Harold Olson
1949-50	13-9	4-8	Osborne Cowles	Whitey Skoog
1950-51	13-9	7-7	Osborne Cowles	Whitey Skoog
1951-52	15-7	10-4	Osborne Cowles	Dick Means
1952-53	14-8	11-7	Osborne Cowles	Bob Gelle
1953-54	17-5	10-4	Osborne Cowles	Ed Kalafat
1954-55	15-7	10-4	Osborne Cowles	Chuck Mencel
1955-56	11-11	6-8	Osborne Cowles	Dave Tucker
1956-57	14-8	9-5	Osborne Cowles	Jed Dommeyer
1957-58	9-12	5-9	Osborne Cowles	George Kline
1958-59	8-14	5-9	Osborne Cowles	Roger Johnson
1959-60	12-12	8-6	John Kundla	Ron Johnson
1960-61	10-13	8-6	John Kundla	Dick Erickson
1961-62	10-14	6-8	John Kundla	Ray Cronk
1962-63	12-12	8-6	John Kundla	Eric Magdanz
1963-64	17-7	10-4	John Kundla	Bill Davis
1964-65	19-5	11-3	John Kundla	Lou Hudson
1965-66	14-10	7-7	John Kundla	Archie Clark
1966-67	9-15	5-9	John Kundla	Tom Kondla
1967-68	7-17	4-10	John Kundla	Tom Kondla
1968-69	12-12	6-8	Bill Fitch	Al Nuness
1969-70	13-11	7-7	Bill Fitch	Larry Mikan
1970-71	11-13	5-9	George Hanson	Jim Brewer
1971-72	**18-7**	**11-3 (1st)**	**Bill Musselman**	**Jim Brewer**
1972-73	21-5	10-4	Bill Musselman	Jim Brewer

1973-74	12-12	6-8	Bill Musselman	Peter Gilcud
1974-75	18-8	11-7	Bill Musselman	Mark Olberding
1975-76	16-10	8-10	Jim Dutcher	Ray Williams
1976-77	24-3 (0-27*)	15-3 (0-18*)	Jim Dutcher	Mychal Thompson
1977-78	17-10	12-6	Jim Dutcher	Mychal Thompson
1978-79	11-16	6-12	Jim Dutcher	Kevin McHale
1979-80	21-11	10-8	Jim Dutcher	Kevin McHale
1980-81	19-11	9-9	Jim Dutcher	Trent Tucker
1981-82	**23-6**	**14-4 (1st)**	**Jim Dutcher**	**Darryl Mitchell**
1982-83	18-11	9-9	Jim Dutcher	Randy Breuer
1983-84	15-13	6-12	Jim Dutcher	Tommy Davis
1984-85	13-15	6-12	Jim Dutcher	Tommy Davis
1985-86	15-16	5-13	Jim Dutcher/Jimmy Williams	John Shasky
1986-87	9-19	2-16	Clem Haskins	Terence Woods
1987-88	10-18	4-14	Clem Haskins	Richard Coffey
1988-89	19-12	9-9	Clem Haskins	Willie Burton
1989-90	23-9	11-7	Clem Haskins	Willie Burton
1990-91	12-16	5-13	Clem Haskins	Kevin Lynch
1991-92	16-16	8-10	Clem Haskins	Arriel McDonald
1992-93#	22-10	9-9	Clem Haskins	Voshon Lenard
1993-94	21-12	10-8	Clem Haskins	Voshon Lenard

** = Helms Foundation National Champions; * = all games forfeited; # = NIT Champions

All-Time Minnesota Individual Career Records

Points Scored .... Mychal Thompson (1,992, 1974-78)
Scoring Average .... Dick Garmaker (22.9, 1953-55)
Games Played .... Randy Breuer (119, 1979-83)
                                                                                        Kevin Lynch (119, 1987-91)
                                                                                        Bob Martin (119, 1988-92)
Field Goals .... Mychal Thompson (823, 1974-78)
Field-Goal Percentage .... Mychal Thompson (.568, 1974-78)
Free Throws Made .... Willie Burton (426, 1986-90)
Free-Throw Percentage .... Phil Saunders (.809, 1973-77)
3-Point Field Goals .... Kevin Lynch (117, 1987-91)
Rebounds .... Mychal Thompson (956, 1974-78)
Assists .... Marc Wilson (375, 1982-86)
Steals .... Melvin Newbern (215, 1987-90)
Blocked Shots .... Kevin McHale (235, 1976-80)
Personal Fouls .... Willie Burton (355, 1986-90)

All-Time Minnesota Individual Season Records

Points Scored .... Mychal Thompson (647, 1975-76)
Scoring Average .... Mychal Thompson (25.9, 1975-76)
Field Goals .... Mychal Thompson (265, 1975-76)
Field-Goal Percentage .... Jim Petersen (.639, 1983-84)
Free Throws Made .... Dick Garmaker (181, 1953-54)
Free-Throw Percentage ....Osborne Lockhart (.870, 1976-77)
3-Point Field Goals.. Voshon Lenard (58, 1992-93)
Rebounds .... Larry Mikan (349, 1969-70)
Rebound Average.. Larry Mikan (14.3, 1969-70)
Assists .... Melvin Newbern (167, 1989-90)
Steals .... Melvin Newbern (101, 1988-89)
Blocked Shots .... Randy Breuer (87, 1982-83)

All-Time Minnesota Individual Single-Game Records

Points Scored .... Eric Magdanz (42 vs. Michigan, 3-5-62)
                                                          Ollie Shannon (42 vs. Wisconsin, 3-6-71)
Field Goals .... Ron Johnson (18 vs. Ohio State, 1-31-59)
Free Throws Made .... Larry Mikan (17 vs. Purdue, 1-25-69)
3-Point Field Goals............................ Tim Hanson (6 vs. Michigan State, 2-28-87)
                                                          Kevin Lynch (6 vs. Iowa, 1-12-91)
Rebounds .... Larry Mikan (28 vs. Michigan, 3-3-70)
Assists .... Ray Williams (13 vs. Indiana, 1-27-77)
Steals .... Melvin Newbern (9 vs. Rider, 1-3-90)
Blocked Shots .... Mychal Thompson (12 vs. Ohio State, 1-26-76)

All-Time Minnesota Coaching Records

Coach	Overall Record	Conference Record	Seasons
L.J. Cooke (1897-1924)	244-135 (.643)	105-99 (.515)	27
Dave MacMillan (1927-42, 45-48)	197-157 (.556)	148-116 (.561)	18
Jim Dutcher (1975-86)	190-113 (.627)	98-89 (.524)	11
Osborne Cowles (1948-59)	147-93 (.613)	86-68 (.558)	11
Clem Haskins (1986-Present)	132-112 (.541)	58-86 (.403)	8
John Kundla (1959-68)	110-105 (.512)	67-59 (.532)	9
Bill Musselman (1971-75)	69-32 (.683)	38-22 (.633)	4
Bill Fitch (1968-70)	25-23 (.521)	13-15 (.464)	2
Harold Taylor (1924-27)	18-30 (.378)	12-24 (.333)	3
Carl Nordly (1942-44)	17-23 (.425)	7-17 (.292)	2
George Hanson (1970-71)	11-13 (.458)	5-9 (.357)	1
Weston Mitchell (1944-45)	8-13 (.381)	4-8 (.333)	1
Jimmy Williams (1986)	2-9 (.182)	2-9 (.182)	Partial

Minnesota All-Americans and All-Big Ten Selections

Consensus All-Americans
Jim McIntyre, Center, 1948
Dick Garmaker, Guard, 1955
Mychal Thompson, Center, 1978

All-Big Ten Selections (since 1948)
Jim McIntyre, Center, 1948
Myer "Whitey" Skoog, Guard, 1950-1951
Charles Mencel, Guard, 1953-1955
Dick Garmaker, Guard, 1954-1955
George Kline, Forward, 1957-1958
Ron Johnson, Center, 1959-1960
Lou Hudson, Forward, 1965
Tom Kondla, Center, 1967
Clyde Turner, Forward, 1972
Ron Behagen, Forward, 1973
Jim Brewer, Center, 1973
Mychal Thompson, Center, 1976-1977-1978
Kevin McHale, Center, 1980
Randy Breuer, Center, 1982-1983
Darryl Mitchell, Guard, 1982
Tommy Davis, Forward, 1985
Willie Burton, Forward, 1990
Voshon Lenard, Guard, 1994

Voshon Lenard, a 1994 All-Big Ten selection, is closing rapidly on Minnesota's all-time career scoring record held by Mychal Thompson. (University of Minnesota photo)

Chapter 7

NORTHWESTERN *Wildcats*

Wildcats Long Lost in Basketball Wilderness

All-Time Record: 751-1,089, .408; **Conference Record:** 394-784, .330

Big Ten Championships — **2** (1931, 1933*) * = Co-Champion

National Championships: None

Greatest Player: Billy McKinney (1974-77)

Career Scoring Leader: Billy McKinney (1,900 Points, 1974-77)

Most Successful Coach: Arthur Lonborg (1928-50), 236-203, .538

All-Time Team: Joe Ruklick (F, 1957-59), Andre Goode (F, 1982-85), Otto Graham (F, 1942-44), Shon Morris (G, 1985-88), Billy McKinney (G, 1974-77)

Best Season: 1930-31 (16-1), Big 10 Champion (Coach: Arthur Lonborg)

University Profile

Location: Evanston, Illinois (pop. 73,750); **Founded:** 1851; **Campus Enrollment:** 7,400 (Undergraduates, 1994); **Started Basketball:** 1904-05. Northwestern University was chartered in 1851, the dream of nine Chicago-based founders with an ambitious purpose of creating an institution "of the highest order of excellence to serve the people of the Northwest Territory." Today's major research and teaching facility houses nearly 17,000 full- and part-time students in 12 academic divisions and maintains one of the most competitive admissions procedures in the entire nation. Distinguished Northwestern alumni include two-time presidential candidate Adlai E. Stevenson, astronaut Joseph Kerwin, ABC sports analyst Brent Musberger, author and sportswriter Rick Telander, film stars Warren Beatty and Charlton Heston, Nobel Prize-winning author Saul Bellow, actresses Cloris Leachman and Shelly Long, pro sports mogul Jerry Reinsdorf and former Chicago mayor Harold Washington.

Team Nickname, Colors and Arena

Nickname: Wildcats (since 1926); **Colors:** Purple and White; **Arena:** Welsh-Ryan Arena (8,117 capacity, opened 1951). While the official school colors of purple and white seem to date back to 1894, the "Wildcats" nickname can be traced only to 1924. The personification of "Willie the Wildcat" took place in two stages. In 1933 the NU athletic department employed a local advertising firm to create the first caricature of Willie, while the first "live" Willie in costume debuted in 1947 as part of an Alpha Delta fraternity homecoming float. The 1924 origin of the "Wildcat" moniker is usually traced to a *Chicago Tribune* article by sports journalist Wallace Abbey which provided a stirring account of the memorable Northwestern-Chicago football contest that autumn in the Windy City. Wrote Abbey: "...football players had not come down from Evanston; wildcats would be a name better suited to Coach Thistlewaite's boys ... Once they (Chicago) had the ball on the 9-yard line and had been stopped dead by a wall of wildcats." The named seemed to be a natural for all athletic teams representing the Evanston campus.

Wildcat Basketball History

On Feb. 5, 1994, rookie Northwestern coach Ricky Byrdsong put on one of the most outrageous bench displays ever witnessed in the history of Big Ten basketball. During the largest portion of a game his team was losing by 14 points at Minnesota's Williams Arena, Byrdsong roamed the aisles behind the team's bench, sat and chatted with fans in the grandstand, disputed with ushers his right to wander among the ticketholders, and waved gleefully to the crowd from a post near one of the building's exits. Such unprecedented antics from the unabashed Wildcat coach seemed to top anything even unpredictable badboy mentor Bob Knight had ever displayed.

Byrdsong next requested a temporary leave of absence which stretched for two and a half weeks and appeared to spur sharp improvement in his unflappable team's on-floor performance. At 0-8 in the Big Ten after the embarrassing Minnesota affair, Northwestern would roar down the stretch to finish 5-5 over the season's final 10 games and earn a rare postseason NIT bid. In the end, Byrdsong claimed that his apparent "madness" had a purposeful method to it, and that his loony displays were pre-planned to aid in the progress of a long-suffering college basketball program desperate for a serious shot in the arm. The idea behind the bizarre theatrics was supposed to have something to do with teaching his team to concentrate under even the most extreme form of distraction. To some small degree, it seemed to work.

Unfortunately, Byrdsong's antics were the most exciting thing happening with Northwestern basketball in at least several decades. Until Penn State's arrival on the conference scene in 1992, Northwestern held undisputed claim to the title of Big Ten basketball doormat. For a number of seasons things had been as bleak as they could possibly be on the Evanston hardwoods. For starters, Byrdsong was taking over a program that had won exactly 15 of its last 144 conference games over the past eight seasons. On the road, the hapless Wildcats could boast of only one conference victory in the last 66 outings. To boot, the Wildcats have now posted 26 straight losing seasons in conference play, by far an all-time unmatched conference low-water mark for ineptitude.

It hadn't always been this way. In the early days of league play Northwestern had been a conference pioneer and leader when it came to basketball wars. Although Northwestern was not one of the seven colleges forming the original Western Conference in November, 1905, the school joined in the fall of 1908, just in time for a fourth season of league competition. The earliest campaigns provided the kind of mediocre Northwestern teams that unfortunately became a regular feature during the last 25 years as well. But there were four straight decent seasons between 1913 and 1916, two under coach Dennis Grady (14-4, 11-6) and two with Fred Murphy (11-8, 14-5) at the helm. The Northwestern club finished second in the league standings twice (1913, 1916) during this spell.

The first real upsurge came in the late '20s with the arrival of Arthur Lonborg. Lonborg would soon become part of the long list of legendary Big Ten coaches but the only member of that list to coach on the Evanston campus. He would eventually join an exclusive club with more than 100 Big Ten coaching victories, although only two other club members (Harold "Bud" Foster of Wisconsin and Dave MacMillan of Minnesota) besides him would in the end lose more conference games than they won. Lonborg's first two seasons in charge (1928, 1929) would produce identical 12-5 ledgers. His first 11 campaigns would also find his team finishing at or above the break-even mark.

Lonborg would last in Evanston for 23 seasons and become something of a full-blown athletic institution. But his most successful outings came very early on in his tenure. After two solid initial campaigns, by his fourth year Lonborg had the Wildcats prowling at the very top of the pack. The season of 1930-31 (16-1) was the greatest in school history. Only a late-year 35-28 stumble on the home floor to Illinois would blemish an otherwise perfect record. The Wildcats would easily outdistance a runner-up trio of Purdue, Michigan and Minnesota (all 8-4) to salt away a first-ever league championship trophy.

There would be one more championship for Lonborg and his crew two seasons later. This second title team was perhaps not quite as potent, dropping games to Notre Dame (28-25), Illinois (27-25), Purdue (42-40) and Marquette (26-24). And the conference bragging rights had to be shared with Ohio State, a better overall ballclub at 17-3 (compared to the Wildcats' 15-4). But the Evanston team was a legitimate league winner nonetheless, and all four defeats had been narrow and on the road in enemy territory. The first Northwestern All-American anchored both championship squads. Joe Reiff was one of the best centers in the country during the early '30s and was the school's first league scoring champ (168 points) since Harold Whittle back in 1914.

After this brief flourish of the early '30s, Lonborg would patch together several more competitive teams across the next decade. But these were interspersed with an equal number of lackluster squads with an emerging pattern of regular losing records. Four of the next nine Northwestern teams would finish below .500 on the Big Ten slate. A second flourish would come during the war years of the early '40s as both the 1943 (7-5, third) and 1944 (8-4, fourth) teams would climb to the middle of the league pack as would the 1946 (8-4, third) outfit. Two more outstanding players were soon featured in purple and white. Football hero and future NFL Hall of Fame quarterback Otto Graham distinguished himself as a basketball All-American as well as a gridiron sensation during this wartime era. Graham would be a consensus All-American in 1944 at forward, the first athlete ever to earn All-American status in both basketball and football. Max Morris, a star forward a couple of years later, was tabbed the first-ever *Chicago Tribune* Big Ten Most Valuable Player. Morris would also serve as league scoring champion in 1945 (15.8 points per game) and 1946 (16.5). Reiff, Graham and Morris remarkably remain the only Northwestern cage All-Americans to date.

The decades of the '50s, '60s and '70s produced a few individual stars at Northwestern but little team success. The first of these stars was Ray Ragelis, a Big Ten scoring champion in 1951 with 421 points and a 19.1 points per game average (19.8 in Big Ten games). Next came another potent point producer named Joe Ruklick in the late 1950s. The 6-foot-9 Ruklick still maintains the highest career scoring average (19.9) in Northwestern history. But Ruklick also maintains a unique set of connections with the greatest legend in basketball. It was Ruklick's odd fate to make a full career out of playing deep in the shadow of basketball's greatest-ever one-man offensive show, Wilt Chamberlain. When Wilt debuted as a Kansas sophomore in 1956 it would be against the Northwestern Wildcats. The 7-footer poured in a collegiate career-best 52 that night against the helpless Ruklick, himself only an untested sophomore. When the Philadelphia Warriors exercised their territorial prerogative to grab Wilt in the NBA draft three years later, it was the same Joe Ruklick who found himself tabbed as the Warriors' second choice that year — a sentence which meant a certain stint at the far end of the bench as Chamberlain's almost never-used backup. And in the final season of Ruklick's brief three-year NBA career it would be the unheralded Northwestern journeyman — in one of his rare on-court moments — who would feed Wilt a crucial pass in the closing seconds of a famous March 1, 1962, game in Hershey, Penn. It was that very pass which resulted in Chamberlain's 99th and 100th points of the night, leaving Ruklick as proud owner of one of the most noteworthy yet long-forgotten assists in professional basketball history.

Ruklick's luster was nearly surpassed a half-dozen seasons later by another frontcourt gunner named Rick Falk. Falk would set a single-game scoring mark of 49 points in 1964 against Iowa, topping Ruklick's one-game record by nine points. And at the end of the '60s, Dale Kelley would set some scoring marks of his own with a brilliant and productive 1969-70 campaign. During that season, Kelley would set new mileposts for total points (582), scoring average (24.3), free throws (164) and field goals (209), that still stand as school records.

The greatest individual star for Northwestern, however, would be a flashy shooting guard who came on the scene in time for the 1973-74 season. Bill McKinney would set a host of school offense records (career points, career field goals, career field-goal attempts) during a Big Ten career that was also staging ground for the journeyman's six-season NBA sojourn at the end of the decade.

But while rare headliners like McKinney, Falk, Ragelis, Ruklick and Kelley provided some feeble cheers in Evanston between the 50's Eisenhower years and the '80s Reagan years, the team itself was never very exciting nor successful. Four 8-6 campaigns (1958, 1959, 1960, 1968) were the only winning years in Big Ten play between 1950 and 1980. A tie for second in 1959 was the highest any Northwestern team finished in the league standings. Behind Joe Ruklick's senior-season 23 points per game scoring that 1959 team was the only one to win as many as 15 ballgames.

The 1980s and 1990s in Evanston have witnessed the longest and most uninterrupted string of dismal losing in conference history. Coaches Rick Falk (the Wildcat scoring hero of

Joe Ruklick, above, holds the school record for rebounds and was Northwestern's all-time leading scorer at one time. At right, Rick Sund goes to the basket in a 1970 game against Western Illinois. (Northwestern University photos)

Shon Morris paced the Wildcats in scoring three times and merits selection on any all-time Northwestern all-star team. (Northwestern University photo)

the mid-60s) and Bill Foster (earlier a successful ACC coach at Clemson) would combine to compile two of the worst overall and conference won-lost records in NCAA hoops history. A record road losing streak eventually reached 62 conference games (stretching back to a late-season 1986 victory in Minnesota) before finally being broken at Purdue in February 1993.

Three Northwestern players were able to supply a modicum of excitement around the campus during the past decade. Jim Stack, a capable scorer in the early '80s, climbed over the 1,500-point barrier into second slot on the all-time school scoring list. Andre Goode, another talented forward, averaged double figures during the final two of his four seasons and earned notice as a defensive specialist who three times paced the Wildcats in blocked shots. And Shon Morris, multi-talented at the frontcourt post in 1986, 1987 and 1988, eventually climbing into third on the school scoring list and first in career free throws. Cedric Neloms, Walker Laimbiotte (his 18.0 scoring average in 1989 was the highest since Billy McKinney's 20.6 in 1977) and Rex Walters also performed admirably. Walters (a rare recruit out of Kansas) was a rangy 6-4 guard and perhaps the most promising player seen at Northwestern in years. But the sharp-shooting and crisp-passing backcourt ace transferred back to the University of Kansas after an outstanding sophomore season in Evanston (17.6 points per game, 125 assists) and was soon leading the Jayhawks and not the Wildcats back into national prominence. Walters would prove good enough in the Big Eight after his transfer to lead an outstanding Kansas team all the way to the 1993 NCAA Final Four. And he would wind up in the NBA as a first-round draft choice with the New Jersey Nets.

Thus, even when Northwestern recruited a star player it was another matter altogether to keep him. Of the less luminous stars who did remain at Northwestern, none was quite good enough to make the all-conference team despite some stellar play in a losing cause. McKinney, the all-time school scoring leader who rang up his final baskets way back in 1977, remains the last Wildcat to boast an All-Big Ten first team honor.

It's been a long and painful sojourn for the Wildcat basketball program across recent decades and there are few signs of immediate improvement. Byrdsong's first season on the job brought more than the usual share of growing pains. His mid-season antics in the Minnesota game and subsequent brief "leave of absence" may have motivated the club in the long run but was hardly an image-booster for the school. Cedric Neloms, one of the most dynamic players in the league and Northwestern's scoring leader during his freshman and sophomore seasons, had difficulty adjusting to Byrdsong's style and languished for much of the campaign. A 5-13 conference record and last-place tie with Iowa were not big signs of progress.

Yet the preseason goal of a postseason appearance was achieved with the first winning season (15-14) in 11 years and an 83-79 second-round NIT loss to Xavier of Ohio. The upswing under Byrdsong is hardly reason for optimism, however. The respectable 1994 team has lost four key starters to graduation including Kevin Rankin (the team's MVP), Patrick Baldwin (the Big Ten's best defensive player in 1993-94) and Todd Leslie (holder of the NCAA record for consecutive three-point baskets). Neloms returns for another season and guard Dio Lee and 7-footer Dan Kreft also indicate a talent upgrade in Evanston. But in the nation's strongest basketball conference, moderate talent upgrades suggest that a noticeable overhaul in Northwestern's fortunes may still be a very long time in coming.

Records and Summaries
Year-by-Year Northwestern Records
(Championship Years in Boldface)

Season	All Games	Conference	Coach(es)	Top Scorer (Points)
1904-05	2-2	None	Tom Holland	No Record
1905-06		*No Games Played*		
1906-07	1-5	None	Louis Gillesby	No Record
1907-08	2-7	None	Louis Gillesby	No Record
1908-09	1-7	1-4	Louis Gillesby	No Record
1909-10	0-9	0-9	Louis Gillesby	No Record

1910-11	4-15	1-12	Stuart Templeton	No Record
1911-12	4-9	0-8	Charles Hammett	No Record
1912-13	14-4	7-2	Dennis Grady	No Record
1913-14	11-6	6-5	Dennis Grady	Harold Whittle (109)•
1914-15	11-8	5-5	Fred Murphy	No Record
1915-16	14-5	9-3	Fred Murphy	No Record
1916-17	3-11	2-10	Fred Murphy	No Record
1917-18	7-4	5-3	Norman Elliott	No Record
1918-19	6-6	6-4	Tom Robinson	No Record
1919-20	3-7	2-6	Norman Elliott	No Record
1920-21	2-12	1-11	Ray Elder	No Record
1921-22	7-11	3-9	Dana Evans	No Record
1922-23	5-10	3-9	Maury Kent	No Record
1923-24	0-16	0-12	Maury Kent	No Record
1924-25	6-10	4-8	Maury Kent	No Record
1925-26	5-12	3-9	Maury Kent	No Record
1926-27	3-14	1-11	Maury Kent	No Record
1927-28	12-5	9-3	Arthur Lonborg	No Record
1928-29	12-5	7-5	Arthur Lonborg	No Record
1929-30	8-8	6-6	Arthur Lonborg	No Record
1930-31	**16-1**	**11-1 (1st)**	**Arthur Lonborg**	**No Record**
1931-32	13-5	9-3	Arthur Lonborg	Joe Reiff (120)•
1932-33	**15-4**	**10-2 (1st-T)**	**Arthur Lonborg**	**No Record**
1933-34	11-8	8-4	Arthur Lonborg	No Record
1934-35	10-10	3-9	Arthur Lonborg	No Record
1935-36	13-6	7-5	Arthur Lonborg	No Record
1936-37	11-9	4-8	Arthur Lonborg	No Record
1937-38	10-10	7-5	Arthur Lonborg	No Record
1938-39	7-13	5-7	Arthur Lonborg	No Record
1939-40	13-7	7-5	Arthur Lonborg	No Record
1940-41	7-11	3-9	Arthur Lonborg	No Record
1941-42	8-13	5-10	Arthur Lonborg	No Record
1942-43	8-9	7-5	Arthur Lonborg	No Record
1943-44	12-7	8-4	Arthur Lonborg	No Record
1944-45	7-12	4-8	Arthur Lonborg	Max Morris (189)•
1945-46	15-5	8-4	Arthur Lonborg	Max Morris (198)•
1946-47	7-13	2-10	Arthur Lonborg	No Record
1947-48	6-14	3-9	Arthur Lonborg	No Record
1948-49	5-16	2-10	Arthur Lonborg	No Record
1949-50	10-12	3-9	Arthur Lonborg	Ray Ragelis (338)
1950-51	12-10	7-7	Harold Olson	Ray Ragelis (421)•
1951-52	7-15	4-10	Harold Olson	Frank Petrancek (313)
1952-53	6-16	5-13	Waldo Fisher	Larry Kurka (273)

1953-54	9-13	6-8	Waldo Fisher	Frank Ehmann (383)
1954-55	12-10	7-7	Waldo Fisher	Frank Ehmann (501)
1955-56	2-20	1-13	Waldo Fisher	Dick Mast (463)
1956-57	6-16	2-12	Waldo Fisher	Joe Ruklick (396)
1957-58	13-9	8-6	William Rohr	Joe Ruklick (414)
1958-59	15-7	8-6	William Rohr	Joe Ruklick (505)
1959-60	11-12	8-6	William Rohr	Willie Jones (410)
1960-61	10-12	6-8	William Rohr	Ralph Wells (309)
1961-62	8-15	3-11	William Rohr	Ralph Wells (312)
1962-63	9-15	6-8	William Rohr	Rich Falk (372)
1963-64	8-13	6-8	Larry Glass	Rich Falk (489)
1964-65	7-17	3-11	Larry Glass	Jim Burns (411)
1965-66	12-12	7-7	Larry Glass	Jim Burns (485)
1966-67	11-11	7-7	Larry Glass	Jim Burns (472)
1967-68	13-10	8-6	Larry Glass	Dale Kelley (312)
1968-69	14-10	6-8	Larry Glass/Brad Snyder	Dale Kelley (416)
1969-70	9-15	4-10	Brad Snyder	Dale Kelley (582)
1970-71	7-17	3-11	Brad Snyder	Barry Moran (420)
1971-72	5-18	3-11	Brad Snyder	Mark Sibley (324)
1972-73	5-19	2-12	Brad Snyder	Mark Sibley (461)
1973-74	9-15	3-11	Tex Winter	Billy McKinney (378)
1974-75	6-20	4-14	Tex Winter	Billy McKinney (473)
1975-76	12-15	7-11	Tex Winter	Billy McKinney (533)
1976-77	9-18	7-11	Tex Winter	Billy McKinney (516)
1977-78	8-19	4-14	Tex Winter	Tony Allen (393)
1978-79	6-21	2-16	Rich Falk	Rod Roberson (282)
1979-80	10-17	5-13	Rich Falk	Jim Stack (348)
1980-81	9-18	3-15	Rich Falk	Rod Roberson (464)
1981-82	9-18	5-13	Rich Falk	Jim Stack (401)
1982-83	18-12	8-10	Rich Falk	Jim Stack (447)
1983-84	14-14	7-11	Rich Falk	Art Aaron (457)
1984-85	6-22	2-16	Rich Falk	Andre Goode (352)
1985-86	8-20	2-16	Rich Falk	Shon Morris (432)
1986-87	7-21	2-16	Bill Foster	Shon Morris (379)
1987-88	7-21	2-16	Bill Foster	Shon Morris (423)
1988-89	9-19	2-16	Bill Foster	William Lambiotte (486)
1989-90	9-19	2-16	Bill Foster	Rex Walters (492)
1990-91	5-23	0-18	Bill Foster	Todd Leslie (392)
1991-92	9-19	2-16	Bill Foster	Cedric Neloms (402)
1992-93	8-19	3-15	Bill Foster	Cedric Neloms (438)
1993-94	15-14	5-13	Ricky Byrdsong	Kevin Rankin (443)

• = League Individual Scoring Champion

All-Time Northwestern Individual Career Records

Points Scored .... Billy McKinney (1,900, 1974-77)
Scoring Average .... Joe Ruklick (19.9, 1957-59)
Games Played .... Andre Goode (113, 1982-85)
Games Started ....Jim Stack (109, 1979-83)
Field Goals .... Billy McKinney (768, 1974-77)
Field-Goal Percentage .... Paul Schultz (.541, 1981-84)
Free Throws Made .... Shon Morris (371, 1985-88)
Free-Throw Percentage ....Jeff Grose (.862, 1986-89)
3-Point Field Goals .... Todd Leslie (126, 1990-94)
Rebounds .... Joe Ruklick (868, 1957-59)
Rebound Average...Jim Pitts (13.3, 1964-66)
Assists .... Shawn Watts (379, 1984-87)
Steals .... Patrick Baldwin (213, 1990-94)
Blocked Shots .... Jim Pitts (123, 1966*)
*No records kept in 1964 and 1965

All-Time Northwestern Individual Season Records

Points Scored .... Dale Kelley (582, 1969-70)
Scoring Average .... Dale Kelley (24.3, 1969-70)
Minutes Played..................................... Gaddis Rathel (1091, 1982-83)
Field Goals .... Dale Kelley (209, 1969-70)
Field-Goal Percentage .... Frank Petrancek (.588, 1951-52)
Free Throws Made .... Dale Kelley (164, 1969-70)
Free-Throw Percentage ....Jim Stack (.900, 1980-81)
3-Point Field Goals .... Todd Leslie (65, 1990-91)
Rebounds ....Jim Pitts (321, 1965-66)
Rebound Average...Joe Ruklick (13.9, 1957-58)
Assists .... Patrick Baldwin (136, 1992-93)
Steals .... Patrick Baldwin (90, 1990-91)
Blocked Shots ....Jim Pitts (123, 1965-66)

All-Time Northwestern Individual Single-Game Records

Points Scored .... Rich Falk (49 vs. Iowa, 1964)
Field Goals .... Rich Falk (19 vs. Iowa, 1964)
Free Throws Made ....Shon Morris (17 vs. Northern Arizona, 1988)
3-Point Field Goals .... Todd Leslie (7 vs. Iowa, 1992)
Rebounds ....Joe Ruklick (31 vs. Kansas, 1958)
Assists ....Patrick Baldwin (14 vs. Youngstown St., 1992)
Steals .... Patrick Baldwin (9 vs. Oakland, 1991)
Blocked Shots ....Jim Pitts (10 vs. Purdue, 1966)

All-Time Northwestern Coaching Records

Coach	Overall Record	Conference Record	Seasons
Arthur Lonborg (1928-50)	236-203 (.538)	138-141 (.495)	23
Rick Falk (1979-86)	80-142 (.360)	34-110 (.236)	8
William Rohr (1958-63)	66-70 (.485)	39-45 (.464)	6
Larry Glass (1964-69)	61-71 (.462)	33-45 (.423)	6
Bill Foster (1987-93)	54-141 (.277)	13-113 (.103)	7
Tex Winter (1974-78)	44-87 (.336)	21-61 (.256)	5
Waldo Fisher (1953-57)	35-75 (.318)	21-53 (.284)	5
Brad Snyder (1970-73)	30-71 (.297)	16-46 (.258)	4
Harold Olson (1951-52)	19-25 (.432)	11-17 (.393)	2
Maury Kent (1923-27)	19-62 (.235)	11-49 (.183)	5
Ricky Byrdsong (1994-present)	15-14 (.517)	5-13 (.278)	1
Dana Evans (1922)	7-11 (.389)	3-9 (.250)	1
Ray Elder (1921)	2-12 (.143)	1-11 (.083)	1
Tom Robinson (1919)	6-6 (.500)	6-4 (.600)	1
Norman Elliot (1918, 1920)	10-11 (.476)	7-9 (.438)	2
Fred Murphy (1915-17)	28-24 (.538)	16-18 (.471)	3
Dennis Grady (1913-14)	25-10 (.714)	13-7 (.650)	2
Charles Hammett (1912)	4-9 (.308)	0-8 (.000)	1
Stuart Templeton (1911)	4-15 (.211)	1-12 (.077)	1
Louis Gillesby (1907-10)	4-28 (.125)	1-13 (.071)	4
Tom Holland (1905)	2-2 (.500)	None	1

Northwestern All-Americans and All-Big Ten Selections

Consensus All-Americans
Joe Reiff, Center, 1931-1932-1933
Otto Graham, Forward, 1944
Max Morris, Forward, 1946

All-Big Ten Selections (since 1948)
Ray Ragelis, Center, 1951
Frank Ehmann, Forward, 1955
Joe Ruklick, Center, 1959
Rick Lopossa, Forward, 1964
Jim Burns, Guard, 1967
Billy McKinney, Guard, 1977

Chapter 8

OHIO STATE *Buckeyes*

Buckeyes, Deadeyes and Best Team Ever Invented

All-Time Record: 1,230-824, .599; **Conference Record:** 600-540, .530

Big Ten Championships —15: (1925, 1933*, 1939, 1944, 1946, 1950, 1960, 1961, 1962, 1963*, 1964*, 1968*, 1971, 1991*, 1992) * = Co-Champion

National (NCAA) Championships —1: (1960)

National Invitation Tournament (NIT) Championships —1: (1986)

Greatest Player: Jerry Lucas (1960-62)

Career Scoring Leader: Dennis Hopson (2,096 Points, 1984-87)

Most Successful Coach: Fred Taylor (1959-76), 297-158, .653

All-Time Team: Jerry Lucas (C, 1960-62), Gary Bradds (C-F, 1962-64), John Havlicek (F, 1960-62), Robin Freeman (G, 1954-56), Jim Jackson (G, 1990-92)

Best Season: 1959-60 (25-3), NCAA Champion (Coach: Fred Taylor)

University Profile
    Location: Columbus, Ohio (pop. 615,000); **Founded:** 1870; **Campus Enrollment:** 52,183 (1994); **Started Basketball:** 1902-03. With a combined student, faculty and staff population of 68,000, OSU's Columbus campus is the nation's largest. Founded 125 years ago as the Ohio Agricultural and Mechanical College, the Big Ten's largest member offers more than 200 master's and doctoral degree programs. The prestigious OSU graduate faculty includes a Nobel Prize winner, members of the National Academy of Sciences, Guggenheim and Fulbright Fellows, Rhodes Scholars and editors of prestigious academic journals.

Team Nickname, Colors and Arena

Nickname: Buckeyes; Colors: Scarlet and Gray; **Arena:** St. John Arena (13,276 capacity, opened 1957). The OSU athletic teams' unique nickname derives from the glossy brown nut from the state tree of the same name. This seems hardly an appropriate symbol for the ferocious competitiveness of today's intercollegiate athletics, especially when compared with the raft of dangerous birds and animals that serve as symbols for most rival universities. But such inanimate representation of school spirit hasn't tarnished the proud OSU athletic tradition for a moment. The Buckeyes lay claim to unique distinction as the first school ever to win national titles in basketball, football, baseball, track and golf.

Buckeye Basketball History

The tradition of Buckeye basketball in the Big Ten reaches back to the 1912-13 season when an Ohio State team coached by second-year-man Lynn St. John became the ninth official member of the Western Conference, the Big Ten's predecessor. Coach St. John would leave a legacy that would be carried on by the stately arena which has been home to Buckeye teams since 1957 and now bears his name. During the eight seasons St. John coached the Buckeyes, however, it was a legacy of losing. His second team was his best in conference play with a 5-1 league mark. All other Big Ten (Western Conference) teams under St. John would be nothing more than hopeless also-rans and lackluster losers.

The quarter century following St. John's departure would be a far brighter era, however, and one which would bear the stamp of 24-year coach Harold Olsen, a stern figure whose reign was among the longest at any Big Ten school. Harold Foster later logged 25 years at Wisconsin. Indiana's Branch McCracken served 24 seasons but not consecutively and current Hoosier coach Bob Knight is now zeroing in on Olsen's mark with 23 seasons and counting.

In only his third year on the job, Olsen would bring the Columbus school its first conference title. His long tenure would result in four more league banners, two in the 1930s and two in the middle of the talent-thin World War II years. There would be many poor and average teams along the way under Olsen's steady if unspectacular leadership, but overall, his record fell squarely on the winning side with 154 conference victories and 255 wins overall. It was one of the best records among conference coaches serving before the modern postwar era.

Pioneering stars for the Buckeyes under Olsen were two consensus All-Americans of the 1930s, guard Wes Fesler in 1931 and forward Jimmy Hull in 1939. Johnny Miner had actually been the school's first All-American selection way back in 1929, but it was Hull who built the most far-ranging and lasting reputation. An early distinction for the program would soon be earned by the 1939 squad paced by Hull and coached by Olsen. That team would win a conference title, then hustle its way to the finals of the first-ever NCAA postseason tournament. That historic title tilt, played in familiar territory on the Northwestern campus in Evanston, Ill., would find the Buckeyes falling to Oregon in a one-sided game distinguished by the typical low scoring of that early era. The final count was 46-33 with Hull scoring 12 points. Ironically, Northwestern's Patten Gym had been settled on as the playoff site when Olsen (organizer and most energetic backer of the first tournament) decided his Buckeyes couldn't afford the financial strain of travel to east- or west-coast venues despite prospects of higher gate revenues.

Ohio State would return to the NCAA tournament three straight times in Olsen's final three seasons but the Buckeyes would lose in the tournament semifinals each time. The first defeat would be at the hands of Dartmouth by a 60-53 count in New York's glamorous Madison Square Garden. The second in 1945 — also staged in the famous indoor arena — would be a hard-fought overtime loss to local favorite New York University, 70-65. The third, also at Madison Square Garden, would come at the hands of North Carolina, 60-57. The 1946 team would end Olsen's career in glorious fashion, however, defeating California for third place in the NCAA postseason carnival. The consolation victory was an easy 63-45 romp paced by future pro center Arnie Risen. The game was staged as a preliminary match to the featured title shootout between North Carolina's Tar Heels and an Oklahoma A&M (now Oklahoma State) team sporting the nation's top player, 7-foot wonder Bob Kurland. This was in the days when the National Invitation Tournament was still king and the NCAA ranked second when it came to year-end championship prestige. But Olsen's three straight trips to the "Final Four" had finally gained the OSU program a measure of true national prominence.

A short four-year tenure for William Dye brought another Big Ten title and another NCAA postseason visit during the 1949-50 season. It also brought the All-American play of Dick Schnittker, a two-time All-Big Ten selection at forward. Backcourt ace Bob Donham, however, was the most valuable player on the 22-4 club. Donham posted the best field-goal shooting mark in the conference that year. But Schnittker, team MVP in 1948 and 1949, also earned consensus All-American and all-league status in 1950. The '47 and '48 teams also featured future NBA scoring champ and hook shot pioneer Neil Johnston at center. Johnston would be one of seven Buckeyes eventually enshrined in the Naismith Basketball Hall of Fame — the sport's highest and most lasting honor. Other Buckeye Hall of Famers would include coaches St. John, Olsen and Fred Taylor, players Jerry Lucas and John Havlicek along with another member of the 1960 national championship team who would earn his major accolades elsewhere in the Big Ten — Indiana University coaching legend Bob Knight.

The 1950s in the unfolding saga of OSU basketball turned into a lengthy holding pattern under eight-year mentor Floyd Stahl. All of Stahl's teams were true middle-of-the-pack outfits; only two (1957, 16-6 and 1957, 14-8) posted winning records. But there were two notable stars of the period who left lasting marks on the school's cage history. The first was 5-foot-11 guard Robin Freeman, whom many longtime Buckeye watchers still select as the most exciting player ever to wear the scarlet and gray uniform. Freeman was the first Ohio State player to specialize in the newly popular jump shot. His novel shooting arsenal made Freeman nearly unstoppable. In 1956 he would be the first player in conference history to average more than 30 points per game for a full season and that same winter became Ohio State's first two-time All-American. His career scoring average (28.0) is still the best in school annals. He was followed in 1956, 1957 and 1958 by bulky forward Frank Howard, another member of the Buckeyes' career 1,000-point club. Howard would later earn greater fame as a home run hitter on the baseball diamond.

The true glory era of OSU basketball arrived with scholarly looking Fred Taylor just in time for the 1958-59 campaign. Taylor would soon recruit and coach the school's greatest individual players, earn its most magnificent regular-season and postseason triumphs, and post the best-ever Buckeye coaching ledger. Taylor's 297 overall victories would outdistance Olsen by 42; his .653 overall winning percentage would be the best in school annals among those who coached more than two seasons. With 158 Big Ten wins when he retired, Taylor would rank behind only Ward Lambert, Branch McCracken and Illinois' Harry Combes. He now stands eighth on the all-time list. His conference winning percentage (.608) is today matched or surpassed by only seven other longtime league mentors.

The Buckeye teams that remained nearly intact for the 1960, 1961 and 1962 seasons under Taylor were arguably the greatest in Big Ten history. Only the 1975 and 1976 Indiana teams come close to the mythical honor. The OSU dream units were anchored by Havlicek and Lucas in the frontcourt, with Mel Nowell and Larry Siegfried (1960-61) at the guards. The fifth starter would be Joe Roberts in 1960, Richie Hoyt in 1961 and Doug McDonald in 1962, with Dick Reasbeck replacing Siegfried in 1962 as well. Key backups would be future coaching legend Bob Knight and, in 1962, future superstar center Gary Bradds.

Lucas was perhaps the greatest single player in Big Ten annals, certainly the finest ever to ply his talents in Columbus. Lucas earned first-team All-American honors three times and did so without posting huge scoring numbers, although he was the nation's leader in field-goal accuracy all three seasons. While Lucas played, the Buckeyes' owned an overall 78-6 record, two of those losses coming in NCAA title matchups with Cincinnati in 1961 and 1962. As a sophomore, Lucas hit an incredible 63.7 percent of his shots and the 6-8 super center graduated as the Buckeyes' all-time leading scorer with 1,990 points (24.3 points per game), a record which would quickly fall to Bradds two seasons later.

Havlicek and Siegfried were stars of almost the same magnitude as Lucas. Although more famous for his Hall of Fame career with the Boston Celtics, "Hondo" Havlicek was nonetheless an all-time All-Big Ten choice and an All-American during his senior season. Siegfried ran the Buckeyes' offense for the first two seasons of the glory era and later enjoyed a stellar NBA career in Boston. And there were other great players on the same team, especially Nowell and the young and promising sophomore, Bradds. Bradds adequately replaced the injured Lucas in the 1962 title game and would be National Player of the Year during his 1964 senior season.

Thus the 1960 OSU team was the highlight moment of a remarkable era. First the young club would breeze through the conference schedule at 13-1 enroute to a 25-3 season which was the best in school history. Only the 1950 team had previuosly broken the 20-victory circle. The four NCAA tournament games that season were hardly a test as Taylor's club would roll over Western Kentucky (98-79), Georgia Tech (86-69), NYU (76-54) and California (75-55) in rapid succession. Few if any teams ever enjoyed an easier time throughout an NCAA playoff schedule. The championship game with California saw the Buckeyes sprint to a 37-19 halftime lead. All five starters (Havlicek, Roberts, Lucas, Nowell and Siegfried) would post double figures in the one-sided contest. California's leading scorer, 6-10 center Darrall Imhoff, was completely blanketed by Lucas and held to single-digit scoring.

The 1960-61 Ohio State team was every bit as good as its predecessor and featured essentially the same lineup, with only Richie Hoyt replacing Joe Roberts at one forward slot alongside Havlicek. Perhaps this unit was even better as the Buckeyes maintained a 20-point margin of victory (85.1 to 65.7) over all opponents throughout the season. The Taylor-coached squad would eventually extend its winning streak to 32 games, a conference record that would stand until the 1974 and 1975 Indiana teams won 34 in a row. Throughout 24 regular-season

Dennis Hopson, right, a 1987 All-Big Ten selection, holds Buckeye records for single-season scoring (958 points) and career scoring (2,096 points). (Ohio State University photo)

and three NCAA games, the record of Lucas, Havlicek, Siegfried and company would remain unblemished. The Bucks did receive a brief scare in their opening NCAA match, however, as the Louisville Cardinals, playing on their home floor, led by five points with three minutes remaining. But Havlicek's long jumper in the closing seconds saved a 56-55 victory.

The question was not so much whether Ohio State was now the best team in the country but seemed more a matter of whether this was perhaps the best team ever invented in any place or any year. In the tournament final, a classic matchup transpired with state rival Cincinnati, a powerhouse outfit which had lost its greatest star, Oscar Robertson, a season earlier but was as strong as ever for its showdown with the Buckeyes. The final overtime thriller between the two juggernauts was one of the great matches in NCAA annals. Cincinnati enjoyed superior rebounding skills (despite the presence of Lucas) with center Paul Hogue and powerful forwards Tom Thacker and Bob Wiesenhahn, and used this edge to slow the Buckeyes' fast-breaking attack. The tense game remained deadlocked into the closing seconds when a driving layup by reserve forward Bobby Knight sealed a 61-61 tie to force overtime.

But in the extra period the surprising Bearcats pulled away for a stunning 70-65 victory and on this memorable night, at least, the Lucas-Havlicek unit was not the best team of all time. Suddenly it seemingly wasn't even the best team in the basketball-rich state of Ohio.

The 1962 squad fully expected to avenge the painful season-wrecking loss suffered against the neighboring Bearcats. A new Big Ten record of 27 straight league victories would soon be reached. It would be a mark that would later fall only to the 37 straight by Indiana from the final game of 1974 through the final conference match of 1976. But as expected, the campaign came down to another dramatic showdown with down-state rival Cincinnati.

Cincinnati had now been strengthened by a warhorse sophomore forward named Ron Bonham. Ohio State had lost Siegfried (Dick Reasbeck filled in but averaged only 7.9 points for the season), but the Buckeyes now also had Bradds, a promising sophomore center, to spell Lucas when needed. While the Buckeyes had suffered only a single upset loss in Wisconsin, the Bearcats entered the finals with an almost equal 25-2 ledger. The turning point this time, however, came when Lucas suffered a knee injury in the semifinal game against Wake Forest, a blow which left him hobbled for the all-important Cincinnati rematch. Bradds would have to carry most of the load in the title game (he paced the Bucks with 15 points), but with Hogue (22) and Thacker (21) leading the Cincinnati onslaught, it wasn't enough. The Bearcats would again prevail, this time even more convincingly to the tune of 71-59 in a game that provided plenty of breathing room for Cincinnati in the closing moments. "We really proved a point this time," boasted Bearcat guard Tony Yates in the postgame celebration. "You don't repeat flukes."

Jerry Lucas and John Havlicek had thus bowed out in what had to be the most disappointing moment of a three-year career that contained few disappointments indeed. It had been a truly glorious era, perhaps the most glorious for any single three-year unit in Big Ten history. Only the UCLA teams featuring first Lew Alcindor and later Bill Walton enjoyed more continuous success and more national prestige. With Lucas and Havlicek gone, the dropoff would not be altogether immediate in Columbus, either. Bradds remained and his star rose dramatically in 1963 and 1964. The 1963 squad (20-4, 11-3) would share a piece of the Big Ten crown with Illinois but sit on the sidelines while the Illini carried the conference banner into NCAA postseason play. Taylor's record fifth-straight conference banner would come in 1964, again a

Clark Kellogg, Big Ten Most Valuable Player in 1982, enjoyed a productive NBA career. (Ohio State University photo)

tie with Michigan, but the final season for Bradds would find the Buckeyes slipping to 16-8 overall and again missing the postseason dance. Bradds, for his part, would establish credentials as one of the great scorers of all time by posting six straight 40-point games in 1964, a mark not even pro-lific-shooting Rick Mount could match (the Purdue ace had four in a row in 1969).

Taylor would remain for 12 seasons after the five straight Big Ten titles. But never again would Taylor's teams reach quite the same zany heights. He would win two more championships and he would have a few later stars like Bill Hosket (the school's first-ever Academic All-American), Dick Ricketts, Dave Sorenson and Jim Cleamons. The 1967-68 ballclub posted 21 victories and was perhaps the best outside of the Lucas-Havlicek era. A conference tie with Iowa that year was broken by an 85-81 OSU victory in a playoff for the NCAA berth. With Hosket lead-ing all conference scorers at 20.1 points per game and Sorenson plugging the center position, that final great Taylor team scratched out an 82-81 regional championship victory over Kentucky to return to the Final Four. But the Buckeyes were no match for North Carolina in the national semi-finals and fell to a balanced Tar Heel attack 80-66, missing a crack at Alcindor and the defend-ing champion UCLA Bruins in the title round. Nothing like the glory of those five seasons of the 1960s was seen again. Not in Columbus, nor anywhere else in the Big Ten.

The Eldon Miller era at OSU, which stretched from 1976 through 1986, was a seem-ingly endless "passion play" of near-misses and late-season frustrations. Plenty of top-notch players wore Buckeye uniforms during this memorable epoch with Clark Kellogg, Herb Will-iams and Dennis Hopson at the top of the heap. There were four Miller-coached teams that won 20 games or more and two others with 19 victories. But there were no close runs at a Big Ten title. Either Indiana (with Isiah Thomas and Mike Woodson) or Purdue (with Joe Barry Carroll) or Michigan (with Mike McGee or Roy Tarpley) was always in the way.

Individual talent during this period, though, was some of the greatest in school history. Kellogg broke into the starting lineup as a freshman and was a 1982 All-Big Ten selection. One of the most popular OSU players ever, he passed up his senior season to enter the NBA hardship draft. Herb Williams was also a pillar of strength at center, starting four seasons and amassing more than 2,000 points and 1,000 rebounds (only Lucas has done this for the Buckeyes before or since). Both Williams and Kellogg eventually enjoyed outstanding pro careers with the Indiana Pacers during the early 1980s. Brad Sellers first was a rebounding star at Wisconsin, then transferred to Columbus and continued his board work during the 1985 and 1986 campaigns. Sellers is, in fact, a unique player in Big Ten history, holding school records for two different Big Ten teams, career and season records for blocked shots at Wisconsin and the single-season mark for blocked shots at Ohio State.

But the gold-medal player of this 1970s-1980s era was clearly Dennis Hopson. Hopson would build a solid, but not spectacular, foundation his first three seasons and then burst upon the national scene to average 29 points per game as a senior and earn UPI Big Ten Player-of-the-Year honors and selection to *Sporting News* All-America team. With a school-record 958 points in his 1987 senior season, Hopson would become the most prolific scorer in school history (2,096 points) and one of the best in the Big Ten. Other records set by "Hop" during his spectacular final year were for most free throws made (217) and three-point baskets (67).

The Eldon Miller tenure would end on an unexpected high note with a 1986 championship in the postseason NIT tournament. The final Miller team sported a lineup of co-captains Hopson and Sellers, alongside Jerry Francis, Keith Wesson and Kip Lomax. It was a team only good enough to post a 15-14 season record and simply didn't measure up in conference play. The Buckeyes finished 8-10 and in seventh place. Against the NIT field, however, Hopson and his teammates reeled off five victories in a row (Ohio University, Texas, Brigham Young, LSU and Wyoming) to become the fourth Big Ten club ever to win the less-prestigious NIT.

The first three seasons of Coach Randy Ayres were packed with plenty of excitement to say the least. Ayres' arrival was a period graced by back-to-back league titles in 1991 and 1992, two of the school's highest victory totals of 27 (1991) and 26 (1992) which matched the record numbers posted by the Lucas-era teams, and the memorable three-year career of Jim Jackson. Jackson led OSU back into conference prominence by starting 93 consecutive games before bypassing his senior season for early entry into the NBA draft. The 6-6 guard-forward was conference Freshman of the Year in 1990 and an easy choice for Big Ten Player of the Year the following two seasons. Jackson was also a two-time All-American and the national Player of the Year his final (junior) campaign. By passing up his senior season, Jim Jackson would remain fifth on the all-time OSU scoring list (1,785 points), but not even Lucas, Kellogg, Hopson or Havlicek had a more solid reputation as a clutch money player in game-breaking situations than did Ohio State's greatest star of the 1990s.

While a number of league schools have constructed new arenas as part of upscale image building during the past decade, Ohio State continues to play its home games in one of the league's oldest and most prestigious venues. Only Minnesota's Williams Arena can match St. John Arena for color, tradition and old-style basketball aura. It's one of the most difficult places for opponents to play. And it's one of the most thrilling locations for a tried and true basketball junkie to take in a thrill-packed and ear-splitting contest.

The Ohio State basketball program has fallen on the hardest of times during the past three seasons under Ayres. Recruiting mistakes and off-court scandals have the current team in a shambles and toppled a once-proud program into the depths of the conference basement. But

Jim Jackson was UPI Player of the Year in 1992 and a two-time All-Big Ten selection. (Ohio State University photo)

if history is any indicator, more great Buckeye hoop stars cannot be far down the road. The program that has featured such legends as Lucas, Havlicek, Freeman, Siegfried, Hosket, Kellogg, Bradds, Hopson and Jim Jackson is not likely to remain on the endangered species list for long.

Records and Summaries
Year-by-Year Ohio State Records
(Championship Years in Boldface)

Season	All Games	Conference	Coach(es)	Buckeye MVP
1902-03	5-2	None	D.C. Huddleston	Not Yet Awarded
1903-04	10-4	None	D.C. Huddleston	Not Yet Awarded
1904-05	12-2	None	No Coach	Not Yet Awarded
1905-06	9-1	None	No Coach	Not Yet Awarded
1906-07	7-5	None	No Coach	Not Yet Awarded
1907-08	5-6	None	No Coach	Not Yet Awarded
1908-09	11-1	None	Thomas Kibler	Not Yet Awarded
1909-10	11-1	None	Thomas Kibler	Not Yet Awarded
1910-11	7-2	None	No Coach	Not Yet Awarded
1911-12	7-5	None	Lynn St. John	Not Yet Awarded
1912-13	13-7	4-5	Lynn St. John	Not Yet Awarded
1913-14	11-4	5-1	Lynn St. John	Not Yet Awarded
1914-15	10-7	3-9	Lynn St. John	Not Yet Awarded
1915-16	9-13	2-8	Lynn St. John	Not Yet Awarded
1916-17	15-11	3-9	Lynn St. John	Not Yet Awarded
1917-18	12-7	5-5	Lynn St. John	Not Yet Awarded
1918-19	7-12	2-6	Lynn St. John	Not Yet Awarded
1919-20	17-10	3-9	George Trautman	Not Yet Awarded
1920-21	4-13	2-10	George Trautman	Not Yet Awarded
1921-22	8-10	5-7	George Trautman	Not Yet Awarded
1922-23	4-11	1-11	Harold Olsen	Not Yet Awarded
1923-24	12-5	7-5	Harold Olsen	Not Yet Awarded
1924-25	**14-2**	**11-1 (1st)**	**Harold Olsen**	**Not Yet Awarded**
1925-26	10-7	6-6	Harold Olsen	Not Yet Awarded
1926-27	11-6	6-6	Harold Olsen	Not Yet Awarded
1927-28	5-12	3-9	Harold Olsen	Not Yet Awarded
1928-29	9-8	6-6	Harold Olsen	Not Yet Awarded
1929-30	4-11	1-9	Harold Olsen	Not Yet Awarded
1930-31	4-13	3-9	Harold Olsen	Not Yet Awarded
1931-32	9-9	5-7	Harold Olsen	Not Yet Awarded
1932-33	**17-3**	**10-2 (1st-T)**	**Harold Olsen**	**Not Yet Awarded**
1933-34	8-12	4-8	Harold Olsen	Not Yet Awarded
1934-35	13-6	8-4	Harold Olsen	Not Yet Awarded
1935-36	12-8	5-7	Harold Olsen	Not Yet Awarded
1936-37	13-7	7-5	Harold Olsen	Not Yet Awarded
1937-38	12-8	7-5	Harold Olsen	Not Yet Awarded

Year	Overall	Conference	Coach	Award
1938-39	**16-7**	**10-2 (1st)**	**Harold Olsen**	**Not Yet Awarded**
1939-40	13-7	8-4	Harold Olsen	Not Yet Awarded
1940-41	10-10	7-5	Harold Olsen	Not Yet Awarded
1941-42	6-14	4-11	Harold Olsen	Not Yet Awarded
1942-43	8-9	5-7	Harold Olsen	Not Yet Awarded
1943-44	**14-7**	**10-2 (1st)**	Harold Olsen	**Not Yet Awarded**
1944-45	15-5	10-2	Harold Olsen	Not Yet Awarded
1945-46	**16-5**	**10-2 (1st)**	**Harold Olsen**	**Paul Huston**
1946-47	7-13	5-7	William Dye	Jack Underman
1947-48	10-10	5-7	William Dye	Dick Schnittker
1948-49	14-7	6-6	William Dye	Dick Schnittker
1949-50	**22-4**	**11-1 (1st)**	**William Dye**	**Bob Donham**
1950-51	6-16	3-11	Floyd Stahl	Jim Remington
1951-52	8-14	6-8	Floyd Stahl	Paul Ebert
1952-53	10-12	7-11	Floyd Stahl	Paul Ebert
1953-54	11-11	5-9	Floyd Stahl	Paul Ebert
1954-55	10-12	4-10	Floyd Stahl	John Miller
1955-56	16-6	9-5	Floyd Stahl	Robin Freeman
1956-57	14-8	9-5	Floyd Stahl	Gene Millard
1957-58	9-13	8-6	Floyd Stahl	Ken Sidle
1958-59	11-11	7-7	Fred Taylor	Larry Siegfried
1959-60#	**25-3**	**13-1 (1st)**	**Fred Taylor**	**Jerry Lucas**
1960-61	**27-1**	**14-0 (1st)**	**Fred Taylor**	**Jerry Lucas**
1961-62	**26-2**	**13-1 (1st)**	**Fred Taylor**	**Jerry Lucas**
1962-63	**20-4**	**11-3 (1st-T)**	**Fred Taylor**	**Gary Bradds**
1963-64	**16-8**	**11-3 (1st-T)**	**Fred Taylor**	**Gary Bradds**
1964-65	12-12	6-8	Fred Taylor	Dick Ricketts
1965-66	11-13	5-9	Fred Taylor	Bob Dove
1966-67	13-11	6-8	Fred Taylor	Bill Hosket
1967-68	**21-8**	**10-4 (1st-T)**	**Fred Taylor**	**Bill Hosket**
1968-69	17-7	9-5	Fred Taylor	Dave Sorenson
1969-70	17-7	8-6	Fred Taylor	Dave Sorenson
1970-71	**20-6**	**13-1 (1st)**	**Fred Taylor**	**Jim Cleamons**
1971-72	18-6	10-4	Fred Taylor	Mark Minor
1972-73	14-10	8-6	Fred Taylor	Allan Hornyak
1973-74	9-15	4-10	Fred Taylor	Bill Andreas
1974-75	14-14	8-10	Fred Taylor	Bill Andreas
1975-76	6-20	2-16	Fred Taylor	Craig Taylor
1976-77	11-16	4-14	Eldon Miller	Larry Bolden
1977-78	16-11	9-9	Eldon Miller	Kelvin Ransey
1978-79	19-12	12-6	Eldon Miller	Herb Williams
1979-80	21-8	12-6	Eldon Miller	Kelvin Ransey
1980-81	14-13	9-9	Eldon Miller	Herb Williams
1981-82	21-10	12-6	Eldon Miller	Clark Kellogg
1982-83	20-10	11-7	Eldon Miller	Tony Campbell

1983-84	15-14	8-10	Eldon Miller	Tony Campbell
1984-85	20-10	11-7	Eldon Miller	Ron Stokes
1985-86**	19-14	8-10	Eldon Miller	Brad Sellers
1986-87	20-13	9-9	Gary Williams	Dennis Hopson
1987-88	20-13	9-9	Gary Williams	Jay Burson
1988-89	19-15	6-12	Gary Williams	Jay Burson
1989-90	17-13	10-8	Randy Ayres	Jim Jackson
1990-91	**27-4**	**15-3 (1st-T)**	**Randy Ayres**	**Jim Jackson**
1991-92	**26-6**	**15-3 (1st)**	**Randy Ayres**	**Jim Jackson**
1992-93	15-13	8-10	Randy Ayres	Lawrence Funderburke
1993-94	13-16	6-12	Randy Ayres	Derek Anderson

= National (NCAA) Champions; ** = NIT Champions.

All-Time Ohio State Individual Career Records

Points Scored .... Dennis Hopson (2,096, 1984-87)
Scoring Average .... Robin Freeman (28.0, 1954-56)
Games Played .... Jerry Francis (133, 1986-89)
Games Started .... Jerry Francis (126, 1986-89)
                                                            Jamaal Brown (126, 1989-92)
Field Goals .... Herb Williams (834, 1978-81)
Field-Goal Percentage .... Jerry Lucas (.624, 1960-62)
Free Throws Made .... Jerry Lucas (438, 1960-62)
Free-Throw Percentage .... Alex Davis (.890, 1990-93)
3-Point Field Goals .... Chris Jent (112, 1989-92)
Rebounds .... Jerry Lucas (1,411, 1960-62)
Rebound Average .... Jerry Lucas (17.2, 1960-72)
Assists .... Kelvin Ransey (516, 1977-80)
Steal .... Jay Burson (204, 1986-89)
Blocked Shots .... Herb Williams (328, 1978-81)

All-Time Ohio State Individual Season Records

Points Scored .... Dennis Hopson (958, 1986-87)
Scoring Average .... Robin Freeman (32.9, 1955-56)
Field Goals .... Dennis Hopson (338, 1986-87)
Field-Goal Percentage .... Jerry Lucas (.637, 1959-60)
Free Throws Made .... Dennis Hopson (215, 1986-87)
Free-Throw Percentage .... Jody Finney (.900, 1968-69)
3-Point Field Goals .... Dennis Hopson (67, 1986-87)
Rebounds .... Jerry Lucas (499, 1961-62)
Rebound Average .... Jerry Lucas (17.8, 1961-62)
Assists .... Curtis Wilson (188, 1987-88)
Steals .... Curtis Wilson (74, 1986-87)
Blocked Shots .... Brad Sellers (97, 1985-86)

All-Time Ohio State Individual Single-Game Records

Points Scored .... Gary Bradds (49 vs. Illinois, 2-10-64)
Field Goals ....Gary Bradds (20 vs. Purdue, 1-25-64)
Free Throws Made .... Gary Bradds (18 vs. Michigan State, 1-27-64)
3-Point Field Goals... Jay Burson (9 vs. Florida, 12-27-88)
Rebounds .... Frank Howard (32 vs. Brigham Young, 1-29-56)
Assists ....Curtis Wilson (14 vs. Purdue, 1-7-88)
Steals .... Troy Taylor (8 vs. St. Joseph's, 12-29-83)

All-Time Ohio State Coaching Records

Coach	Overall Record	Conference Record	Seasons
Fred Taylor (1959-76)	297-158 (.653)	158-102 (.608)	18
Harold Olsen (1923-46)	255-192 (.570)	154-135 (.533)	24
Eldon Miller (1977-86)	176-118 (.599)	96-84 (.533)	10
Randy Ayres (1990-Present)	98-52 (.653)	54-36 (.600)	5
Floyd Stahl (1951-58)	84-92 (.477)	51-65 (.440)	8
Lynn St. John (1912-19)	81-69 (.540)	24-43 (.358)	8
Gary Williams (1987-89)	59-41 (.590)	24-30 (.444)	3
William Dye (1947-50)	53-34 (.609)	27-21 (.563)	4
George Trautman (1920-22)	29-33 (.468)	10-26 (.278)	3
Thomas Kibler (1909-10)	22-2 (.917)	None	2
D.C. Huddleson (1903-04)	15-6 (.714)	None	2

Ohio State All-Americans and All-Big Ten Selections

Consensus All-Americans
Jimmy Hull, Forward, 1939
Wes Fesler, Guard, 1941
Dick Schnittker, Forward, 1950
Robin Freeman, Guard, 1956
Jerry Lucas, Center, 1960-1961-1962
Gary Bradds, Center, 1964
Jim Jackson, Guard-Forward, 1992

All-Big Ten Selections (since 1948)
Dick Schnittker, Forward, 1949-1950
Bob Donham, Forward, 1950
Paul Ebert, Center, 1952-1954
Robin Freeman, Guard, 1955-1956
Frank Howard, Forward, 1957-1958
Jerry Lucas, Center, 1960-1962

John Havlicek, Forward, 1961-1962
Larry Siegfried, Guard, 1961
Gary Bradds, Center, 1963-1964
Bill Hosket, Forward, 1967-1968
Dave Sorenson, Center, 1969-1970
Jim Cleamons, Guard, 1971
Luke Witte, Center, 1971
Allan Hornyak, Guard, 1971-1972-1973
Kelvin Ransey, Guard, 1978-1979-1980
Herb Williams, Center, 1980
Clark Kellogg, Forward, 1982
Tony Campbell, Forward, 1983-1984
Brad Sellers, Center, 1986
Dennis Hopson, Forward, 1987
Jay Burson, Guard, 1989
Jim Jackson, Guard-Forward, 1991-1992

Chapter 9

PENN STATE *Nittany Lions*

Overmatched Novice in a Land of Giants

═══════════════════════

All-Time Record: 1,097-777, .585; **Conference Record:** 8-28, .220

Big Ten Championships: None

National Championships: None

Greatest Player: Jesse Arnelle (1952-55)

Career Scoring Leader: Jesse Arnelle (2,138 Points, 1952-55)

Most Successful Coach: Burke Hermann (1916-17, 1920-32), 148-74, .667

All-Time Team: Jesse Arnelle (C, 1952-55), Ron Brown (F, 1972-74), DeRon Haynes (F, 1990-93), Freddie Barnes (G, 1989-92), Bob Weiss (G, 1963-65)

Best Season: 1953-54 (18-6), NCAA Final Four (Coach: Elmer Gross)

═══════════════════════

University Profile

Location: University Park (State College), Pennsylvania (pop. 41,317); **Founded:** 1855; **Campus Enrollment:** 30,500 (1994); **Started Basketball:** 1896-97. Penn State's 4,767-acre campus in the Nittany Valley is one of the most charming settings in the nation. Although most famous for its annual parade of powerhouse football teams, Penn State also boasts unmatched campus pride and holds the distinction of sponsoring the largest student-run fund-raising event in the nation — the annual Interfraternity Council Dance Marathon, a popular 48-hour test of endurance. In 1992, the event raised $1.14 million to benefit childhood cancer victims.

Team Nickname, Colors and Arena

Nickname: Nittany Lions (since 1906); **Colors:** Blue and White; **Arena:** Rec Hall (6,846 capacity, opened 1928). In its basketball media guide, Penn State stakes a claim as the first college to have a lion as an athletic team mascot. True or not, it certainly can be attested that PSU's mascot tradition stretches far into the past as one of the oldest in the nation. It was an undergraduate student named H.D. (Joe) Mason who launched a successful one-man campaign in 1906 to choose a school mascot after he had witnessed the Princeton tiger in action during an intercollegiate baseball trip to the rival New Jersey campus. The Nittany Lion moniker comes from legends surrounding a fierce mountain lion which supposedly roamed the region of Mount Nittany during the late 19th century.

Nittany Lions Basketball History

It's a perfect piece of irony that the best overall record in Penn State basketball history was compiled during an early 19-year stretch (1897-1915) when the Nittany Lions played without an official coaching staff. The record for this early stretch was a solid 131 wins and 64 losses, a .672 winning percentage that outdistances all performances of any schools in modern-era Big Ten play. Even the best Penn State coaches themselves — Burke Hermann (148-74, .667, 1916-32) tops the list — have never been able to outstrip that mark compiled when a long succession of team "playing captains" called practices, ran primitive offensive sets and drew no salary for their spirited volunteer services. It is a unique circumstance that must give all hardened hoop cynics sufficient pause for glee.

Not that the Big Ten's latest newcomer has been anything like a basketball patsy through subsequent years. It may be true that Penn State is far better known the past 25 years for perennial football powerhouse teams under the direction of Coach Joe Paterno. But the Nittany Lions have also posted an overall winning record in the wintertime roundball sport and built a solid cage tradition that stands fair comparison with most of the other Big Ten schools. Penn State's 1,097 all-time victories, for example, rank ahead of longtime Big Ten members Michigan State, Wisconsin and Northwestern. And the Lions have already accomplished something that two of the basketball-rich Big Ten schools (Minnesota and Northwestern) have never accomplished — making it to the Final Four of the glamorous NCAA postseason tournament.

The 98-year saga of Dr. Naismith's sport on the western Pennsylvania campus has other considerable boasting points. Two former Penn State bench bosses have made it to the big time as successful NBA mentors — John Bach, coach of the Golden State Warriors (1983-86), and Dick Harter, first coach for the expansion Charlotte Hornets. Jesse Arnelle (Helms, First Team, 1954), John Barr (Converse Second Team, 1941), Mark DuMars (UPI Honorable Mention, 1959-1960), and Bob Weiss (AP Honorable Mention, 1965) head a small, but distinguished, contingent of Nittany Lion hoopsters earning All-American honors. Bob Weiss (Chicago Bulls) and Frank Brickowski (Seattle, San Antonio, Milwaukee) have carried the school's banner as NBA players of note. Weiss also served coaching assignments with San Antonio, Atlanta and the Los Angeles Clippers. Finally, diminutive guard Craig Collins posted a 1985 season-long free-throw percentage mark (95.9) which was still standing 10 years later as an unchallenged NCAA all-time record.

The prime boasting points of the century-old PSU hoops tradition, however, are found in the school's 11 postseason championship shootouts. There have actually been two Final Four appearances for the teams from State College, the one in the NCAA tournament and the other in the somewhat less prestigious NIT (1990). In addition to two Final Four entrants, Penn State clubs in 1942 (vs. Dartmouth), 1952 (vs. Kentucky) and 1955 (vs. Iowa) have reached and ultimately lost in the NCAA tournament's regional semifinal round. Nittany Lions teams in 1965 (first round, Princeton) and 1991 (second round, Eastern Michigan) were also early NCAA casualties. NIT entrants from State College bowed out in the first round in 1966 against San Francisco, 1980 against Alabama and 1992 at the hands of arch-rival Pittsburgh, and in the second round in 1989 against Villanova.

The first 20 years of the new winter sport at Penn State found an informal team operating without benefit of any salaried full-time coach. But there were plenty of successes, including a 10-4 record in 1908 and a 10-3 squad in 1915. Alumnus Burke Hermann would become the first sanctioned head coach in 1916 and a year later was lead-

Jesse Arnelle (1952-55) may have been the greatest student-athlete in Penn State history. The basketball All-American also lettered four times in football and was president of the student body. (Penn State University photo)

ing his charges to a solid 12-2 record. This was the same "Dutch" Hermann who had already served one term as head man while an undergraduate playing captain back in 1910 and who would maintain a faculty position as a university professor of history for decades until he retired in 1956. Hermann remained as head coach into the early 1930s. Sixty years later his overall won-lost record is still the best in Penn State history. One highlight of the early seasons under Hermann was the 36-point scoring outburst by Frank Wolf in January 1919 against state rival Susquehanna College. That surprising effort came during a lost epoch when such prolific scoring was rare and thus would remain a school record for 33 years until freshman sensation Jesse Arnelle — a 6-foot-5 powerhouse center, who also doubled as a two-way football end — began his own scoring rampages in the early 1950s.

The first inroads for Penn State on the national basketball scene came at the outset of the 1940s under Coach John Lawther. Between 1937 and 1949 Lawther's clubs compiled a solid 150-93 record and featured outstanding individual players and some truly milestone games. John Barr was a Converse second-team All-American in 1941 and became the first cager in the school's modern era to top 500 career points. The 1941 team captained by Barr was 15-5 and narrowly missed being selected for the NCAA tournament. Neighboring Pittsburgh got the bid in the highly subjective selection process. The teams had split a home-and-away season series that winter. But the following year, the Nittany Lions, sporting an 18-3 record, could not be overlooked and would thus enjoy their first-ever NCAA bid. Lawther's unit finished the season with a 10th-place national ranking in the Dunkel Index helping to seal the team's selection to compete in the tourney, at the time an exclusive eight-school event. In a strange foreshadowing of things to come many seasons down the road, the Lions finished third in the East Regional at New Orleans when they defeated the highly touted and nationally renowned Whiz Kids team from Illinois (41-34), the reigning Big Ten champions.

But true national exposure would only come a decade later with Elmer Gross at the helm (Lawther had stepped down in 1949) and All-American Jesse Arnelle playing the starring role. Between 1952 and 1955, Arnelle would set a career scoring record (2,138 points over four seasons) as well as posting career records for field goals and points, and season records in scoring and field goals that have never been matched. The bulky 6-5 center would also prove to be the most proficient rebounder in school history and would be the only first-team All-American selection in Penn State basketball history. A true student-athlete, Arnelle served as student body president and was a four-year football letter winner. His record for pass receptions (33 in 1952) would stand for 13 seasons at the football-rich school.

Behind the hot-shooting Arnelle, the Lions advanced straight to the NCAA Final Four in 1954 with an 18-6 mark. They defeated Toledo, LSU and Notre Dame in preliminary rounds of postseason play but would finally be derailed 69-54 by surprise champion La Salle College of Philadelphia, an overachieving Cinderella outfit built around national player-of-the-year Tom Gola. Arnelle scored 18 points for the Lions but could not quite match the potent La Salle combo of Gola and sophomore forward Frank Blatcher, who both netted 19 for the more balanced Explorers. Arnelle (25 points) and his teammates rebounded a night later, however, to topple Southern California, 70-61, and bring home the proud prize of a third-place national finish. As reward for its brilliant 1953-54 campaign, Penn State was handed a ninth-place ranking in the final Associated Press collegiate poll. Arnelle, only a junior when he earned a spot on the 1954 NCAA Final Four All-Star team, would be back with a vengeance for a superb senior season a year later and would become one of the first 10 players in collegiate history to score 2,000 career points. The all-time PSU great reached this final milestone Feb. 23, 1955, against rival Rutgers.

Success continued for the next 14 seasons under new head coach John Egli who led his first squad back to the NCAA tournament the following March. This time, Arnelle and company would manage to fight past first-round opponent Memphis State (59-55) but would then suffer a pair of lopsided season-ending setbacks to Big Ten upstart Iowa (82-55) and perennial Southeastern Conference powerhouse Kentucky (84-59 in the Eastern Regional consolation game). Under Egli, the Lions would return to the NCAA battlefield 10 years later in 1965 only to suffer a disheartening 60-58 opening-night loss to All-American Bill Bradley's Princeton Tigers. There would also be a 1966 trip to the NIT where San Francisco turned back the Penn Staters and their high-scoring forwards Carver Clinton and Jeff Persson, 89-77, in still another opening-round game.

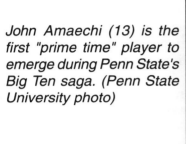

John Amaechi (13) is the first "prime time" player to emerge during Penn State's Big Ten saga. (Penn State University photo)

Greg Bartram (22), famed for his role in a 1993 double-overtime game against Indiana, guards the Hoosiers' Damon Bailey in a 1994 game. (Penn State University photo)

One additional rare highlight of the 1960s was the explosive single-game scoring performance of forward Gene Harris during the December 1961 Quaker City Classic in Philadelphia. Harris pumped in a school-record 46 points against Holy Cross, a mark that was an astounding 27 points better than his 18.7 points per game average. Harris would continue to score regularly throughout his final campaign and climb into the school's exclusive 1,000-point career scoring club, whose only other members at the time were Arnelle and Mark DuMars.

Dick Harter, a future successful NBA mentor, would begin a positive string of seasons at Penn State when he took over as the school's eighth head coach in 1979. Harter would post a 79-61 log in five seasons that would feature a return to the NIT in 1980. A 53-49 first-round loss to Alabama came on the heels of an 18-9 regular season celebrating the school's first postseason appearance in 14 years. Future NBA journeyman Frank Brickowski would pace both the 1980 and 1981 Nittany Lions in scoring, rebounds and field-goal percentage, and was the team's 1980 MVP, but narrowly missed reaching the exclusive 1,000-point career plateau.

But no period in PSU basketball history has enjoyed more boundless growth and progress than that launched when State College native Bruce Parkhill returned to PSU as head coach in 1983. The successor to Dick Harter graduated in 1967 from State College Area High School, was a three-sport star at nearby Lock Haven University and was head coach at William and Mary College for six seasons. While only one of Parkhill's first five teams at Penn State could muster a winning record (15-12 in 1987), four recent editions (1989-92) have all won 20 games or more and made postseason appearances to cap their upbeat seasons. Parkhill was named Atlantic 10 Conference Coach of the Year in 1990 and guided his charges to an Atlantic 10 title the next season.

Despite a rude inauguration into the Big Ten style of basketball during Penn State's first two seasons in the league, Parkhill's teams have always shown steady improvement. During the 1984-85 season (Parkhill's second), sharpshooting backcourt ace Craig Collins highlighted an 8-19 campaign with his national record for single-season free-throw shooting accuracy (94 of 98). Freshman backcourt ace Tony Ward would debut that same season, launching a four-year career that would eventually vault him into the school's 1,000-point club and into the record books with the best single-season mark for three-point field goals (.495 in 1987).

Parkhill's reign has resulted in three additional NIT visits, beginning with a 1989 climb to the tournament's second round and an 11-point defeat at the hands of ancient rival Villanova. In 1990, the Nittany Lions roared to a semifinal match with Vanderbilt where the SEC team outlasted Parkhill's squad for a 75-62 victory in Madison Square Garden. The Lions would quickly rebound from the Vanderbilt loss to capture a consolation matchup with New Mexico, an overtime thriller to settle third-place honors. The 25-9 ledger at the end of the 1990 campaign was the finest in school history and the third-place NIT finish was good enough to match the legendary 1954 team for best postseason performance.

Parkhill's apparent magic spell also brought a return trip to the NCAA tournament for the first time in nearly three decades with a stirring 81-75 defeat of George Washington in the conference tournament finale. This came on the strength of Penn State's first-ever Atlantic 10 championship in 1991 during the school's eighth and final league season. PSU's 21-11 club would celebrate with an opening-round 74-69 triumph over longtime basketball "big wig" UCLA at the Syracuse Carrier Dome. Unfortunately, the March Madness party would not last very long for the overachieving Penn Staters as the Nittany Lions were tripped up in overtime (71-68) by an unheralded but talented team from Eastern Michigan University. Ace of this championship PSU outfit was sophomore forward DeRon Hayes, conference freshman-of-the-year choice in 1990 and an all-league selection in 1991. Hayes would become the first junior since Jesse Arnelle to crack the 1,000-point barrier (1992) and would close his career (1993) as the second leading scorer in school history.

In the end, the crowning glory of Parkhill's tenure has come with admission of Penn State into the glamorous Big Ten Conference. Since joining college basketball's elite "grandaddy league" the Nittany Lions are already making some impressive noise and rattling more than their fair share of unwary visitors to noisy Rec Hall, suddenly the league's most intimidating snake-pit arena. During their first two seasons of Big Ten action, Parkhill's Nittany Lions have enjoyed little overall success in the win-loss column (2-16 and 6-12), yet they have served almost immediate notice of gritty future play with several surprisingly competitive performances. One was the dramatic and controversial 88-84 double-overtime loss to No. 1-ranked Indiana during the first season of league action. That memorable February 1993 PSU-Indiana game is already being canonized as "the greatest ever played at Rec Hall" and it was a contest that brought a significant boost to the PSU program in the form of a huge ESPN national television audience. Nonetheless, it was a bitter defeat, one that seemed to turn crucially on a number of referees' "missed" calls in the closing moments which PSU partisans (and many neutral observers as well) felt clearly favored the nationally ranked Hoosiers.

Penn State basketball is hardly to be compared favorably with Penn State football at this juncture. But neither is the short-term outlook necessarily gloomy. With 6-10 John Amaechi (a native of Manchester, England), a senior in 1995, Penn State can boast one of the strongest and most entertaining inside scorers, rebounders and shot blockers in the conference. The future in University Park looks bright when it comes to the building of a promising new basketball tradition smack in the heart of Joe Paterno's Pennsylvania football country.

Records and Summaries
Year-by-Year Penn State Records

Season	All Games	Conference	Coach(es)	Top Scorer (Points)
1896-97	1-1	None	M.R. Stevenson*	No Record
1897-98	2-1	None	Clay Sprechter*	No Record
1898-99	2-3	None	M.R. Stevenson*	No Record
1899-00	7-1	None	J.S. Ruble*	No Record
1900-01	5-1	None	E.T. McCleary*	No Record
1901-02	9-2	None	C.W. Ruble*	No Record
1902-03	3-5	None	G.V. Sborisi*	No Record
1903-04	5-4	None	Mather Dunn*	No Record
1904-05	6-2	None	Mather Dunn*	No Record
1905-06	6-4	None	W.Y. Heaton*	No Record
1906-07	5-6	None	H.B. Waha*	No Record
1907-08	10-4	None	E.G. DuBarry*	No Record
1908-09	7-6	None	F.G. Funston*	No Record
1909-10	8-6	None	Burke Hermann*	No Record
1910-11	9-4	None	F.H. Blythe*	No Record
1911-12	8-5	None	H.E. Shore*	No Record
1912-13	8-3	None	B.L. Hartz*	No Record
1913-14	8-4	None	W.G. Binder*	No Record
1914-15	10-3	None	J.F. Park*	No Record
1915-16	8-3	None	Burke Hermann	No Record
1916-17	12-2	None	Burke Hermann	No Record
1917-18	12-1	None	No Coach	No Record
1918-19	11-2	None	Hugo Bezdek	No Record
1919-20	12-1	None	Burke Hermann	No Record
1920-21	14-2	None	Burke Hermann	No Record
1921-22	9-5	None	Burke Hermann	J.N. Reed (190)
1922-23	13-1	None	Burke Hermann	J.N. Reed (242)
1923-24	13-2	None	Burke Hermann	J.N. Reed (151)
1924-25	12-2	None	Burke Hermann	E.O. Gerhardt (144)
1925-26	7-7	None	Burke Hermann	Harold Von Neida (83)
1926-27	14-4	None	Burke Hermann	Michael Hamas (223)
1927-28	10-5	None	Burke Hermann	L.D. Reilly (111)
1928-29	10-9	None	Burke Hermann	Neil Stahley (NA)
1929-30	5-9	None	Burke Hermann	Fred Brand (108)
1930-31	3-12	None	Burke Hermann	Fred Brand (120)
1931-32	6-9	None	Burke Hermann	Ed McMinn (141)
1932-33	7-4	None	Earl Leslie	Norrie McFarlane (114)
1933-34	8-4	None	Earl Leslie	Norrie McFarlane (169)
1934-35	8-9	None	Earl Leslie	John Stocker (121)
1935-36	6-11	None	Earl Leslie	Sol Miehoff (121)
1936-37	10-7	None	John Lawther	Sol Miehoff (125)

1937-38	13-5	None	John Lawther	Sol Miehoff (175)
1938-39	13-10	None	John Lawther	Charlie Prosser (195)
1939-40	15-8	None	John Lawther	John Barr (231)
1940-41	15-5	None	John Lawther	John Barr (200)
1941-42	18-3	None	John Lawther	Herschel Baltimore (179)
1942-43	15-4	None	John Lawther	Dave Hornstein (139)
1943-44	8-7	None	John Lawther	Don McNary (146)
1944-45	10-7	None	John Lawther	Irwin Batnick (113)
1945-46	7-9	None	John Lawther	Walt Hatkevich (216)
1946-47	10-8	None	John Lawther	Jack Biery (218)
1947-48	9-10	None	John Lawther	Jack Biery (260)
1948-49	7-10	None	John Lawther	Milt Simon (177)
1949-50	13-10	None	Elmer Gross	Marty Costa (299)
1950-51	14-9	None	Elmer Gross	Lou Lamie (319)
1951-52	20-6	None	Elmer Gross	Jesse Arnelle (492)
1952-53	15-9	None	Elmer Gross	Jesse Arnelle (408)
1953-54	18-6	None	Elmer Gross	Jesse Arnelle (507)
1954-55	18-10	None	John Egli	Jesse Arnelle (731)
1955-56	12-14	None	John Egli	Earl Fields (354)
1956-57	15-10	None	John Egli	Ron Rainey (377)
1957-58	8-11	None	John Egli	Ron Rainey (292)
1958-59	11-9	None	John Egli	Mark DuMars (337)
1959-60	11-11	None	John Egli	Mark DuMars (468)
1960-61	11-13	None	John Egli	Gene Harris (369)
1961-62	12-11	None	John Egli	Gene Harris (431)
1962-63	15-5	None	John Egli	Earl Hoffman (434)
1963-64	16-7	None	John Egli	Bob Weiss (392)
1964-65	20-4	None	John Egli	Carver Clinton (411)
1965-66	18-6	None	John Egli	Carver Clinton (453)
1966-67	10-14	None	John Egli	Jeff Persson (422)
1967-68	10-10	None	John Egli	Jeff Persson (339)
1968-69	13-9	None	John Bach	Tom Daley (313)
1969-70	13-11	None	John Bach	Tom Daley (366)
1970-71	10-12	None	John Bach	Bill Kunze (367)
1971-72	17-8	None	John Bach	Ron Brown (434)
1972-73	15-8	None	John Bach	Randy Meister (309)
1973-74	14-12	None	John Bach	Ron Brown (451)
1974-75	11-12	None	John Bach	Randy Meister (345)
1975-76	10-15	None	John Bach	Chris Erichsen (436)
1976-77	11-15	None	John Bach	Jeff Miller (345)
1977-78	8-19	None	John Bach	Jeff Miller (505)
1978-79	12-18	None	Dick Harter	Mike Edelman (343)
1979-80	18-10	None	Dick Harter	Frank Brickowski (320)
1980-81	17-10	None	Dick Harter	Frank Brickowski (311)

1981-82	15-12	None	Dick Harter	Mike Lang (272)
1982-83	17-11	None	Dick Harter	Mike Lang (366)
1983-84	5-22	None	Bruce Parkhill	Wally Choice (223)
1984-85	8-19	None	Bruce Parkhill	Craig Collins (401)
1985-86	12-17	None	Bruce Parkhill	Paul Murphy (293)
1986-87	15-12	None	Bruce Parkhill	Tom Hovasse (352)
1987-88	13-14	None	Bruce Parkhill	Tom Hovasse (388)
1988-89	20-12	None	Bruce Parkhill	Tom Hovasse (516)
1989-90	25-9	None	Bruce Parkhill	Ed Fogell (520)
1990-91	21-11	None	Bruce Parkhill	DeRon Hayes (479)
1991-92	21-8	None	Bruce Parkhill	Monroe Brown (422)

Big Ten Conference

| 1992-93 | 7-20 | 2-16 | Bruce Parkhill | DeRon Hayes (376) |
| 1993-94 | 13-14 | 6-12 | Bruce Parkhill | John Amaechi (423) |

* = Team Captain (no official coaches, 1897-1915)

All-Time Penn State Individual Career Records

Points Scored .... Jesse Arnelle (2,138, 1952-55)
Scoring Average .... Jesse Arnelle (21.0, 1952-55)
Games Played .... Freddie Barnes (127, 1989-92)
                                                                                            Monroe Brown (127, 1989-92)
Games Started .... DeRon Hayes (120, 1990-93)
Minutes Played .... Freddie Barnes (4,038, 1989-92)
Field Goals .... Jesse Arnelle (738, 1952-55)
Field-Goal Percentage .... Ed Fogell (.539, 1986-90)
Free Throws Made .... Jesse Arnelle (662, 1952-55)
Free-Throw Percentage .... Craig Collins (.866, 1982-85)
3-Point Field Goals .... Tom Hovasse (172, 1986-89)
Rebounds .... Jesse Arnelle (1,238, 1952-55)
Rebound Average .... Jesse Arnelle (12.1, 1952-55)
Assists .... Freddie Barnes (600, 1989-92)
Steals .... Ron Brown (252, 1972-74)
Blocked Shots .... Ed Fogell (90, 1986-90)

All-Time Penn State Individual Season Records

Points Scored .... Jesse Arnelle (731, 1954-55)
Scoring Average .... Jesse Arnelle (26.1, 1954-55)
Minutes Played .... Freddie Barnes (1123, 1989-90)
Field Goals .... Jesse Arnelle (244, 1954-55)
Field-Goal Percentage .... Eric Carr (.626, 1991-92)
Free Throws Made .... Jesse Arnelle (243, 1954-55)

Free-Throw Percentage .... Craig Collins (.959*, 1984-85)
3-Point Field Goals .... Tom Hovasse (74, 1988-89)
Rebounds .... Jesse Arnelle (428, 1954-55)
Rebound Average .... Jesse Arnelle (15.3, 1954-55)
Assists .... Freddie Barnes (177, 1991-92)
Steals .... Ron Brown (97, 1975-76)
Blocked Shots .... John Amaechi (65, 1992-93)
* = NCAA Record

All-Time Penn State Individual Single-Game Records

Points Scored .... Gene Harris (46 vs. Holy Cross, 12-27-61)
Field Goals .... Jesse Arnelle (20 vs. Bucknell, 1-5-55)
Free Throws Made .... Bill Mullan (22 vs. Pittsburgh, 2-28-20)
3-Point Field Goals .... Tom Hovasse (7 vs. George Washington, 1-12-89)
Rebounds .... Jesse Arnelle (27 vs. Temple, 1-29-55)
Assists .... Tom Doaty (15 vs. Syracuse, 1-29-75)
Steals .... Tom Doaty (8 vs. West Virginia, 2-18-70)
Monroe Brown (8 vs. Rhode Island, 1-3-91)
Blocked Shots .... John Amaechi (5 vs. Illinois, 1-21-93; vs. Wisconsin,
3-3-93; vs. Purdue, 3-11-93)

All-Time Penn State Coaching Records

Coach	Overall Record	Conference Record	Seasons
John Egli (1955-68)	187-135 (.581)	None	14
Bruce Parkhill (1984-Present)	160-158 (.503)	8-28 (.220)	11
John Lawther (1937-49)	150-93 (.617)	None	13
Burke Hermann (1916-17, 1920-32)	148-74 (.667)	None	15
No Coach (1897-1915, 1918)	*131-64 (.672)*	*None*	*20*
John Bach (1969-78)	122-121 (.501)	None	10
Elmer Gross (1950-54)	80-40 (.667)	None	5
Dick Harter (1979-83)	79-61 (.564)	None	5
Earl Leslie (1933-36)	29-28 (.509)	None	4
Hugo Bezdek (1919)	11-2 (.846)	None	1

Penn State All-Americans and All-Big Ten Selections

Consensus All-Americans
Jesse Arnelle, Forward, 1954

All-Big Ten Selections (since 1992)
None

Chapter 10

PURDUE *Boilermakers*

Best Kept Secret in the World of Hoopdom

═══════════════════════════

All-Time Record: 1,287-724, .640; **Conference Record:** 706-505, .580

Big Ten Championships — 19: (1911*, 1912*, 1921*, 1922, 1926*, 1928*, 1930, 1932, 1934, 1935*, 1936*, 1938, 1940, 1969, 1979*, 1984*, 1987*, 1988, 1994) * = Co-Champion

National Championships: None

National Invitation Tournament (NIT) Championships — 1: (1974)

Greatest Player: Rick Mount (1968-70)

Career Scoring Leader: Rick Mount (2,323 Points, 1968-70)

Most Successful Coach: Ward "Piggy" Lambert (1917, 1919-45), 371-152, .709

All-Time Team: Joe Barry Carroll (C, 1977-80), Glenn Robinson (F, 1992-94), Terry Dischinger (F, 1960-62), Rick Mount (G, 1968-70), John Wooden (G, 1930-32)

Best Season: 1968-69 (23-5), NCAA Runner-Up (Coach: George King)

═══════════════════════════

University Profile

Location: West Lafayette, Indiana (pop. 21,247); **Founded:** 1869; **Campus Enrollment:** 35,161 (1994); **Started Basketball:** 1896-97. Billed as the "Home of the Astronauts" and a "world-class institution," Purdue is Indiana's link in the nationwide chain of 68 land-grant colleges and universities. Once known as an engineering and agriculture school, Purdue now offers nearly 7,000 undergraduate and graduate courses in more than 200 academic specializations. It has one of the largest enrollments of women and minority engineering students and houses one of the premier schools of veterinary medicine. Twenty graduates (including Neil Armstrong, the first person to walk on the moon) have been selected for the NASA space program. Through 1994, Purdue alumni have flown on 30 of the 86 U.S. manned space flights.

Team Nickname, Colors and Arena

Nickname: Boilermakers (since 1889); **Colors:** Old Gold and Black; **Arena:** Mackey Arena (14,123 capacity, opened 1967). Purdue's "Boilermaker" nickname, one of the oldest in the land, had a colorful origin. The term was originally one of several similar epithets applied to Purdue by supporters of neighboring Wabash College after a lopsided 18-4 football loss to the West Lafayette school in 1889. Wabash was strictly a liberal arts college while archrival Purdue owned a reputation as a school devoted to practical arts like engineering and agriculture. Demonstrating social snobbery common to the times, Wabash boosters bitterly referred to the more talented athletes from Purdue as boilers, blacksmiths, cornfield sailors, pumpkin shuckers, hayseeds, farmers and rail splitters, even spreading a rumor that Purdue had stooped to enrolling eight actual boilermakers from the Monon Railroad shops just in time for fall football season. Like so many derogatory terms of similar fashion, this one particularly struck the fancy of the West Lafayette footballers themselves. It soon was being used widely on the Purdue campus, thus becoming a self-imposed moniker.

Boilermaker Basketball History

When talk inevitably turns to basketball within the Hoosier state — arguably the nation's premier hotbed for schoolboy and collegiate versions of Dr. Naismith's peach-basket game — the folks in West Lafayette must own something of an inferiority complex by now. Despite so many true glory seasons under Gene Keady, including two built around the incessant hype that came with college basketball's No. 1 player, Glenn Robinson; despite the long string of championships stretching from Ward Lambert in the '30s to Rose and Keady in the '70s and '80s; and despite a program second to none, the folks at Purdue still can't seem to get their fair share of attention — even in their home state.

For the past quarter century, downstate rival Indiana has always seemed to do the Boilermakers one better and then some. Keady's has racked up four Big Ten banners in his tenure but Bob Knight has already bagged that many postseason titles (three in the NCAA and one in the NIT) for the charmed Hoosiers. On the national scene, images of Hoosier basketball conjure up Bobby Knight and seemingly little else. Knight's Indiana teams seem to own the Hoosier state lock, stock and barrel. Given these facts, the Purdue saga of continued cage successes, both in and out of Big Ten play, is even the more remarkable.

The argument can be made without embarrassment that Purdue's tradition is the loftiest in the Big Ten and ranks among the nation's finest half-dozen programs, especially if one looks across the full nine decades of conference play. The most sensational (albeit one-dimensional) offensive player in league history, Rick Mount, hailed from Purdue. The remarkable legacy of three-decade coach Ward "Piggy" Lambert (1916-1945) was instrumental in formulating the wide-open, fast-breaking playing style which defines the modern-era game. Lambert's program was also cradle to perhaps the finest individual basketball mind and greatest coaching success story in the sport's history — Westwood Wizard John Wooden, a Purdue All-American of the early '30s. Tallying total wins in conference play, Purdue (706) stands atop the heap, though admittedly occupying a dead heat with Illinois (705) and Indiana (704). And in conference titles (outright and shared) the Boilermakers are again in a virtual deadlock with the Hoosiers — 19 for Indiana, 19 for Purdue. It is only in the national championship arena where the Boilers have slipped a considerable length behind their hated state rivals, almost all of the damage done under Knight and during the past two decades.

The '80s and '90s under Gene Keady have continued a long-standing legacy of stellar basketball achievement on the West Lafayette campus. There have been two outright Big Ten titles (1988, 1994) and two ties (1984, 1987) for the championship. Keady has built one of the best overall coaching records in victory-rich Purdue history. There have been three Keady-led trips to the NIT — exactly half of the school's total appearances in the nation's No. 2 postseason classic. Under Keady, Purdue has surged into a large lead in NIT victories among Big Ten schools. The Boilers now rest at 18-5 overall in NIT play since 1971; Ohio State owns a 13-5 mark, Michigan is 9-3, Indiana checks in at 8-1, with Minnesota standing at 11-5 and Illinois at 5-2. The Boilermakers, under Keady, also have appeared in NCAA postseason play 10 times, once climbing into the regional finals (1994) and reaching the regional semifinal round in 1988. The 1987-88 team which featured Troy Lewis, Everette Stephens and Todd Mitchell and recorded a landmark 29 victories (matched only by the 1994 squad) was one of the finest in the school's proud athletic history.

Several luminous stars have been spawned in the Keady era — Glenn Robinson, Russell Cross, Troy Lewis and Steve Scheffler. The 6-foot-11 Cross (1981-83, 1,529 points) might have been the best Boilermaker ever, but a knee injury hobbled his collegiate career and ruined his pro prospects. Lewis (1985-88, 2,038 points) ranks among Purdue's finest pure shooters, recalling the great Rick Mount with his long-range arsenal of deadly jumpers. But whereas Mount flopped in his brief pro career (five unproductive ABA seasons), Lewis never even got a shot at the NBA wars. A fine marksman (18.5 points per game his sophomore and junior seasons), Lewis was not quick enough or athletic enough for the pro version of the game. Scheffler (1987-90, 1,155 points) was perhaps the most unheralded star in school history. His scoring numbers were not huge (16.8 points per game his senior season) and his play was not packed with the leaping and dunking flair demanded in the modern era. But he was a blue collar workman who etched his name in the collegiate record book with the highest career field-goal percentage (.685) in NCAA history. Scheffler has parlayed his talents into a lasting journeyman NBA stint with the Charlotte Hornets and Seattle SuperSonics.

Purdue University Photo

Glenn Robinson

But the cream of the crop was the much-ballyhooed Glenn Robinson. Robinson didn't stick around in Big Ten play long enough to write his name indelibly among the league's greatest all-time stars. There were no inroads on the league's career offensive records and there were no Final Fours for the player who came to be known as "The Big Dog" and captured a fistful of national player-of-the-year awards in 1994. Yet the 1993-94 Purdue team paced by Robinson's scoring (30.3) nearly matched the memorable 1988 team victory-for-victory and achievement-for-achievement. And Robinson himself compiled an impressive list of credentials to cap his abbreviated two-season career — 15th player in NCAA Division I history to score 1,000 points in a season, first player in Big Ten history to reach the 1,000-point mark in conference games in only two seasons, the only Purdue player ever to record at least 1,000 career points, 500 rebounds, 100 steals, 100 assists and 50 blocked shots.

It was the season of 1987-88, however, that marked one of the greatest achievements and also some of the deepest disappointments for Gene Keady and the numerous Boilermaker backers. It was a season that started out on the highest possible note with the Boilermakers holding a preseason No. 2 national ranking (No. 1 in several polls). Mackey Arena was sold out in advance for the entire season's schedule, with the brilliant recruiting class of Troy Lewis, Everette Stephens and Todd Mitchell ("The Three Amigos") now matured as battle-worn seniors. There were also some shadows looming, especially when Lewis suffered a broken foot in a pickup game in late August and when Mitchell underwent arthroscopic knee surgery in October.

But the starters were in the lineup for the opening bell. After an early-season upset in Mackey at the hands of Iowa State (104-96), the Boilers roared through the year as expected with win streaks of 16 and nine games surrounding a three-point road loss to Indiana (82-79) at the end of January. The Indiana defeat came only after the Boilers fell behind by 21 in the first half, roared back to take a last-second lead before the game was finally lost on a missed Mitchell free throw and a clutch basket by Hoosier center Dean Garrett. A month later, junior center Mel McCants garnered 24 points and 10 rebounds to pace a victory over Michigan which clinched Purdue's first outright Big Ten title in 19 years. The season's final pre-NCAA ledger would show a school-record 27-3 mark, the only other loss coming on the road at Ohio State in the year's penultimate contest.

The 1988 Big Ten champs roared into tournament play with perhaps the loftiest and most legitimate national title hopes in school annals. Things got off to a smooth enough start in the Midwest Regional tourney at South Bend as the Boilers cruised against Fairleigh-Dickinson (94-79) and Memphis State (100-73) in easy tune-ups for regional semifinal action at the Pontiac Silverdome. But any premature dreams of a run to the top were rudely squelched by a tough Big Eight club from Kansas State. K-State featured a talented outfit led by future NBA star Mitch Richmond, but one that Purdue had manhandled 101-72 three months earlier at Mackey Arena. Handed a second crack at the Boilermakers, Richmond (a 1988 Olympic team member and 1989 NBA rookie-of-the-year) and his teammates were primed to give the Boilers more than they could handle. Several crucial Purdue turnovers in the final moments proved disastrous and K-State's Wildcats held on for a 73-70 upset victory which scuttled all Purdue plans for a Final Four trip to the NCAA party in Kansas City.

Purdue remained highly competitive immediately after the great team of Lewis, Stephens and Mitchell (plus juniors Kip Jones and Mel McCants) had departed. Rumors which circulated hot and heavy during the 1988 Final Four weekend that Gene Keady would leave Purdue to assume the head coaching slot at the University of Texas quickly proved entirely ill-founded. Subsequent Boilermaker teams would feature future NBAers McCants (1989 high scorer at 13.4 points per game), Scheffler (1990 pacesetter at 16.8) and Jimmy Oliver (19.2 in 1991). But for several subsequent years, the Keady program always seemed to be one superstar player

Glenn Robinson (13) generated a great deal of excitement during a short two-year career as a Purdue basketball player. He was an All-American and national player-of-the-year but his talents couldn't take the Boilermakers to the NCAA Final Four. (Purdue University photo)

away from the highest rung of achievement. That dream player would finally arrive for the fall season of 1992, however, and his name would be Glenn Robinson. Robinson, a 6-8 leaper and deadeye shooter out of Gary Roosevelt High School, shared national high school player of the year honors with future Michigan Fab Five star Chris Webber. He would sit out his freshman season (1991-92) while gaining academic eligibility. But from Robinson's first days in West Lafayette, excitement built to fever pitch around a player who was immediately celebrated as one of the best and one of the most hyped in Purdue history.

As a sophomore, Robinson debuted with a 24.1 points per game average, a Big Ten scoring title (25.5) and selection as a finalist for John Wooden United States Basketball Writers Association Player of the Year. The crown jewel of Robinson's short stay in West Lafayette was the 1993-94 season, like 1988 a year of considerable expectations and but minimal fulfillment. The Boilers did themselves proud with 29 wins, an undisputed league title and a march to the NCAA regional title game. But they never quite lived up to the hype surrounding Robinson or alumni visions of a national title for the Robinson-led squad. Robinson would rake in all possible personal honors, the most prominent being the Wooden, Naismith and AP/Rupp player of the year trophies, and a national scoring title. The multi-talented athlete was thus the school's first national scoring leader since Dave Schellhase in 1966 (Mount had the misfortune of overlapping his own career with that of Pete Maravich). Keady's charges nearly made it to the final ceremonies this time around, but Purdue would again be left standing disappointed at the altar in a 69-60 Southeast Regional title-game loss to Duke.

The great Purdue teams under Keady extended a tradition stretching back to the first powerhouse squads performing in the shadows of World War I under legendary coach Ward "Piggy" Lambert. Lambert had inherited a Purdue program already rich in tradition but suffering through the worst times in the school's proud athletic history. Purdue had been one of the co-founders of the Western Conference in 1905 when they joined forces with Minnesota, Wisconsin, Indiana, Chicago and Illinois to inaugurate league play. They had produced two very solid teams under Ralph Jones in 1911 and 1912. These were teams that featured court-length passing and quick upcourt movement during an era largely dominated by deliberate offense and slow-paced dribbling. The 1911 outfit backed into a league title when four losses in the final five games were not enough to prevent a tie for the top slot with Minnesota. The 1912 squad was actually undefeated at 12-0 (10-0 in the conference), yet lost out on an undisputed championship since Wisconsin (15-0, 12-0) played a more complete schedule. After three stellar seasons in West Lafayette, Jones transferred his employment to Illinois (where his Fighting Illini teams would stand 12-4 against Purdue in future seasons). Under Jones' replacement, R. E. Vaughn, the Purdue program had quickly fallen on hard times, which included three straight losing seasons on the eve of Lambert's welcomed arrival.

By the early '20s, Ward Lambert had his Purdue Boilermaker teams headed full speed in an exciting new direction. Lambert was a rare innovator who immediately bucked the established style of Big Ten and national cage play. The established style was introduced and proven successful by Doc Meanwell at Wisconsin and later modified by disciples like Doc Carlson at Pittsburgh. Carlson's "continuity offense" patterns consisted of three-man figure-eight offensive weaves and depended more on elaborate drilling than on athleticism. Meanwell's forte was controlled pattern play, also featuring set offensive patterns and sharp, crisp short-range crisp short-range passing attacks. Under Lambert there would be a new style of play — a quick-breaking offense geared to run all-out each time the ball changed hands. And with the right "horses" that were about to arrive on the scene, Lambert's program would soon prove a magical formula for oncourt success.

At first Lambert's formula bore little fruit without the proper steeds to implement the reckless running style of play. But with the arrival of 6-6 Charles "Stretch" Murphy to clear the boards and ignite the floor-length offensive breaks, the pendulum suddenly swung in Lambert's favor. The 1928 team at 15-2 was Lambert's first great squad, averaging nearly 40 points per game and losing only to Indiana and Wisconsin. With both losses on the road and four straight victories to close the campaign, this team tied Everett Dean's Hoosiers for the conference crown. A season later the Boilermakers remained more than respectable at 13-4 and trailed both Wisconsin and Michigan by a single game in conference play; Murphy won his only league scoring title and earned the first of two consensus All-American selections. But Lambert's greatest teams came in the next three seasons (1930-32) behind the floor leadership of fleet guard John Wooden out of Martinsville, Indiana. A three-time All-American and Big Ten scoring leader his senior season, Wooden's Purdue legacy as stellar playmaker and floor general remains almost as great — if less celebrated — as his later UCLA legacy as a Hall of Fame coach and master of NCAA tournament play.

Lambert's career at the helm would stretch another dozen seasons after the great teams of the early '30s. His legacy would include five more Big Ten titles, two additional stellar All-Americans in 1934 league scoring champ Norm Cottom and back-to-back (1937-38) Big Ten scoring pacesetter Jewell Young and a 1938 championship team that posted a then-school-record 18 victories. There would not be a single Lambert-coached Purdue team with a losing record between 1919 and 1943 when a war-era club slumped to 9-11 but still broke even in Big Ten play. Throughout his long tenure Lambert would combine a low-key personal approach with his racehorse offensive schemes to build legendary status among Purdue fans and players alike. He would quickly climb to the top of the list of winningest Purdue coaches and in the process post the second highest victory total (overtaken only by Bob Knight in the mid-80s) in Big Ten history. In the end, Lambert could boast 11 league championships, 10 consensus All-Americans and nine league scoring champions who played under him.

Purdue basketball seemed to fall into a state of hibernation for a couple of decades following Lambert's retirement in January 1946. As Lambert's immediate successor, long-time assistant Mel Taube would survive less than five seasons and post a sub-.500 ledger (45-46) before being forced to resign at the end of the 1950 campaign. Replacement Ray Eddy fared only slightly better for 15 seasons (1951-65) during which the Boilers often enjoyed moderate successes (such as the high-scoring feats of sensational All-Americans Terry Dischinger and Dave Schellhase) yet never returned to past championship prominence.

One infamous moment marred the immediate post-Lambert years. The West Lafayette campus entered a new athletic era with the dedication of a spacious new Purdue Fieldhouse (8,500 initial capacity) in January of 1938. Purdue had defeated Wisconsin 40-34 before a packed house in the festive game to dedicate the building and it would not be until just before Christmas at the end of that same year that Lambert's crew would lose its first game (35-30 to Southern California) in the new facility. But tragedy would strike the renamed Lambert

Fieldhouse 10 years later. On Feb. 24, 1947, Purdue and Wisconsin were locked in a battle that meant a possible conference crown for the visiting Badgers. At halftime, the newly installed wooden bleachers of the east grandstand buckled under the overflow crowd of more than 11,000 and suddenly collapsed, crushing three student spectators and injuring hundreds of others. One bizarre result of the shocking event was that the game itself would be suspended for more than two weeks. The second half of the ill-fated game was completd miles from either campus in a neutral site at Evanston (Illinois) Township High School. Outscoring Purdue 39-26 during the renewed second half, Wisconsin took a belated 72-60 victory in perhaps the most unusual game of conference history. Ironically, the win earned Wisconsin the league title, an accomplishment it has not repeated since.

Eddy's Purdue teams, which stretched across the '50s, were never very distinguished despite several winning campaigns. But in the first half of the '60s, Eddy and Purdue would revive suddenly with the fortuitous debuts of two of the finest players in school history. First 6-7 center Terry Dischinger paced both the team and the league for three seasons, piling up All-American honors (1961-1962) and claiming most existing school scoring and rebounding marks. Dischinger would eventually emerge in the national limelight as NBA rookie-of-the-year with the 1963 Chicago Zephyrs and as perhaps the finest Purdue-bred professional player ever produced. Next, 6-3 forward Dave Schellhase would inherit Dischinger's mantle in time for the 1964, 1965 and 1966 seasons. Schellhase would outstrip even Dischinger's scoring pace (becoming the first Boilermaker to climb above 2,000 career points) and win a national scoring title during his senior season of 1966. No other Purdue or Big Ten conference sharpshooter would be able to outpace the nation's best scorers until Glenn Robinson arrived on the scene. But despite Schellhase's big scoring outbursts, the 1966 Purdue outfit would finish only an embarrassing 8-16 under new coach George King.

Dischinger was only the second player in Big Ten history to average more than 30 points per game for an entire season. He also was one of the finest all-around athletes of his era, a Terre Haute prep school standout in both football and track as well as basketball. And as one of the fastest men in the country for his size, Dish would also be one of three consecutive Big Ten stars (sandwiched between Indiana's Walt Bellamy and Ohio State's Jerry Lucas) to reign as NBA rookies of the year. Purdue had two fine teams during Dischinger's three seasons. The 1961 and 1962 teams both finished third in the conference wars and posted respectable 16-7 and 17-7 overall records. But this was the era of Jerry Lucas and John Havlicek and Ohio State dominated the conference and the national hoops scene as well.

Dischinger and Schellhase launched the stratospheric scoring barrages of '60s-era uptempo basketball in West Lafayette. It was an era of great pointmakers, at Purdue, in the Big Ten (Cazzie Russell, Gary Bradds, Jimmy Rayl) and throughout the basketball scene everywhere (Wilt Chamberlain, Oscar Robertson, Jerry West). But the real scoring onslaught at Purdue came at the very end of the decade with the arrival of the greatest pure shooter in league history and perhaps in all college basketball history as well.

The achievements of Rick Mount remain legendary. There were of course his massive point totals — the four sharpshooters who have now surpassed him (Indiana's Calbert Cheaney and Steve Alford, and Michigan's Glen Rice and Mike McGee) all required four full seasons to edge ahead of the point totals Mount amassed in only three. Mount's Big Ten single-game, single-season and points-per-game standards remain unchallenged. And there were also his stellar long-range shooting displays which would certainly have brought countless more points in the era of the three-point field goal. Mount may well have failed when he took his one-dimensional game to the ABA professional arenas — his deadly eye was not accompanied by the quick release needed against athletic pro defenders. But in Big Ten play alone, Mount remains the most sensational offensive player in conference history.

With Mount filling the nets and former NBA star George King entrenched on the coach's end of the bench, Purdue enjoyed one of its finest teams ever at the end of the 1960s. The 1969 lineup of Mount, Billy Keller and Herm Gilliam (all future pro stars) marched directly to the NCAA title game against a powerful UCLA dynasty squad coached by former Boilermaker hero John Wooden. It would be Purdue's first appearance in the prestigious Final Four and its only crack ever at the championship game. The memorable moment came at the end of Mount's high-scoring (33.3) junior season and matched the 23-5 Big Ten champs against a 29-1 Bruins squad seeking its third straight in a record string of seven eventual national titles. Lew Alcindor outshot Mount 37-28 and UCLA cruised effortlessly in Louisville's Freedom Hall to a one-sided 92-72 championship victory.

Another highlight of the Rick Mount era was the inaugural "Dedication Game" staged on Dec. 2, 1967, in newly constructed Mackey Arena. The opponent, fittingly, was again Wooden and his UCLA Bruins led by Alcindor. The game was one that has perhaps never been topped in the colorful history of the now 25-year-old showcase building. Alcindor was indisputably America's best collegiate player, yet the massive pivotman was held to a total of 35 points in a pair of season-opening games against the tenacious Boilermakers. During the 1967 West Lafayette clash, Alcindor's meager 17 points were nonetheless enough to key an exciting 73-71 victory that kept alive a 35-game win streak for the nation's top team. Mount canned a game-high 28, but his last-second effort at a tie rimmed out in painfully dramatic fashion. The most stellar moment of Mount's career came two years later, however, in a record-smashing 61-point game against Iowa at Mackey Arena. Again, it was a dramatic performance executed in a losing cause as the high-scoring Iowa contingent of Fred Brown and John Johnson held on for a 108-107 win that gave the Hawkeyes the 1970 Big Ten title.

George King stayed on at the helm for seven seasons before heading up to the front office as full-time athletic director. King's tenure was in turn followed by a half-dozen seasons under former Los Angeles Lakers coach Fred Schaus. The latter mentor brought with him from the pro ranks a fast-breaking action game certain to entertain West Lafayette fans, as well as a stingy approach to defense geared to frustrate many of Purdue's Big Ten opponents. There were no further league titles under either King or Schaus but there was a bevy of solid teams and individual stars such as Frank Kendrick (all-Big Ten in 1974 and current assistant under Keady), John Garrett (a 20 points per game scorer as a junior in 1974), Eugene Parker (1978 NBA draft choice of the San Antonio Spurs) and Walter Jordan (sixth on the all-time Purdue point list with 1,813). Schaus also would guide his Boilermakers to three postseason tournament appearances highlighted by an 87-81 NIT championship victory over Utah in 1974. Paced by the combined scoring of Kendrick and Garrett (49 points between them) and clutch bench play of reserves Mike Steele and Gerald Thomas, Purdue became the first Big Ten school ever to capture an NIT crown.

The end of the '70s brought on the scene two giant figures in Purdue cage history. Seven-footer Joe Barry Carroll started slowly (7.9 points per game as a freshman) but eventually emerged as the finest post player in school annals. Coach Lee Rose would enjoy the most successful brief tenure of any Purdue basketball mentor. Rose arrived in 1978 from UNC-Charlotte where two seasons earlier he had directed an NCAA Final Four team starring future NBA workhorse Cedric "Cornbread" Maxwell. Carroll piled up points during his junior and senior seasons at a record rate surpassed only by Mount. Together they provided two stellar seasons in West Lafayette during 1979 and 1980.

The 1979 Purdue team — the first under Rose's coaching direction — would compile the largest victory total (27-8) in school history, surpassing the 23 wins by the Rick Mount-led Boiler team of a decade earlier. (Keady's teams would eventually raise the standard to 29 in both 1988 and 1994.) And the 1979 Rose-coached team would duplicate several other feats of the 1969 George King-led squad as well. One would be to bring the Big Ten crown back to West Lafayette after a 10-year absence, although this time it would be only a partial title shared three ways with Iowa and eventual NCAA champion Michigan State. And Rose's team, like King's, would fight its way into a season-ending national championship game, albeit the less-glamorous NIT versus state-rival Indiana.

The new Purdue head man provided a complete departure from his predecessor. Rose opted for a systematic, controlled offense, with senior backcourt ace Jerry Sichting and trans-fer guard Brian Walker working the ball to Carroll as hub of the Boiler attack. Carroll aver-aged 22.8 points per game and received an able assist around the basket from slashing sopho-more cornerman Drake Morris (7.9 average, 21 points in an upset victory over Nebraska). In early season action, Purdue battled Indiana State and Larry Bird — the eventual NCAA run-ners-up — to a near standoff in West Lafayette. While Purdue fell by a final 63-53 count, Carroll and Bird competed on equal terms (22 points each, with Bird holding a 15-14 rebound-ing edge). The team also grabbed a morale-boosting victory in the Rainbow Classic in Hawaii at mid-season by defeating Boston College, Arizona State and Utah.

Passed over by the NCAA at season's end in favor of Michigan State and Iowa, the Boilers' NIT journey included victories over Central Michigan, Dayton, Old Dominion and Alabama. But it was the final matchup with the rival Hoosiers which provided the true season's highlight — even in last-minute defeat. The nail-biting shootout between two bitter opponents came down to two final images etched for years to come in the memories of Big Ten fans. First there was Indiana's Butch Carter hitting a game-winning jumper from long range with only seconds remaining. Then there was Jerry Sichting sending up a similar arching shot from the left corner at the buzzer, a desperate missile which rolled off the rim in a final moment of gripping drama.

Joe Barry Carroll and the Purdue team enjoyed a quality follow-up season under Rose in 1979-80. The results would even top the first Rose campaign in terms of postseason creden-tials if not in overall record (23-10) or final conference standings (3rd, 11-7). Four of the five starters from Rose's first roster returned in 1980 with Carroll still entrenched at center, Morris and Arnette Hallman at the forwards, and Brian Walker as the ballhandling guard. Replacing Sichting (soon an NBA fixture with the Indiana Pacers and Boston Celtics) would be a prom-ising offense-minded sophomore named Keith "Iceman" Edmonson. Edmonson would im-

Center Joe Barry Carroll was an All-American in 1980 and a first overall NBA draft choice. (Purdue University photo)

prove steadily until he became one of the league's top scorers two seasons later (21.2 points per game in 1982), but as a sophomore he performed in the long shadow of Joe Barry Carroll, as did the entire Boiler lineup. Carroll averaged 26 (with a season-high 41 against Southeastern Louisiana) as Purdue started 7-0 and cracked the top 10 in the national polls by Jan. 1.

A hard-fought loss to nationally ranked Syracuse in Mackey Arena kicked off the second half of the 1980 season as the Boilers eventually wore down in the latter stages of league play. Carroll also slumped in the late going and saw a 59-game streak of double-figure scoring halted with a lackluster performance at Iowa. Purdue finally dropped out of the conference race in the season's final week with a miserable 39-percent shooting performance during a bitter 64-60 homecourt loss to Ohio State. Yet the conference season ended on an upbeat note with victory over Michigan State that clinched an NCAA bid for the third-place Big Ten squad. The Boilers had benefited immensely from two NCAA policy changes — an expansion of the tourney field to 48 teams and the dropping of earlier restrictions permitting only two tournament entries from a single conference.

The 1980 Final Four affair was a hometown party for the Boilermakers. The fortuitous events of schedule-making placed the event in Indianapolis in the very season when the Boilers were making their first serious postseason run in a decade. Little matter that the party was brief in duration and that dreams of a national title were quickly put to rest by a UCLA Bruins club coached by much-travelled Larry Brown and featuring freshman guards Rod Foster and Michael Holton alongside veteran frontcourt stars Kiki Vandeweghe and Mike Sanders. The Bruins coasted 67-62 in the semifinal shootout leaving the Boilers to content themselves with a third-place consolation-round triumph over Iowa. The failure to thrill the hometown faithful with a Final Four victory in Market Square Arena was nothing to be embarrassed about, however. Carroll had closed out an All-American career as a school record holder (first all-time in rebounding and second in scoring) and as a No. 1 overall pick in the NBA draft. But Rose was already unhappy at the West Lafayette campus — he had complained publicly about overemphasis on football and about his recruiting failures within the state of Indiana — and at season's end the successful coach would depart for a similar post at South Florida.

Rose's hasty departure looked like it might well leave the Purdue program strapped and even in shambles. Only Ralph Jones back in the century's second decade had posted a better short-term ledger than had Rose. And if Lee Rose had won big for two seasons, he had seemingly failed to recruit fresh talent for upcoming campaigns. Yet the move turned out to be a huge stroke of good fortune covered in thin disguise. The decade and the coach that would follow Rose would both prove to be the most successful in school history. The upcoming Keady era was destined to be the most victory-rich in Purdue annals judged by almost any measure except perhaps the ultimate success of an NCAA tournament championship. Keady has so far been unable to follow his immediate predecessor back into the magical Final Four. But his victory total in the '80s has outstripped that of any Purdue coach from any past decade. Keady has now rolled into the '90s and into the post-Glenn Robinson era with every sign pointing straight toward a future bright with continued successes.

Records and Summaries
Year-by-Year Purdue Records
(Championship Years in Boldface)

Season	All Games	Conference	Coach(es)	Boilermaker MVPs
1896-97	1-1	None	F. Homer Curtis	Not Awarded
1897-98		*No Games Played*		
1898-99		*No Games Played*		
1899-00	0-1	None	Alpha Jamison	Not Awarded
1900-01	12-0	None	Alpha Jamison	Not Awarded
1901-02	10-3	None	C.M. Besy	Not Awarded
1902-03	8-0	None	C.I. Freeman	Not Awarded
1903-04	11-2	None	No Coach	Not Awarded
1904-05	3-6	None	James L. Nufer	Not Awarded
1905-06	4-7	3-6	C.B. Jamison	Not Awarded
1906-07	7-8	2-6	C.B. Jamison	Not Awarded

1907-08	5-9	0-8	C.B. Jamison	Not Awarded
1908-09	8-4	6-4	E.J. Stewart	Not Awarded
1909-10	8-5	5-5	Ralph Jones	Not Awarded
1910-11	**12-4**	**8-4 (1st-T)**	**Ralph Jones**	**Not Awarded**
1911-12	**12-0**	**10-0 (1st-T*)**	**Ralph Jones**	**Not Awarded**
1912-13	7-5	6-5	R.E. Vaughn	Not Awarded
1913-14	5-9	3-9	R.E. Vaughn	Not Awarded
1914-15	5-8	4-8	R.E. Vaughn	Not Awarded
1915-16	4-10	2-10	R.E. Vaughn	Not Awarded
1916-17	11-3	7-2	Ward Lambert	Not Awarded
1917-18	11-5	5-5	J.J. Maloney	Not Awarded
1918-19	8-6	4-7	Ward Lambert	Not Awarded
1919-20	16-4	8-2	Ward Lambert	Not Awarded
1920-21	**13-7**	**8-4 (1st-T)**	**Ward Lambert**	**Not Awarded**
1921-22	**15-3**	**8-1 (1st)**	**Ward Lambert**	**Not Awarded**
1922-23	9-6	7-5	Ward Lambert	Not Awarded
1923-24	12-5	7-5	Ward Lambert	Not Awarded
1924-25	9-5	7-4	Ward Lambert	Not Awarded
1925-26	**13-4**	**8-4 (1st-T)**	**Ward Lambert**	**Not Awarded**
1926-27	12-5	9-3	Ward Lambert	Not Awarded
1927-28	**15-2**	**10-2 (1st-T)**	**Ward Lambert**	**Not Awarded**
1928-29	13-4	9-3	Ward Lambert	Not Awarded
1929-30	**13-2**	**10-0 (1st)**	**Ward Lambert**	**Not Awarded**
1930-31	12-5	8-4	Ward Lambert	Not Awarded
1931-32	**17-1**	**11-1 (1st)**	**Ward Lambert**	**Not Awarded**
1932-33	11-7	6-6	Ward Lambert	Not Awarded
1933-34	**17-3**	**10-2 (1st)**	**Ward Lambert**	**Not Awarded**
1934-35	**17-3**	**9-3 (1st-T)**	**Ward Lambert**	**Not Awarded**
1935-36	**16-4**	**11-1 (1st-T)**	**Ward Lambert**	**Not Awarded**
1936-37	15-5	8-4	Ward Lambert	Not Awarded
1937-38	**18-2**	**10-2 (1st)**	**Ward Lambert**	**Not Awarded**
1938-39	12-7	6-6	Ward Lambert	Not Awarded
1939-40	**16-4**	**10-2 (1st)**	**Ward Lambert**	**Not Awarded**
1940-41	13-7	6-6	Ward Lambert	Not Awarded
1941-42	14-7	9-6	Ward Lambert	Not Awarded
1942-43	9-11	6-6	Ward Lambert	Not Awarded
1943-44	11-10	8-4	Ward Lambert	Not Awarded
1944-45	9-11	6-6	Ward Lambert	Paul Hoffman
1945-46	10-11	4-8	Ward Lambert/Mel Taube	Rudy Lawson
1946-47	9-11	4-8	Mel Taube	Paul Hoffman
1947-48	11-9	6-6	Mel Taube	Bill Berberian
1948-49	13-9	6-6	Mel Taube	Howie Williams
1949-50	9-13	3-9	Mel Taube	Howie Williams
1950-51	8-14	4-10	Ray Eddy	Carl McNulty

1951-52	8-14	3-11	Ray Eddy	Carl McNulty
1952-53	4-18	3-15	Ray Eddy	Jack Runyan
1953-54	9-13	3-11	Ray Eddy	Dennis Blind
1954-55	12-10	5-9	Ray Eddy	Don Beck
1955-56	16-6	9-5	Ray Eddy	Joe Sexson
1956-57	15-7	8-6	Ray Eddy	Lamar Lundy
1957-58	14-8	9-5	Ray Eddy	Wilson Eison
1958-59	15-7	8-6	Ray Eddy	Willie Merriweather
1959-60	11-12	6-8	Ray Eddy	Terry Dischinger
1960-61	16-7	10-4	Ray Eddy	Terry Dischinger
1961-62	17-7	9-5	Ray Eddy	Terry Dischinger
1962-63	7-17	2-12	Ray Eddy	Mel Garland
1963-64	12-12	8-6	Ray Eddy	Dave Schellhase
1964-65	12-12	5-9	Ray Eddy	Dave Schellhase
1965-66	8-16	4-10	George King	Dave Schellhase
1966-67	15-9	7-7	George King	Herm Gilliam
1967-68	15-9	9-5	George King	Herm Gilliam/Billy Keller
1968-69#	**23-5**	**13-1 (1st)**	**George King**	**Rick Mount**
1969-70	18-6	11-3	George King	Rick Mount
1970-71	18-7	11-3	George King	Larry Weatherford
1971-72	12-12	6-8	George King	Bob Ford
1972-73	15-9	8-6	Fred Schaus	Frank Kendrick
1973-74**	22-8	10-4	Fred Schaus	Frank Kendrick
1974-75	17-11	11-7	Fred Schaus	John Garrett
1975-76	16-11	11-7	Fred Schaus	Eugene Parker
1976-77	20-8	14-4	Fred Schaus	Walter Jordan
1977-78	16-11	11-7	Fred Schaus	Walter Jordan
1978-79	**27-8**	**13-5 (1st-T)**	**Lee Rose**	**Joe Barry Carroll**
1979-80	23-10	11-7	Lee Rose	Joe Barry Carroll
1980-81	21-11	10-8	Gene Keady	Brian Walker
1981-82	18-14	11-7	Gene Keady	Keith Edmonson
1982-83	21-9	11-7	Gene Keady	Russell Cross
1983-84	**22-7**	**15-3 (1st-T)**	**Gene Keady**	**Jim Rowinski/Ricky Hall**
1984-85	20-9	11-7	Gene Keady	James Bullock
1985-86	22-10	11-7	Gene Keady	Mack Gadis
1986-87	**25-5**	**15-3 (1st-T)**	**Gene Keady**	**Doug Lee**
1987-88	**29-4**	**16-2 (1st)**	**Gene Keady**	**Everette Stephens/Troy Lewis**
1988-89	15-16	8-10	Gene Keady	Tony Jones
1989-90	22-8	13-5	Gene Keady	Steve Scheffler/Ryan Berning
1990-91	17-12	9-9	Gene Keady	Jimmy Oliver
1991-92	18-15	8-10	Gene Keady	Woody Austin
1992-93	18-10	9-9	Gene Keady	Glenn Robinson
1993-94	**29-5**	**14-4 (1st)**	**Gene Keady**	**Glenn Robinson**

= NCAA Runners-Up; ** = NIT Champs

Billy Keller, who shared team MVP honors with Herm Gilliam in the 1967-68 season, splits the defense in a 1966 game against the Washington Huskies. (Purdue University photo)

All-Time Purdue Individual Career Records

Points Scored .... Rick Mount (2,323, 1968-70)
Scoring Average .... Rick Mount (32.3, 1968-70)
Games Played..Drake Morris (126, 1978-81)
Minutes Played.. Troy Lewis (3,859, 1985-88)
Games Started ....Melvin McCants (121, 1986-89)
Dunks ....Joe Barry Carroll (158, 1977-80)
Field Goals .... Rick Mount (910, 1968-70)
Field-Goal Percentage .... Steve Scheffler (.685, 1987-90)
Free Throws Made .... Terry Dischinger (713, 1960-62)
Free-Throw Percentage .... Jerry Sichting (.867, 1976-79)
3-Point Field Goals .... Troy Lewis (151, 1987-88)
Rebounds ....Joe Barry Carroll (1,148, 1977-80)
Rebound Average.. Terry Dischinger (13.6, 1960-62)
Assists .... Bruce Parkinson (690, 1973-77)
Steals .... Brian Walker (187, 1979-81)
Blocked Shots ....Joe Barry Carroll (349, 1977-80)

All-Time Purdue Individual Season Records

Points Scored .... Rick Mount (932, 1968-69)
Scoring Average .... Rick Mount (35.4, 1969-70)
Minutes Played...Joe Barry Carroll (1,235, 1978-79)
Dunks .... Joe Barry Carroll (70, 1978-79)
Field Goals .... Rick Mount (336, 1968-69)
Field-Goal Percentage .... Steve Scheffler (.708, 1987-88)
Free Throws Made .... Terry Dischinger (292, 1961-62)
Free-Throw Percentage .... Henry Ebershoff (.907, 1965-66)
3-Point Field Goals .... Troy Lewis (100, 1987-88)
Rebounds ....Joe Barry Carroll (352, 1978-79)
Rebound Average.. Terry Dischinger (14.3, 1959-60)
Assists .... Bruce Parkinson (207, 1974-75)
Steals .... Brian Walker (88, 1978-79)
Blocked Shots ....Joe Barry Carroll (105, 1977-78)

All-Time Purdue Individual Single-Game Records

Points Scored .... Rick Mount (61 vs. Iowa, 2-28-70)
Field Goals .... Rick Mount (27 vs. Iowa, 2-28-70)
Free Throws Made .... Terry Dischinger (21 vs. Iowa, 2-27-61)
Rebounds .... Carl McNulty (27 vs. Minnesota, 2-19-51)
Assists .... Bruce Parkinson (18 vs. Minnesota, 3-8-75)
Steals .... Bruce Parkinson (7 vs. Indiana, 2-20-77)
Blocked Shots ....Joe Barry Carroll (11 vs. Arizona, 12-10-77)

All-Time Purdue Coaching Records

Coach	Overall Record	Conference Record	Seasons
Ward Lambert (1917, 1919-46)	371-152 (.709)	227-105 (.684)	29
Gene Keady (1981-Present)	297-135 (.688)	161-91 (.639)	14
Ray Eddy (1951-65)	176-164 (.518)	92-122 (.430)	15
George King (1966-72)	109-64 (.630)	61-37 (.622)	7
Fred Schaus (1973-78)	106-58 (.646)	65-35 (.650)	6
Lee Rose (1979-80)	50-18 (.735)	24-12 (.667)	2
Mel Taube (1946-50)	45-46 (.495)	22-33 (.400)	5
Ralph Jones (1910-12)	32-9 (.780)	23-9 (.719)	3
R.E. Vaughn (1913-16)	21-32 (.396)	15-32 (.319)	4
C.B. Jamison (1906-08)	16-24 (.400)	5-20 (.200)	3
Alpha Jamison (1900-01)	12-1 (.923)	None	2
J.J. Maloney (1918)	11-5 (.688)	5-5 (.500)	1
C.M. Besy (1902)	10-3 (.769)	None	1
E.J. Stewart (1909)	8-4 (.667)	6-4 (.600)	1
C.I. Freeman (1903)	8-0 (1.000)	None	1
James L. Nufer (1905)	3-6 (.333)	None	1
F. Homer Curtis (1897)	1-1 (.500)	None	1

Purdue All-Americans and All-Big Ten Selections

Consensus All-Americans
Charles Murphy, Center, 1929-1930
John Wooden, Guard, 1930-1931-1932
Norman Cottom, Forward, 1934
Robert Kessler, Forward, 1936
Jewell Young, Forward, 1937-1938
Terry Dischinger, Center, 1961-1962
Dave Schellhase, Forward, 1966
Rick Mount, Guard, 1969-1970
Joe Barry Carroll, Center, 1980
Glenn Robinson, Forward, 1994

All-Big Ten Selections (since 1948)
Howard Williams, Guard, 1949
Carl McNulty, Center, 1952
Willie Merriweather, Guard, 1959
Terry Dischinger, Center, 1960-1962
Mel Garland, Guard, 1963
Dave Schellhase, Forward, 1964-1966
Rick Mount, Guard, 1968-1970
Herm Gilliam, Forward, 1969
Bob Ford, Forward, 1972
Frank Kendrick, Forward, 1974
Bruce Parkinson, Guard, 1975
John Garrett, Center, 1975
Walter Jordan, Forward, 1977-1978
Joe Barry Carroll, Center, 1979-1980
Keith Edmondson, Guard, 1982
Russell Cross, Center, 1983
Jim Rowinski, Center, 1984
James Bullock, Forward-Center, 1985
Troy Lewis, Guard, 1987-88
Todd Mitchell, Forward, 1988
Steve Scheffler, Center, 1990
Jimmy Oliver, Forward, 1991
Woody Austin, Guard, 1992
Glenn Robinson, Forward, 1993-1994

Chapter 11

WISCONSIN *Badgers*

Lost Outpost of a Forgotten Basketball Pioneer

=========

All-Time Record: 1,050-942, .527; **Conference Record:** 548-679, .447

Big Ten Championships — 14: (1907*, 1908*, 1912*, 1913, 1914, 1916, 1918, 1921*, 1923*, 1924*, 1929*, 1935*, 1941, 1947) * = Co-Champion

National (NCAA) Championships — 1 (1941)

Greatest Player: Claude Gregory (1977-1981)

Career Scoring Leader: Danny Jones (1,854 Points, 1987-90)

Most Successful Coach: Walter Meanwell (1912-17, 1921-34), 246-99, .712

All-Time Team: Claude Gregory (F, 1978-81), Trent Jackson (F, 1986-89), Michael Finley (G-F, 1992-95), Wes Matthews (G, 1978-80), Rick Olson (G, 1983-86)

Best Season: 1940-41 (20-3), NCAA Champion (Coach: Harold Foster)

=========

University Profile

Location: Madison, Wisconsin (pop. 185,000); **Founded:** 1848; **Campus Enrollment:** 39,300 (1994); **Started Basketball:** 1898-99. Faculty and alumni of one of the nation's most prestigious universities account for a dozen Nobel and 17 Pulitzer Prizes, plus 54 Presidential Young Investigator Awards among the current faculty members alone. Notable alumni: actor Don Ameche, novelist Joyce Carol Oates, Exxon chairman Lee Raymond, journalists Jeff Greenfield and Edwin Newmann, and Washington Post sports editor Len Shapiro. According to a 1983 study by the *Surveys of Science Resource Series*, University of Wisconsin scientists rank third as the most frequently cited from any academic institution in the world.

Team Nickname, Colors and Arena

Nickname: Badgers; **Colors:** Cardinal and White; **Arena:** University of Wisconsin Field House (11,500 capacity, opened 1930). It is indeed dangerous to make too much out of the appearance of such a frivolous appendage as a school mascot. But one can not help but wonder if the tame approach to basketball, along with the languid performances of so many Wisconsin teams of the past century, is not somehow related to the lovable and even cuddly appearance down through the years of mascot Bucky Badger. No ferocious Wolverine, warlike Indian chief, proud Spartan warrior, snarling Wildcat or stalking Nittany Lion here, to be sure. But then if it's not the mascot to blame, the explanation certainly must lie somewhere.

Badger Basketball History

Ironically, Wisconsin basketball started out at the very top of the heap and at the very front of the pack. The Madison school was one of six original Western Conference founders who gathered on Thanksgiving Day of 1905 to draw up official operating rules for the new affiliation that would begin formal basketball competitions that winter. The Wisconsin team which entered the new association in January 1906 could — along with rival Minnesota — already boast the best tradition of the lot from the game's first two rapid-growth decades. The previous season the Badgers won 10 games in 18 outings, including two victories by more than 60 points. A winter earlier they posted an outstanding 11-4 mark against an assorted collection of colleges, athletic clubs and YMCA teams.

Even before legendary Walter "Doc" Meanwell arrived in Madison in 1912, the very first of a long line of innovative Western Conference coaching geniuses, and even before the Western Conference was officially formed, Wisconsin could boast of a pioneering powerhouse team that was among the very best in the Midwest if not in the entire country. It was in the first season of conference play, however, that the Badgers launched their early domination of the new indoor sport. During the inaugural conference campaign, Wisconsin would post a solid 12-2 overall mark with a 6-2 conference ledger. This trailed by only a shade the Minnesota club that had played and lost a game less. The Badgers were coached that first season by student-athlete Emmett Angell, who also paced the conference in individual scoring with 96 points (6.9 points per game). It would be the only time that an individual would both coach and star simultaneously in Big Ten conference play.

Over the next several seasons — two more with Angell acting as coach and three with Haskell Noyes manning the bench — Wisconsin would launch its best epoch of conference play, a proud era which ran with few interruptions through the mid-20s. Over a 13-year stretch that ended in 1918, the Badgers would not know a single losing campaign and would post double figures in the victory column 10 times. Between 1912 and 1918 the overall record stood at 106-12 for Wisconsin basketballers, an incredible .898 winning percentage. And this early pre-World War I era also featured a memorable high scoring star to boost local enthusiasms. In one lopsided 80-10 victory over Beloit College on Jan. 7, 1905, lanky Chris Steinmetz became a Midwest sensation by netting 44 points for Angell's charges.

But it was Meanwell who would soon dominate the first third of the century when it came to winter athletics on the Madison campus. Meanwell came on board as Wisconsin coach in

1912. His first team went 12-0 to claim a conference title, the third for the already powerful Badgers. (Purdue also was undefeated but played two fewer games.) Forward Otto Stangel, who tallied a then-record 177 points during conference play, led the team. Meanwell would win four titles in his first five seasons, two of his first three teams would finish undefeated (the only two teams in school history to do so) and his first three years would boast an almost incomprehensible 44-1 overall record. No college coach anywhere, in any era, has ever enjoyed a more auspicious career start. It would prove to be anything but beginner's luck; Meanwell's next three teams were 13-4, 20-1 and 15-3.

In the annals of college basketball's earliest days, Doc Meanwell's lasting niche is based on more than sterling won-lost ledgers. For Meanwell was one of the important trend-setting pioneers of the new collegiate cage game. Doc preached a stern doctrine of teamwork and patterned offense based on a then-revolutionary precision passing game. His deftly designed and thoroughly drilled set-offense type of controlled play set standards of efficiency for all college teams up to that time. The style caught on in the Western Conference and along much of the East Coast as well. It was a style that would reign unchallenged

Center Don Rehfeldt was a two-time Big Ten scoring champion and Wisconsin's first All-Big Ten selection in 1949 and 1950. (University of Wisconsin photo)

throughout the teens and eventually be supplanted only when the fast-breaking game began to take hold in the '20s under the direction of rival Midwest coaches like Ward Lambert at Purdue and Eastern coaches like Frank Keaney of Rhode Island College and Bill Reinhart (Red Auerbach's mentor) at George Washington.

Meanwell's early successes began to slide somewhat once the game itself evolved onto another level. Once Ward Lambert had the "horses" — like All-Americans "Stretch" Murphy and Johnny Wooden — to staff his high-powered running game and others around the league followed suit, the patterned-style and lesser talent at Wisconsin could no longer keep pace. Meanwell would continue to produce winning teams throughout the '20s and win four more titles — all ties for the crown — during that decade. But by the early '30s the Badgers had slipped from the role of contender and Doc Meanwell's final four seasons produced only one

Big Ten winning record. In both 1932 and 1933 the Badgers slipped all the way to eighth place. The 13 losses in 1933 were the most in the first 40 years of Wisconsin hoop history. But when the books closed on Meanwell's career in 1934 the indelible record showed only five losing seasons in 20 years at the helm. And fittingly, the greatest coach in school history bowed out with a 1934 squad which finished 14-6 and tied for second in conference play.

There would be only one true burst of national glory for Wisconsin basketball once Meanwell left the scene. And that moment would come with the Harold Foster-coached 1941 miracle team, a talented outfit which scrapped its way to the first 20-victory season since Meanwell's 1916 squad and capturing the school's only national championship. When the best team in the East, the undefeated Seton Hall Pirates with star backcourt man Bob Davies (inventor of behind-the-back passing and dribbling), accepted a bid to the more prestigious National Invitational Tournament, this suddenly cleared the way for two unheralded and less respected teams from the West — Wisconsin and Washington State — to work their way into the finals of the newer but increasingly competitive NCAA postseason tourney. The NCAA Finals of 1941 were a historic moment for the basketball world, marking the exact end to the sport's first half-century of play. Yet nowhere would it be more historic than in the basketball annals of the newly crowned NCAA champion Wisconsin Badgers.

The 1940-41 team was unquestionably the finest — judged strictly against its competition — in Wisconsin history. It was the only Wisconsin team ever to make serious inroads on the national level. Gene Englund and John Kotz were the stars of that well-balanced unit which also featured guard Ted Strain and forward Charlie Epperson. But after outdistancing defending NCAA champion Indiana by a single game in conference play, the Badgers nearly lost their opening NCAA postseason match. Two clutch free throws by sophomore Kotz in the closing seconds were enough to preserve a tense 51-50 victory against Ivy League power Dartmouth. The tournament was still an eight-team affair at the time, so the Dartmouth victory placed the Badgers in a semifinal matchup with Pittsburgh which fell to the Big Ten team 36-30. In the finals, center Englund scored 13 points and Kotz 12 to account for 65 percent of the offense in the tight 39-34 victory against Washington State. Kotz would be the tourney MVP and Englund would be named an All-American, an honor which would fall to Kotz the following season. The 1941 club under Bud Foster had not only won the school's only national hoops title, but it had featured the school's only two consensus All-Americans.

The 1941 team would forever remain the crowning achievement of Foster's Wisconsin coaching career, a career that lasted throughout the 1940s and 1950s. The remainder of the 1940s had only one highlight and that was the 1946-47 team which captured the school's final Big Ten crown. At the heart of the team was three-year star Bob Cook who would pace the conference in scoring that year by averaging a modest 15.6 points per game, the last league scoring champ to net fewer than 200 points.

The final decade of Foster's tenure was as bleak as any period in school hoops history, trailing off into four dismal campaigns with conference records of 4-10, 3-11, 3-11 and 1-13. The 1958-59 team was 3-19 overall, arguably the weakest unit in school history. And that is saying something in a program with few boasting points and no championships in 47 seasons.

With the 1960s came Coach John Erickson, but little else would change in Madison beyond perhaps the names and revolving personalities. In Erickson's nine seasons there would

Guard Wes Matthews, above, who played for Wisconsin from 1977-80, is one of the few Badgers to have a successful career in the NBA. Current star Michael Finley, right, also is likely to end up in the NBA after his senior season. Finley, one of only three Wisconsin players to average more than 20 points per game in a season, is the school's first legitimate All-American candidate in 50 years. (University of Wisconsin photos)

be four campaigns with an overall record above .500, but only the 1962 team posted a winning Big Ten ledger. Joe Franklin in 1968 was Wisconsin's only All-Big Ten selection of the decade and the last until well into the 1990s. Basketball doldrums in Madison had arrived in a big way. The 1970s could offer only more of the same. Clarence Sherrod produced the best offensive season in school history in 1970-71, averaging 23.8 points per game and moving into fifth place on Wisconsin's all-time scoring list. But the Badgers would win but four conference games that season and finish only one slot out of the league basement.

By the 1980s, the Badgers were at least featuring some talented frontline players but still weren't having much success during the annual conference wars. Danny Jones became the career scoring leader at the end of the decade by piling up 1,854 points over four seasons. Yet Jones was never an all-league performer and could muster but a single season (20.4 points per game, 1989) that ranks in the top 10 of Badger history. Rick Olson (1983-86, 1,736 points) and Trent Jackson (1986-89, 1,545 points) worked their way into the third and fourth slots in career scoring during this period and onto any mythical all-time Badger all-star team.

But perhaps the finest all-around player to wear Badger scarlet would be four-year performer Claude Gregory. Gregory (1978-81) was hardly deemed sensational and never made a large enough impact on the league as a whole to earn all-conference honors. He ranks as the school's career leader in just one important category — total rebounds. But the numbers he compiled over the seasons nonetheless argue for strong support as best all-around Badger performer. The talented forward remains fifth in games started, seventh in scoring average (15.9), third all time in field goals, and only recently lost the top spot in career points (he scored 1,745) to Jones. Gregory will continue to have his backers for all-time Badger hero at least until the final season of Michael Finley's unfolding career has been completed.

No school in the conference, of course, owns a basketball past quite so devoid of individual superstar players — not even newcomer Penn State with Jesse Arnelle in the '50s and John Amaechi in the '90s. Wisconsin's only two consensus All-Americans came off the same 1941 and 1942 teams and the school also boasts the fewest all-conference selections as well — five. Paul Tompkins (1991) and Finley (1993, 1994) have been the only two chosen for conference honors since the late 1960s. Wes Matthews is so far the only player in school history to make even a small impact upon the NBA scene. But Finley and 6-foot-11 sophomore center Rashard Griffith now suggest that such notable weaknesses in star player attraction may be about to shift somewhat, if not disappear altogether.

The 1990s — split between Steve Yoder and Stu Jackson in the coach's slot — have seen something of a long-overdue turnaround in cage fortunes at Madison. In three of the last four seasons, Wisconsin has reached the .500 mark in overall record. Two of those years ended only a victory shy of a .500 record in league play. This wouldn't be much to brag about elsewhere, but in Wisconsin it might seem like outrageous good fortune indeed.

Jackson — an import from the pro ranks and the New York Knicks — lasted only two seasons before heading back to the NBA as general manager of an expansion club for Vancouver. Jackson's departure came amidst a storm of controversy surrounding his handling of Griffith, a temperamental star who spent much of the 1994 off-season sulking about playing time and threatening transfer. Yet Jackson had put the 1993 Badgers (18-11) back in the NCAA tourney for the first time in 46 seasons. For all its turmoil, the short-lived Jackson era had been the most exciting in many a winter on the Madison campus. Jackson's pro-style running offense produced a superb player in Finley, a preseason consensus All-American heading into his senior 1995 season. Badger fans only hope that Finley is the first of perhaps many star-quality players so common at other Big Ten venues but so rare in Madison.

Records and Summaries
Year-by-Year Wisconsin Records
(Championship Years in Boldface)

Season	All Games	Conference	Coach(es)	Top Scorer (Points)
1898-99	0-3	---	James Elsom	No Record
1899-00	1-1	---	James Elsom	No Record
1900-01	1-1	---	James Elsom	No Record
1901-02	7-3	---	James Elsom	No Record
1902-03	5-2	---	James Elsom	No Record
1903-04	11-4	---	James Elsom	No Record
1904-05	10-8	---	James Elsom	No Record
1905-06	12-2	6-2	Emmett Angell	Emmett Angell (96)•
1906-07	**11-3**	**6-2 (1st-T)**	**Emmett Angell**	**No Record**
1907-08	**10-2**	**7-1 (1st-T)**	**Emmett Angell**	**No Record**
1908-09	8-4	5-4	Haskell Noyes	No Record
1909-10	9-5	7-5	Haskell Noyes	No Record
1910-11	9-6	6-6	Haskell Noyes	No Record
1911-12	**15-0**	**12-0 (1st-T)**	**Walter Meanwell**	**Otto Stangel (177)•**
1912-13	**14-1**	**11-1 (1st)**	**Walter Meanwell**	**No Record**
1913-14	**15-0**	**12-0 (1st)**	**Walter Meanwell**	**No Record**
1914-15	13-4	8-4	Walter Meanwell	George Levis (140)•
1915-16	**20-1**	**11-1 (1st)**	**Walter Meanwell**	**No Record**
1916-17	15-3	9-3	Walter Meanwell	No Record
1917-18	**14-3**	**9-3 (1st)**	**Guy Lowman**	**No Record**
1918-19	5-11	3-9	Guy Lowman	No Record
1919-20	15-5	7-5	Guy Lowman	No Record
1920-21	**13-4**	**8-4 (1st-T)**	**Walter Meanwell**	**No Record**
1921-22	14-5	8-4	Walter Meanwell	No Record
1922-23	**12-3**	**11-1 (1st-T)**	**Walter Meanwell**	**No Record**
1923-24	**11-5**	**8-4 (1st-T)**	**Walter Meanwell**	**No Record**
1924-25	6-11	3-9	Walter Meanwell	No Record
1925-26	8-9	4-8	Walter Meanwell	No Record
1926-27	10-7	7-5	Walter Meanwell	No Record
1927-28	13-4	9-3	Walter Meanwell	No Record
1928-29	**15-2**	**10-2 (1st-T)**	**Walter Meanwell**	**No Record**
1929-30	15-2	8-2	Walter Meanwell	No Record
1930-31	8-9	4-8	Walter Meanwell	No Record
1931-32	8-10	3-9	Walter Meanwell	No Record
1932-33	7-13	4-8	Walter Meanwell	No Record

1933-34	14-6	8-4	Walter Meanwell	No Record
1934-35	**15-5**	**9-3 (1st-T)**	**Harold Foster**	**No Record**
1935-36	11-9	4-8	Harold Foster	No Record
1936-37	8-12	3-9	Harold Foster	No Record
1937-38	10-10	5-7	Harold Foster	No Record
1938-39	10-10	4-8	Harold Foster	Dave Dupee (154)
1939-40	5-15	3-9	Harold Foster	Gene Englund (199)
1940-41#	**20-3**	**11-1 (1st)**	**Harold Foster**	**Gene Englund (304)**
1941-42	14-7	10-5	Harold Foster	John Kotz (325)•
1942-43	12-9	6-6	Harold Foster	John Kotz (308)
1943-44	12-9	9-3	Harold Foster	Ray Patterson (295)
1944-45	10-11	4-8	Harold Foster	Ray Patterson (225)
1945-46	4-17	1-11	Harold Foster	Bob Cook (289)
1946-47	**16-6**	**9-3 (1st)**	**Harold Foster**	**Bob Cook (323)•**
1947-48	12-8	7-5	Harold Foster	Bob Cook (235)
1948-49	12-10	5-7	Harold Foster	Don Rehfeldt (381)•
1949-50	17-5	9-3	Harold Foster	Don Rehfeldt (436)•
1950-51	10-12	7-7	Harold Foster	Ab Nicholas (366)
1951-52	10-12	5-9	Harold Foster	Ab Nicholas (361)
1952-53	13-9	10-8	Harold Foster	Paul Murrow (352)
1953-54	12-10	6-8	Harold Foster	Dick Cable (301)
1954-55	10-12	5-9	Harold Foster	Dick Cable (442)
1955-56	6-16	4-10	Harold Foster	Dick Miller (429)
1956-57	5-17	3-11	Harold Foster	Bob Litzow (355)
1957-58	8-14	3-11	Harold Foster	Bob Litzow (324)
1958-59	3-19	1-13	Harold Foster	Bob Barneson (259)
1959-60	8-16	4-10	John Erickson	Tom Hughbanks (312)
1960-61	7-17	4-10	John Erickson	Tom Hughbanks (301)
1961-62	17-7	10-4	John Erickson	Ken Siebel (392)
1962-63	14-10	7-7	John Erickson	Jack Brens (425)
1963-64	8-16	2-12	John Erickson	Ken Gustafson (359)
1964-65	9-13	4-10	John Erickson	Mark Zubor (345)
1965-66	11-13	6-8	John Erickson	Ken Gustafson (333)
1966-67	13-11	8-8	John Erickson	Chuck Nagle (463)
1967-68	13-11	7-7	John Erickson	Joe Franklin (544)
1968-69	11-13	5-9	John Powless	James Johnson (462)
1969-70	10-14	5-9	John Powless	Clarence Sherrod (538)
1970-71	9-15	4-10	John Powless	Clarence Sherrod (570)
1971-72	13-11	6-8	John Powless	Leon Howard (378)
1972-73	11-13	5-9	John Powless	Leon Howard (431)
1973-74	16-8	8-6	John Powless	Kim Hughes (367)
1974-75	8-18	5-13	John Powless	Bruce McCauley (418)
1975-76	10-16	4-14	John Powless	Dale Koehler (505)
1976-77	11-16	7-11	Bill Cofield	James Gregory (429)
1977-78	8-19	4-14	Bill Cofield	Arnold Gaines (294)
1978-79	12-15	6-12	Bill Cofield	Wes Matthews (499)

1979-80	15-14	7-11	Bill Cofield	Wes Matthews (549)
1980-81	11-16	5-13	Bill Cofield	Claude Gregory (550)
1981-82	6-21	3-15	Bill Cofield	Brad Sellers (378)
1982-83	8-20	3-15	Steve Yoder	Cory Blackwell (511)
1983-84	8-20	4-14	Steve Yoder	Cory Blackwell (529)
1984-85	14-14	5-13	Steve Yoder	Scott Roth (513)
1985-86	12-16	4-14	Steve Yoder	Rick Olson (571)
1986-87	14-17	4-14	Steve Yoder	J.J. Weber (469)
1987-88	12-16	6-12	Steve Yoder	Trent Jackson (546)
1988-89	18-12	8-10	Steve Yoder	Danny Jones (611)
1989-90	14-17	4-14	Steve Yoder	Danny Jones (548)
1990-91	15-15	8-10	Steve Yoder	Patrick Tompkins (423)
1991-92	13-18	4-14	Steve Yoder	Tracy Webster (537)
1992-93	14-14	7-11	Stu Jackson	Michael Finley (620)
1993-94	18-11	8-10	Stu Jackson	Michael Finley (592)

= National (NCAA) Champions; • = League Individual Scoring Champion

All-Time Wisconsin Individual Career Records

Points Scored .... Danny Jones (1,854, 1987-90)
Scoring Average .... Clarence Sherrod (19.6, 1969-71)
Games Played .... Tim Locum (118, 1988-91)
                                                                                    Danny Jones (118, 1987-90)
                                                                                    Kurt Portmann (118, 1987-90)
Games Started .... Rick Olson (112, 1983-86)
Field Goals .... Rick Olson (729, 1983-86)
Field-Goal Percentage .... Patrick Tompkins (.573, 1988-91)
Free Throws Made .... Claude Gregory (433, 1978-81)
Free-Throw Percentage .... Rick Olson (.870, 1983-86)
3-Point Field Goals .... Tim Locum (227, 1988-91)
Rebounds .... Claude Gregory (904, 1978-81)
Rebound Average .... Joe Franklin (11.9, 1966-68)
Assists .... Mike Heineman (388, 1984-87)
Steals .... Trent Jackson (151, 1986-89)
Blocked Shots .... Brad Sellers (120, 1982-83)

All-Time Wisconsin Individual Season Records

Points Scored .... Michael Finley (620, 1992-93)
Scoring Average .... Clarence Sherrod (23.8, 1970-71)
Field Goals .... Rick Olson (237, 1985-86)
Field-Goal Percentage .... Patrick Tompkins (.636, 1990-91)
Free Throws Made .... Clarence Sherrod (168, 1969-70)
Free-Throw Percentage .... Brian Good (.905, 1989-90)

3-Point Field Goals .... Tracy Webster (75, 1991-92)
Rebounds .... Jim Clinton (344, 1950-51)
Rebound Average .... Jim Clinton (15.6, 1950-51)
Assists .... Tracy Webster (179, 1992-93)
Steals .... Tracy Webster (66, 1992-93)
Blocked Shots .... Brad Sellers (68, 1982-83)

All-Time Wisconsin Individual Single-Game Records

Points Scored .... Ken Barnes (42 vs. Indiana, 3-8-65)
Field Goals .... Rick Olson (17 vs. San Francisco State, 12-2-85)
Free Throws Made .... Dale Koehler (17 vs. Loyola-Chi., 12-6-75)
3-Point Field Goals .... Larry Hisle (7 vs. Texas-Arlington, 12-22-90)
                                                        Tim Locum (7 vs. Rollins, 12-15-89)
                                                         Tim Locum (7 vs. Butler, 12-5-87)
                                                     Trent Jackson (7 vs. Ohio State, 1-17-87)
Rebounds .... Paul Morrow (30 vs. Purdue, 1-3-53)
Assists .... Tracy Webster (13 vs. Michigan, 2-26-92)
                                                      Wes Matthews (13 vs. Army, 12-30-79)
Steals .... Michael Finley (10 vs. Purdue, 2-13-93)
Blocked Shots .... Brad Sellers (9 vs. Toledo, 11-29-82)

All-Time Wisconsin Coaching Records

Coach	Overall Record	Conference Record	Seasons
Harold Foster (1935-59)	265-267 (.498)	143-182 (.440)	25
Walt Meanwell (1912-17, 21-34)	246-99 (.712)	158-80 (.660)	20
Steve Yoder (1983-92)	128-165 (.437)	50-130 (.278)	10
John Erickson (1960-68)	100-114 (.467)	52-74 (.413)	9
John Powless (1969-76)	88-108 (.449)	42-78 (.350)	8
Bill Cofield (1977-82)	63-101 (.384)	32-76 (.296)	6
Emmett Angell (1905-08)	43-15 (.741)	19-6 (.760)	4
Guy Lowman (1918-20)	34-19 (.642)	19-17 (.528)	3
Stu Jackson (1993-94)	32-25 (.561)	15-21 (.417)	2
Haskell Noyes (1909-11)	26-15 (.634)	18-15 (.541)	3
James Elsom (1899-1904)	25-14 (.641)	None	6

Wisconsin All-Americans and All-Big Ten Selections

Consensus All-Americans
Gene Englund, Forward, 1941
John Kotz, Forward, 1942

All-Big Ten Selections (since 1948)
Don Rehfeldt, Center, 1949-1950
Ab Nicholas, Guard, 1951-1952
Joe Franklin, Forward, 1968
Patrick Tompkins, Center, 1991
Michael Finley, Forward-Guard, 1993-1994

II

Coaches, Teams and Players

Chapter 12

THE DOZEN GREATEST COACHES

Indiana University's 1993-94 *Basketball Media Guide* listing of all-time Hoosier coaching records contends that Bob Knight leads all Big Ten coaches, past and present, with a career in-conference record of 517 wins against only 164 losses. Knight indeed ranks atop the all-time list of Big Ten coaches in league games won, but his actual victory total, while still a substantial 293, is slightly more than half of what the university publication has claimed. (The 517 victories are Knight's entire Indiana output, non-conference matches included). It is undoubtedly a harmless enough typographical error, but one which reflects the truth-bending history of Robert Montgomery Knight. There is little question that Knight remains the most successful coach in league annals. But at the same time, the Indiana coach's documented history has always had a rough time keeping pace with his colorful legend.

But Knight is not the only Big Ten coach of past or present eras whose legend seems to overwhelm considerable real-life achievement. At the beginning of conference history there were Doc Meanwell — a pacesetter in the disciplined ball-control style of play — and Ward "Piggy" Lambert, who replaced Meanwell's tradition with a revolutionary fast-breaking style of basketball. At Bloomington, Branch McCracken became a legend long before Bob Knight came on the scene. And in West Lafayette, Gene Keady is presently constructing an ongoing legacy that threatens to rival that of both IU's Knight and even Keady's earlier Purdue forerunner, Lambert. Meanwhile in Champaign-Urbana, Harry Combes constructed a two-decade career surpassed for longevity and success only by Knight, Meanwell and McCracken. But just as Knight has overhauled the records of McCracken and Keady has challenged those of Lambert, so has Combes nearly been outstripped by current long-term Illini mentor Lou Henson. Like Knight, Henson boasts a career victory total that has climbed above 600 and a league victory mark that will soon make him a member of the exclusive 200-win club (alongside Knight, Lambert and McCracken).

Of course, all of the coaching legends at Indiana, Purdue and Illinois, the league's three most successful year-in and year-out cage programs, have not yet been written. In Columbus, Ohio, Fred Taylor remains the only coach with five straight league titles and three straight trips to the Final Four. Ohio State also was home to Harold Olsen, whose 24-year tenure matches Knight's and McCracken's and trails only Lambert's and that of Bud Foster at Wisconsin. Foster was, of course, another of the memorable Big Ten pioneers. In 1941 it was Foster who claimed the second NCAA crown ever captured by a Big Ten school. And when boasting of conference coaching legends one would have to review the careers of close to a dozen other immortals as well — Doug Mills at Illinois, L.J. Cooke at Minnesota, Arthur Lonborg at Northwestern, and Johnnie Orr and Bill Frieder (and of course Steve Fisher) at Michigan.

A larger-than-life legend, Indiana's Bob Knight owns nearly all of the Big Ten's milestones of success. (Indiana University photo)

If Big Ten cage history is as rich as that of any conference in the country, then this is in large part due to the traditions of the men who have organized the programs, pioneered strategies, molded the championship teams, and drawn the crucial x's and o's during nearly a century of league play. To single out the dozen or so most enduring legends is both quite easy and, at the same time, most difficult. There are a half-dozen mentors (Knight, Meanwell, Lambert, McCracken, Taylor, Keady) who have called the Big Ten home for the bulk of their careers and who would rank atop any imaginable survey of the sport's greatest collegiate coaches and teachers; this handful of coaching legends stands with any half-dozen figures from any conference or any epoch of the sport's 100-year history.

The next half-dozen nominees for the mythical Big Ten coaching Hall of Fame would be a much closer call. The achievements of modern era coaches — often with NCAA or NIT titles to their credit — tend to overshadow the dimly remembered pioneers who shaped the league and sport in an era before television and without the aura of March Madness. Jud Heathcote or Steve Fisher or Lee Rose or Lute Olson have recently seized the limelight with glamorous Final Four achievements during an era of the sport's highest popularity. But we also must make room for men like Meanwell, Lambert, Mills and Combes who nurtured Big Ten basketball in its often rocky formative years, leaving a legacy upon which all future generations could build. Theirs, too, is a story of championship cage play — Big Ten style.

Bob Knight (Indiana, 1972-Present, 538-173, .757 Pct.)

Bob Knight never played a moment of professional basketball nor has he ever coached at the play-for-pay level. Nonetheless, Knight holds a close association with the only two teams — both from the Big Ten — ever to send an entire starting five into the NBA/ABA ranks. First there was the national champion Ohio State team of 1960 (Lucas, Havlicek, Siegfried, Mel Nowell and Joe Roberts) on which Knight was the unheralded "sixth man" contributor. And later there was of course the undefeated 1976 Indiana NCAA championship outfit (Scott May, Kent Benson, Tom Abernethy, Quinn Buckner and Bobby Wilkerson) which Knight coached to the only perfect season in modern Big Ten history. These two teams are without debate the two greatest in league history. And both wear the clear stamp of Bob Knight's presence.

Knight was not a star on the 1960 OSU national championship club. His playing career was limited to a narrowly defined role; but in that role Knight already was able to display the telltale marks of a winner. His one moment for glory was a moment which he seized and converted into near-victory of the most dramatic sort. As a junior reserve with only a four-point scoring average, Knight came off the bench to sink a key driving bucket with 1 minute, 41 seconds remaining in the 1961 NCAA title game against downstate rival Cincinnati, temporarily rescuing the defending champions and sending the game into tense overtime. In the end, Knight's heroics were wasted as the Buckeyes wilted during the final stanza and lost the first of two disappointing title shootouts with the Bearcats. Knight's only two points of NCAA championship play were nonetheless the biggest points of his undistinguished career and an early sign of his penchant for NCAA postseason heroics.

But it is clearly as a coach that Knight has made his lasting mark. Since The General's arrival in Bloomington a quarter-century back, the Indiana basketball program has been a national symbol for winning excellence. The greatest boasting points of Knight's career are, of course, the overall winning percentage (now at .757), the near-dozen Big Ten titles, three national championships, and the rapid climb up the ladder toward the highest victory total in collegiate basketball history. Knight has climbed that ladder with amazing speed, being among the youngest coaches to obtain the 200-, 300-, 400-, 500- and 600-victory plateaus. Victory 200 (93-56, Georgia, 1976) would come at age 35; his 300th win (83-69, Northwestern, 1980) would be owned by age 40; four years later the 400th victory would also be pocketed (81-68, Kentucky, 1984); by 48 Knight owned 500 wins (92-76, Northwestern, 1989) and by 52 he had reached 600 (75-67, Iowa, 1993). At his young age (he is the youngest ever to win 600) Knight seems almost certain to become the winningest coach in college basketball history.

Knight's legacy within the league is eternally assured. Ironically, it was in a game against arch-rival Purdue (74-73, 1989) that Knight became the winningest coach in conference annals, surpassing the mark held by the Boilermakers' Ward Lambert. And in terms of winning percentage, Bob Knight is in a league of his own; his current .724 mark makes him the only coach in league history to stand above a 70 percent winning level. Knight's current marks for winning efficiency have no challengers from the past epochs of Big Ten play; it's hardly likely they will face any serious challenges for a long, long time to come.

But there is more to the Knight story than league and NCAA title banners and the endless string of basketball games won. There is the side of Knight and his program often buried by the enthusiasms of alumni and fans over victories, or by the barrage of criticisms from detractors who harp on Knight's outburst with the press and his stern discipline with his own players. This is the side of a man and coach who represents lofty principles of excellence in education as well as in athletics, and who teaches lessons of loyalty and honor as well as those of skilled basketball play. This side of Knight is seen in the exemplary graduation rates of his players; it is also measured by the personal and business successes of so many of his ex-players after college graduation. And there is also the deep bond between former and current Knight athletes which makes IU basketball one of the nation's most special sportsworld stories. In every way, basketball tradition at Indiana has become the stuff of legend under Bob Knight. And this has miraculously transpired in spite of the fact that Coach Knight himself has always remained the largest legend of all.

Bob Knight's Coaching Record and Career Milestones

Years .... 29 (Indiana 23, Army 6)
NCAA Championships... 3 (1976, 1981, 1987)
Big Ten Championships........................... 11 (1973, 1974*, 1975, 1976, 1980, 1981, 1983, 1987*, 1989, 1991*, 1993)
Big Ten Won-Lost Record .... 291-111 (.724)
Indiana Won-Lost Record... 538-173 (.757)
Total Won-Lost Record .... 640-223 (.742)
Consensus All-Americans .... 8 (Scott May, 1975-76; Kent Benson, 1976-77; Isiah Thomas, 1981; Steve Alford, 1986-87; Calbert Cheaney, 1993)
*First-Place Tie

Walter Meanwell (Wisconsin, 1912-17, 1921-34, 246-99, .712 Pct.)

No one ever launched a coaching career with a faster route to the top of the heap than Walter "Doc" Meanwell. Not even Michigan's Steve Fisher — winner of an NCAA title game before he ever copped a regular-season victory as a head coach — can boast of a quicker jump out of the blocks. Nine of Meanwell's first dozen seasons (seven at Wisconsin interrupted with two at Missouri) resulted in conference titles; his first three years on the job translated into Western Conference crowns for Wisconsin and the Badgers lost only one game in the process (a road game at Chicago on the final date of the 1912 campaign). Meanwell's coaching record was an astounding 44-1 after just three winters on the job.

Like Fisher, Meanwell would also coach a national championship club in his rookie campaign. For Meanwell, it was a Helms Foundation national title, one that rang of slightly less authority since there was no tournament at that time to settle the issue of the nation's best cage squad. Meanwell's impressive victory skein continued for much of the next two decades in Wisconsin, though the championship pace abated somewhat after the first dozen seasons. In all, Meanwell's teams would claim the Western Conference championship banner in nine of his 20 seasons at Madison, nearly a .500 average.

But like Ward "Piggy" Lambert at Purdue, it was more than winning championships that etched Meanwell's nationwide reputation, though admittedly it was the year-in and year-out winning that first drew attention to his renowned coaching philosophies. In short order, Doc Meanwell was established as the most influential coach in the land. His methods were copied by other head coaches from East Coast to West Coast and everywhere in-between. Meanwell's game was one of disciplined offensive patterns built around crisp short passing and precisely rehearsed set offensive plays. It was Meanwell in Wisconsin more than any other figure who entrenched the earliest notions of the basketball coach as artistic choreographer.

Ironically, Doc Meanwell's greatest legacy to the modern game of basketball in the end involved the battle he lost with the sport's national rule-making body and the dramatic backward-looking overhaul of the sport which he tried but failed to provide. Although Lambert's fast-breaking style at Purdue was beginning to hold sway by the late '20s, Meanwell would make one last-ditch effort to move the game back in the direction of the pass-oriented sport he admired. In what has become known to basketball historians as "the last great dribble debate" of 1927, Meanwell convinced the Collegiate Joint Rules Committee to vote by a slim margin (9-8) in favor of eliminating the dribble as a league offensive maneuver. After adjourning to witness a professional championship game in which the famed Original Celtics defeated the Cleveland Rosenblums by using a perfected version of Meanwell's passing style, the committee reconvened to hear an impassioned plea from CCNY coach Nat Holman, himself a player on the Original Celtics. Holman's message that college players needed the dribbling game to successfully compete convinced the august committee to reverse its earlier stand and seal modern basketball's futuristic direction.

Walter Meanwell's Coaching Record and Career Milestones

Years	22 (Wisconsin 20, Missouri 2)
NCAA Championships	None (no tournament held)
Helms National Champions	3 (1912, 1914, 1916)
Big Ten Championships	8 (1912, 1913, 1914, 1916, 1921*, 1923*, 1924*, 1929*)
Big Ten Won-Lost Record	158-80 (.660)
Wisconsin Won-Lost Record	246-99 (.712)
Total Won-Lost Record	280-101 (.735)
Consensus All-Americans	None

*First-Place Tie

Ward "Piggy" Lambert (Purdue, 1917, 1919-45, 371-152, .709 Pct.)

Nearly a half-century after his retirement in 1946, Ward Lambert's glowing basketball record is still largely unchallenged. For years, Lambert owned seemingly unapproachable records for Big Ten coaching excellence: 29 seasons, 228 conference wins, 371 overall victories at a conference school, 11 Big Ten (then Western Conference) titles, a stable of nine consensus All-American players. Before Bob Knight, only Branch McCracken had joined Lambert at the conference 200-victory plateau. In recent seasons Knight has begun overhauling Lambert's records — foremost those for career (538 at Indiana) and conference (291) wins and for league championships (they are now tied at 11 each). Today it is Knight as symbol of the modern era and Lambert as standard-bearer for the past who remain the greatest symbols of winning in Big Ten basketball history.

But Lambert's legacy had to do with more than just winning countless games and a near-dozen league titles. Piggy Lambert was one of that small contingent of most influential pioneers who worked to shape the modern-era game of racehorse basketball. When Lambert first came on the Purdue scene in the receding shadows of World War I, it was the "pass-and-plan" philosophy of Wisconsin's Walter Meanwell which still ruled the world of collegiate play. Lambert had a different vision of court tactics, however, and once he could recruit athletes good enough to learn and execute his freer vision of the game, basketball was on its way to being radically changed forever.

Lambert's game would soon come to be known as racehorse basketball and was built on a delicate balance of size (for controlling the defensive boards) and speed (for running the ball up the court without set plays and careful shot selections). All-Americans John Wooden and Lloyd Kemmer (the speedsters) and Charles "Stretch" Murphy (the rebounder) soon enabled Lambert to take racehorse basketball off the drawing board and put it directly onto the hardwood. The era of Doc Meanwell was suddenly at a close and that of Piggy Lambert was now off the ground. Although Lambert would know lean seasons from time to time over the next quarter century he would never go more than three seasons without a Western Conference championship until the final five years of his lengthy career. But Lambert had also launched more than a winning tradition for Purdue; he had launched a revolutionary style of play that would eventually give birth to Red Auerbach and Bob Cousy and to all the slam-dunking stars of today's more athletic version of James Naismith's once painfully slow-moving indoor game.

Ward Lambert's Coaching Record and Career Milestones

Years .... 29 (Purdue 29)
NCAA Championships .... None (no tournament held)
Big Ten Championships 11 (1921*, 1922, 1926*, 1928*, 1930, 1932,
                                                                                 1934, 1935*, 1936*, 1938, 1940)
Big Ten Won-Lost Record .... 228-105 (.685)
Total Won-Lost Record .... 371-152 (.709)
Consensus All-Americans .... 9 (Charles Murphy, 1929-30; John Wooden, 1930-
          31-32; Norm Cottom, 1934; Robert Kessler, 1936; Jewell Young, 1937-38)
*First-Place Tie

Doug Mills (Illinois, 1937-47, 151-66, .696 Pct.)

On the surface record alone it would seem that Doug Mills hardly merits rank among the greatest Big Ten coaches or even among the greatest mentors representing the Fighting Illini of the University of Illinois. Mills, for one thing, doesn't boast half the victory total of either Lou Henson or Harry Combes. And his tenure didn't stretch even half as long as the two greatest Illini coaching legends. But there was a certain amazing economy and admirable compactness to the Mills tenure that cannot go entirely ignored. In half as many seasons, Mills tripled Henson's Big Ten title output and fell only one short of Combes on the championship ledger. Also, of the five consensus All-American awards earned by Illini players, four came during Mills' stay on the job. And then there was the matter of the 1942-43 "Whiz Kids" team, probably the greatest man-for-man outfit in Illinois basketball history.

Mills and his famed Whiz Kids unit never got a chance to fully demonstrate their prowess on the national scene (their story is told in a subsequent chapter), and that fact alone largely accounts for the short shrift now given to the coaching accomplishments of Doug Mills. The '43 Illini team (Andy Phillip, Ken Menke, Art Mathisen, Jack Smiley and Gene Vance) was acknowledged everywhere to be the best in the land. This memorable squad racked up a second straight conference crown, averaged nearly 58 points per game in an era when other clubs scored less than 40, finished with a 12-0 conference slate, and lost only when Coach Mills played his subs in a meaningless December contest with an Army unit from Camp Grant. Mills believed an intentional early-season loss would prevent overconfidence during upcoming regular-season conference combat. But the Whiz Kids for all their winning and scoring never got the chance to pursue the national title that might have been theirs. Events of World War II intervened in late season; the team passed up postseason NCAA play and disbanded on March 1 as all five starters headed off for wartime duty. Mills would never get another shot at glory once the events of wartime America dismantled the brilliant team that he had somehow managed to assemble.

Doug Mills' Coaching Record and Career Milestones

Years	11 (Illinois 11)
NCAA Championships	None
Big Ten Championships	3 (1937*, 1942, 1943)
Big Ten Won-Lost Record	88-47 (.642)
Total Won-Lost Record	151-66 (.696)
Consensus All-Americans	4 (Bill Hapac, 1940; Andy Phillip, 1942-43; Walton Kirk, 1945)

*First-Place Tie

Gene Keady (Purdue, 1981-Present, 297-135 .688 Pct.)

Gene Keady is a battler and his coaching philosophy has always demanded mental toughness from his overachieving players. Mental toughness has been the byword in West Lafayette because Keady has had a tough row to hoe and a series of tough acts to follow. First there is the matter of the shadow cast by Bob Knight throughout the Hoosier State and throughout the entire present-day Big Ten as well. Over the past decade, Keady has constructed some of the best teams, recruited some of the best athletes (Troy Lewis, Everette Stephens, Steve Scheffler, Glenn Robinson), and enjoyed some of the best seasons (25-5, 29-4, 29-5) in league play. But while Keady has kept the Boilermakers at the top of the conference heap, he has never been "No. 1" in the hearts of a vast majority of Hoosier cage fanatics. Keady admittedly wins his share of league titles. But it is Knight and his Hoosiers that live for the Final Four and grab the truly big prizes in the form of NCAA titles.

Keady has had another long shadow to escape closer to home as well. This is the still-

Purdue's Gene Keady has had to labor in the shadows of both Indiana's Bob Knight and former Purdue coach Ward "Piggy" Lambert but has produced a record that backs him as perhaps Purdue's most glamorous coach ever. (Purdue University photo)

looming legend of the greatest of all Boilermaker coaches, Ward Lambert. Lambert, with his tradition of All-American players and conference banners, still hovers over Purdue basketball and his own 29-year reign was truly the stuff of magic. And there are also a couple of other Purdue coaching giants as well whose short tenures brought postseason accomplishment that Keady has never been able to reach. George King took a Rick Mount-led team to the national title game with UCLA and Lew Alcindor in 1969, and Lee Rose barely missed doing the same exactly a decade later. But Keady's greatest teams, by contrast, never seem to quite get over the hump in postseason play, reaching the regional championship level on only one occasion (1994) and getting bumped in the opening round an embarrassing five times.

Nonetheless, Gene Keady has built a record for the ages. It is a record which now places him seventh on the all-time conference winning list (just ahead of Fred Taylor) and fifth in overall winning percentage (behind only Knight, Lambert, Meanwell and Mills). Entering the post-Glenn Robinson era, that record is still far from complete.

Gene Keady's Coaching Record and Career Milestones

Years .... 16 (Purdue 14, Western Kentucky 2)
NCAA Championships .... None
Big Ten Championships 4 (1984*, 1987*, 1988, 1994)
Big Ten Won-Lost Record .... 161-91 (.639)
Purdue Won-Lost Record .... 297-135 (.688)
Total Won-Lost Record .... 335-154 (.690)
Consensus All-Americans .... 1 (Glenn Robinson, 1994)
*First-Place Tie

Harry Combes (Illinois, 1948-67, 316-150, .678 Pct.)

Only three coaches have taken Big Ten teams on three separate trips into the prestigious NCAA Final Four. One is Bob Knight, the master of postseason festivities who has been there five times and owns three national titles. Another is OSU's Fred Taylor, who guided his once-in-a-lifetime "dream team" of Lucas and Havlicek and Gary Bradds into three straight Final Four outings.

The third name on this illustrious list is that of Illinois legend Harry Combes. Combes would get his first crack at the national title in 1949 when his young team surprised the eastern powers with their title run before a semifinal drubbing (76-47) by Kentucky, then finished third by defeating Oregon State in the consolation matchup. Combes' early '50s outfit, with future NBA great John "Red" Kerr entrenched at center, would arrive at the big dance two times running. Both title-round visits found Illinois once more losing the semifinal game to eventual champ Kentucky (76-74) in '51 and St. John's (61-59) in '52. Two straight years a single bucket had been all that separated Combes and the Illini from a shot at the national title game.

The highlight of Combes' coaching career would be those two sterling teams of 1951 (22-5) and 1952 (22-4), plus the all-around play of second-team All-American Johnny Kerr and new school scoring record holder Don Sunderlage. Only once more in his second decade of coaching at Illinois would Combes have a team that would rise to the top of the Big Ten heap and return to the NCAA wars. The 1963 Illini (20-6) earned a tense share of the conference crown on the season's final day and then made it to the second round of NCAA play before being pasted by eventual champ Loyola of Chicago, 79-64.

Combes was a playing as well as a coaching legend for the Illini. The quick-footed forward was an all-league second team selection in 1936 and a first teamer in 1937; it was during the latter season that Combes teamed with fellow all-leaguer Robert Riegel and future baseball Hall of Famer Lou Boudreau to key an Illini outfit under rookie coach Doug Mills that would tie Minnesota for the league championship. But it was as coach of three NCAA Final Four squads that Harry Combes eventually wrote his name permanently in the Big Ten history books.

Harry Combes' Coaching Record and Career Milestones

Years .... 20 (Illinois 20)
NCAA Championships .... None (3 times in Final Four)
Big Ten Championships 4 (1949, 1951, 1952, 1963*)
Big Ten Won-Lost Record .... 174-104 (.626)
Total Won-Lost Record .... 316-150 (.678)
Consensus All-Americans .... 1 (Rod Fletcher, 1952)
*First-Place Tie

Branch McCracken (Indiana, 1935-43, 1947-65, 364-174, .677 Pct.)

Branch McCracken still owns one record that can never be snatched from his resume. It was McCracken (a Naismith Hall of Famer and the school's first All-American player in 1930) who coached the very first NCAA championship team to emerge out of the Big Ten Conference, guiding IU to a lopsided 60-48 triumph against Kansas in only the second year (1940) of the infant tournament's existence. Ohio State had been to the very first postseason title fray in 1939 and had come home a 46-30 loser to Oregon. But McCracken and his Hoosiers did the nation's oldest conference proud a single season later. Jay McCreary, Marv Huffman and Curly Armstrong combined for more than half the scoring output as McCracken's free-wheeling offense overwhelmed Kansas' controlled "pass-and-wait-for-the-perfect-shot" style of play. McCracken believed in putting the ball straight in the bucket and not in the hands of his playmakers, and it would be another decade before any team would again top the 60-point plateau during an NCAA title game. In the interim, McCracken's teams remained at the top of the Western Conference (as it was still called) for almost all of the 1940s wartime era (second for five straight seasons between 1939 and 1943) and the immediate postwar epoch (second in '47 and '51) as well.

But despite his earliest successes, McCracken was never able to capture a conference crown during his first decade-plus of service in the league. That changed in the '50s — when the conference expanded by adding Michigan State University and officially renaming itself "The Big Ten," and when McCracken landed an unheralded prize Hoosier State recruit named Don Schlundt. The wiry 6-foot-9 player was able to shoot with either hand, used his elbows with recklessness under the basket, and was the most mobile big man the league so far had known. Behind Schlundt (a better than 25 points per game scorer over his final three seasons) the supercharged Indiana team became an immediate powerhouse and McCracken soon earned his string of conference titles (1953, 1954, 1957, 1958) and another NCAA crown to boot. The national title would come at the conclusion of Schlundt's sophomore season, with forward-guard Bob Leonard sharing the offensive load (16.9 points per game) and Kansas again providing the futile opposition for the breathtaking 69-68 championship game decision.

Branch McCracken's Coaching Record and Career Milestones

Years .... 32 (Indiana 24, Ball State 8)
NCAA Championships... 2 (1940, 1953)
Big Ten Championships 4 (1953, 1954, 1957*, 1958)
Big Ten Won-Lost Record .... 210-166 (.644)
Total Won-Lost Record .... 450-231 (.661)
Consensus All-Americans .... 3 (Ernie Andres, 1939; Ralph Hamilton, 1947; Don Schlundt, 1954)

*First-Place Tie

Lou Henson (Illinois, 1976-Present, 386-199, .660 Pct.)

Lou Henson has built a memorable record at Illinois and today stands poised to surpass some of the league's and the NCAA's most prestigious milestones — 200 Big Ten victories, 400 wins at Illinois, 650 career victories. Among active college coaches, Henson trails only Knight (by only a slim margin) in overall career winning numbers. Henson, like Knight, can look forward to retiring among the handful of winningest coaches in the history of the sport. Henson has also overhauled all the school and league victory records of the legendary Harry Combes as well.

But for all his triumphs, the current Illini mentor remains one of those successful coaches who can never quite satisfy the victory-starved alumni nor squelch the legions of second guessers. For Lou has not yet made a serious run at a national title (though he did reach the NCAA semifinals in 1989); his Big Ten championship portfolio is slim (one first-place tie in 19 campaigns); and in recent seasons some of his best teams on paper have turned out to be huge disappointments — especially in the eyes of overzealous Illini supporters. No one can question what Henson has accomplished. But plenty question what he has so far left largely undone.

Among league coaches, Lou Henson of Illinois trails only Bob Knight in the number of total career coaching victories. (University of Illinois photo)

Henson's biggest curse is that, although he has always kept Illinois near the top of the heap, he has also always lacked that truly great player and that truly great team. Despite some potent scorers (Nick Anderson, Kendall Gill, Deon Thomas) and deft playmakers (Derek Harper, Bruce Douglas) there has never been a consensus All-American during his tenure that now stretches to 20 seasons. And when there have been very good teams at Illinois (like the 31-5 club in '89 which lost by two points to Michigan in the NCAA semifinal) there have always been better ones at Indiana or Michigan or Purdue or Ohio State. Henson has nonetheless done the lion's share of the recent work in keeping Illinois in a near dead heat with Purdue and Indiana as the winningest program in Big Ten Conference history.

Lou Henson's Coaching Record and Career Milestones

Years .... 32 (Illinois 19, New Mexico State 9, Hardin-Simmons 4)
NCAA Championships.. None
Big Ten Championships... 1 (1984*)
Big Ten Won-Lost Record .... 197-145 (.576)
Illinois Won-Lost Record .... 386-199 (.660)
Total Won-Lost Record.. 626-306 (.672)
Consensus All-Americans .... None
*First-Place Tie

L.J. Cooke (Minnesota, 1897-1924, 244-135, .643 Pct.)

The name of L.J. Cooke is largely lost to collegiate basketball legend and lore. When reviewing pioneering Big Ten Conference coaches, discussion inevitably seems to turn first to Ward Lambert, who championed the fast-breaking game during the sport's pre-modern era. Next in line are Walter Meanwell and perhaps Branch McCracken, owner of two NCAA titles at Indiana and spiritual godfather to Bob Knight. Meanwell built the earliest traditions of Midwestern cage play and in the early '20s was the guru of tightly organized and efficient styles of patterned offense. McCracken jump-started the league's finest winning tradition at Indiana University when he captured the league's first-ever national tournament crown. But Cooke should not be forgotten among these pioneering giants. His Minnesota teams were among the league's most powerful in its first two decades. He brought home five Western Conference titles, something only a handful of the league's coaches have done.

But Cooke's true legacy is the gigantic shadow he casts upon the program of a single league institution. No other Big Ten coach so exclusively owns almost all of an individual school's basketball boasting rights. Arthur Lonborg comes close at Northwestern, outdistancing all successors in games won and years on the job; yet Lonborg stood out due more to lack of competition than to his own performance and fell distinctly short when it came to league championships. L.J. Cooke, in turn, stands head and shoulders above all the other Minnesota coaches of the modern era who have followed less successfully in his considerable wake. With five conference titles, one undefeated campaign (1919), the third longest league coaching tenure (behind Lambert and Knight), and a lifetime winning percentage well above .600, there is little reason to question Cooke's spot among the conference coaching immortals.

L.J. Cooke's Coaching Record and Career Milestones

Years .... 27 (Minnesota 27)
NCAA Championships.. None (no tournament held)
Big Ten Championships..................................... 5 (1906, 1907*, 1911*, 1917*, 1919)
Big Ten Won-Lost Record .... 105-99 (.515)
Total Won-Lost Record.. 244-135 (.643)
Consensus All-Americans .... None
*First-Place Tie

Fred Taylor (Ohio State, 1959-76, 297-158, .653 Pct.)

Three feats distinguish Fred Taylor's illustrious 18-year career at OSU, and all came early in his remarkable Columbus tenure. The first was earning a national championship banner for the school and for the Big Ten, as well as achieving a berth in the Final Four shootout three consecutive seasons. The second of Taylor's lasting monuments was the winning of five straight Big Ten titles, something no other Big Ten coach has managed to accomplish. And the third landmark was Taylor's handling of both the greatest all-around team (1960) and the greatest individual star (Jerry Lucas) in Big Ten annals.

It was the unparalleled contingent of Lucas, John Havlicek, Larry Siegfreid, Mel Nowell and Gary Bradds that would cement Taylor's reputation for postseason successes and build his string of landmark conference titles. Behind two-time player-of-the-year Jerry Lucas (1961-62), the Buckeyes charged to a surprising national title in 1960 and then fell ever so short of repeating during the next two seasons. It was a streak of unmatched Big Ten glory.

The five-year reign of Taylor and his Buckeyes over the rest of the Big Ten during the first half of the 1960s is the closest thing to a dynasty period found anywhere within the Big Ten story. Over the course of three seasons the Bucks dominated the conference in all facets of team play, losing but two league games over the three-year span. This domination occurred despite a number of other quality clubs — a 20-4 Indiana contingent with Walt Bellamy in 1960 and Purdue teams featuring Terry Dischinger throughout the same three-year span. Any team with Lucas was just too strong

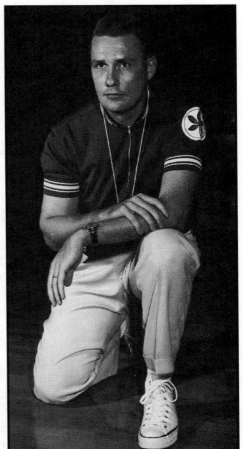

Former Ohio State coach Fred Taylor is the only Big Ten coach to win five straight conference championships. (Ohio State University photo)

for league opponents (and anyone else in the country, save downstate rival Cincinnati). Despite NCAA championship-game losses to Cincinnati in 1961 and 1962, the Buckeyes were clearly the nation's class team for three years running.

When Lucas and Havlicek finally departed, Taylor was still not quite done with his winning ways. His 1963 and 1964 clubs with Gary Bradds (the nation's top performer in '64) tied for conference crowns. And he was back again with league champions in both 1968 and 1971 as well. By career's end, Taylor had climbed atop the all-time list of OSU coaches, surpassing Harold Olsen in overall wins (297-255), league victories (158-154) and winning percentage (.753- .570). Taylor still sits firmly on top today, almost 20 years after giving up his coaching reins after a rare last-place finish in 1976.

Fred Taylor's Coaching Record and Career Milestones

Years .... 18 (Ohio State 18)
NCAA Championships.. 1 (1960)
Big Ten Championships............... 7 (1960, 1961, 1962, 1963*, 1964*, 1968*, 1971)
Big Ten Won-Lost Record .... 158-102 (.608)
Total Won-Lost Record... 297-158 (.653)
Consensus All-Americans .... 5 (Jerry Lucas, 1960-61-62; Gary Bradds, 1964;
Jimmy Jackson, 1992)

*First-Place Tie

Johnny Orr (Michigan, 1969-80, 209-111, .653 Pct.)

Johnny Orr never won a national title at Michigan but he did once come tantalizingly close with a trip to the championship contest versus conference foe Indiana in 1976. Orr's club, featuring backcourt ace Rickey Green and frontcourt star Phil Hubbard, gamely battled the undefeated Hoosiers in the NCAA Finals but was overwhelmed 86-68 by one of the most potent Final Four teams of all time. More surprising, perhaps, Orr managed to capture only one outright Big Ten title (1977) during his dozen-year Michigan tenure. He came close on several occasions, trailing Ohio State by a game in 1971 and tying Indiana for the crown in 1974. It was the balanced '74 Michigan club featuring Big Ten MVP and scoring leader Campy Russell (23.7 points per game) that was perhaps the best overall squad Orr ever put out on the floor. Only a heartbreaking 72-70 defeat in the regional championship round to eventual NCAA runner-up Marquette blocked a direct path into the Final Four.

It is the era of Campy Russell that stands out as the highlight of Orr's Michigan reign. Russell was one of the most complete forwards (second in the conference in rebounding his second and final season) in league history and around him Orr built a formidable team. Michigan's winningest coach had other great stars in All-American Rudy Tomjanovich (30 points, 15 rebounds per game in 1970 and the school's career rebound leader), Henry Wilmore (two-time All-American forward), and Green, another two-year phenomenon. In the end, this stable of stars was never quite enough to bring a slew of championship banners to the program Orr ran so successfully for a dozen winters. But it was a full enough stable to bring Orr more victories than any other coach who has ever served a tenure for the maize and blue.

Johnny Orr's Coaching Record and Career Milestones

Years .... 29 (Michigan 12, Iowa State 14, UMass 3)
NCAA Championships.. None
Big Ten Championships... 2 (1974*, 1977)
Big Ten Won-Lost Record .... 120-72 (.625)
Michigan Won-Lost Record .... 209-113 (.649)
Total Won-Lost Record .... 466-346 (.574)
Consensus All-Americans .... 5 (Rudy Tomjanovich, 1970; Henry Wilmore, 1971-
72; Campy Russell, 1974; Rickey Green, 1977)

*First-Place Tie

Steve Fisher (Michigan, 1989-Present, 123-45, .730 Pct.)

With a tenure of only a half-dozen seasons as head coach, Steve Fisher would hardly seem to qualify for distinction among verified coaching legends. Legends, after all, are the stuff of oft-repeated successes, not of comet-like momentary bursts. And yet the past six seasons with Fisher at the controls of the Wolverine cage program have known more lofty successes within a shorter period of time than can been found with perhaps any other head coach in collegiate basketball history. This is certainly the case if the standard for excellence is merely a berth in the Final Four at the season-ending NCAA tournament. Fisher has coached in the Final Four showdown three times now and missed being there a fourth time by a single game; no league coach as visited championship play so often — save Bob Knight — no matter how many seasons or decades he has served at the job.

Fisher's head-coaching career began with a rare piece of good fortune when he was handed the reins of a team in March of 1989 that was already holding onto an NCAA berth. But when Michigan officials dismissed Bill Frieder — who prematurely announced he was heading to Arizona State for the upcoming season — and installed longtime assistant Fisher in his slot, it was Fisher, not Frieder, who got the job done under extraordinary pressure. What might have been a demoralized 1989 Michigan club was suddenly inspired to a postseason run which brought the Wolverines their only national title celebration. A mere three seasons later, Steve Fisher was back with a vengeance on the wings of his Fab Five club of talented newcomers. Under Fisher, the much-heralded unit of Chris Webber, Jalen Rose and company twice survived Big Ten disappointments and inconsistent mid-season play to storm into NCAA title games. Twice Fisher and his five phenoms fell flat against Atlantic Coast Conference juggernauts with a national title squarely on the line. Yet if the Fab Five failed in their bid to be national champion they nonetheless demonstrated beyond any doubt the tournament skills of a Michigan coaching newcomer who already owns the best lifetime won-lost mark (20-4, .833 Pct.) in NCAA postseason history.

Fisher has now had two great teams in only a handful of seasons. One was handed to him by a stroke of fate and the other was of his own ingenious making. The issue will now be if this heady start will hold up under the test of time. But whatever happens, Steve Fisher can boast of a record coming out of the starting gate that few if any coaches are ever likely to match.

Steve Fisher's Coaching Record and Career Milestones

Years .... 6 (Michigan 6)
NCAA Championships 1 (1989)
Big Ten Championships .... None
Big Ten Won-Lost Record .... 58-32 (.644)
Total Won-Lost Record .... 123-45 (.732)
Consensus All-Americans .... 1 (Chris Webber, 1993)

Dr. Tom Davis coached Iowa to five seasons of 20 or more victories in less than 10 years. (University of Iowa photo)

Clem Haskins, right, is on pace to become one of the most successful coaches in Minnesota's colorful basketball history. Below, Penn State coach Bruce Parkhill's legacy is just getting started, but he already is looked upon as one of the Big Ten's most promising young coaches.

University of Minnesota photo

Penn State University photo

University of Wisconsin photo

Michigan State University photo

Harold Foster, above, led Wisconsin to the 1941 national championship, while Jud Heathcote, right, led Michigan State to a national title in 1979.

Others could, of course, be mentioned here who have also labored nobly in years past to construct additional chapters of the league's unchallenged coaching legacies. Jud Heathcote, for one, guided his Magic Johnson-led charges into the most dramatic and ballyhooed NCAA title game ever played by a Big Ten standard-bearer. There were also names like Lute Olson, Tom Davis and Bucky O'Connor in Iowa; George King and Fred Schaus at Purdue; Arthur Lonborg, who held the reins at Northwestern for 27 seasons and tripled the victory output of his nearest coaching rival on the Wildcat scene; and Harold "Bud" Foster, who packed away the second-ever NCAA championship earned by a league member when he piloted the 1941 Wisconsin Badgers to ultimate tournament success. But in the end it is the above dozen, those whose careers are capsulized here, who will always most likely be discussed — above all the others — when talk turns to the true legends of Big Ten basketball coaching.

Chapter 13

THE TWENTY-FIVE GREATEST PLAYERS OF THE BIG TEN

It is the favored pastime of just about every armchair sports fanatic. And every self-appointed "expert" comes well-armed with reams of iron-clad statistical support, hours of well-reasoned subjective evaluations, and obvious defining biases provided by hometown fervor. The Purdue fan will talk your ear off in support of Glenn Robinson — or Rick Mount and Terry Dischinger if his roots reach deeper than the college hoops boom-era of the '80s and '90s. The IU faithful hear of nothing else but Steve Alford and Calbert Cheaney and are likely to find support for a full five-man roster (including Scott May, Kent Benson and Isiah Thomas) of mythical league all-stars all wearing Hoosier cream and crimson. Even the Northwestern booster can make his case for Otto Graham or Shon Morris, and the Michigan State alumnus will opt for Scott Skiles and Greg Kelser. Everyone loves to name the all-time greats and construct his own honor roll of sure-bet all-time all-stars.

It is perhaps the richest source of nostalgia for a sport which all too often forgets its legendary past. And it is also surely the quickest route to a heated argument — even among knowledgeable fans whose rooting interests attach to the same schools and whose own undergraduate days harken the same lost era. Ask any five fans to name their personal all-time All-Big Ten team and results are guaranteed to provide five different (yet nonetheless potent) rosters.

The selections offered here are, admittedly, tilted firmly in the direction of the modern-era (post-1970) ballplayer. Such is the nature of the hoops game itself: basketball has evolved with incredible speed and changed its face drastically from the set-pattern offensive styles of its formative years to the high-flying "hangtime" game which now dominates the American sports scene. Giants from the earliest eras, like Charles "Stretch" Murphy of Purdue ('20s-'30s), Joe Reiff of Northwestern ('30s), Andy Phillip of Illinois ('40s) and Dick Schnittker of Ohio State ('50s) no longer stand even loose comparisons with stars of later generations. Lumbering, lead-footed postmen and immobile set-shooting guards who dominated earlier decades would likely not even qualify for roster spots on Big Ten squads of the latter-day television era. Nevertheless, the time-honored achievements of a small handful of pioneering players such as John Wooden (the league's first three-time consensus All-American) or Murray Wier (first official NCAA scoring champion in 1948) merit at least token tribute to the game's dim past.

All-Time Big Ten First Team

Jerry Lucas (Ohio State)

He may well have been the most dominant collegiate player of all-time — at least outside of Bill Walton, Tom Gola and Bill Russell. We are not here talking about huge offensive numbers á la Pete Maravich or Glenn Robinson; nor is future pro stardom a yardstick, as in the case of Magic Johnson or Isiah Thomas. At issue here is the rare combination of skilled, crowd-pleasing offensive and defensive play coupled with the ability to lift the team around

him to championship heights. For three seasons, the Ohio State Buckeyes (despite their talented supporting cast of Havlicek, Siegfried and others) largely rode the shooting and rebounding of Jerry Lucas — and they rode it all the way to the NCAA championship game three straight years, winning the title in 1960. Only Walton and Alcindor carried their teams to equal championship heights in quite the same fashion.

Lucas' collegiate numbers are solid enough, yet they are more moderate than outstanding. For three seasons he averaged more than 20 points per game. He owns no school or Big Ten scoring records, however. The latter fact is attributed to the coincidence that Terry Dischinger was in the league at exactly the same time. Rebounding was Lucas' true forte and he paced the nation in that department for two seasons running. For three seasons he was a unanimous first team All-American and for two years the nation's clear-cut player of the year. Only a handful of roundball's greatest stars share the first distinction.

Ohio State star Jerry Lucas still ranks as the Big Ten's greatest player. (Ohio State University photo)

Only Alcindor, Oscar Robertson (thrice), Walton and David Thompson divide the latter honor.

But perhaps the truest (and most costly) measure of the impact of Jerry Lucas at Ohio State came with the most disappointing game in Buckeye cage history. The national title won by OSU during Lucas' sophomore season was rudely ripped away by an inspired Cincinnati club in a tense overtime match a year later. Poised to regain their crown during the senior season of Lucas and Havlicek, the Buckeyes rode the scoring and rebounding prowess of the nation's top player through a 26-1 campaign into an expected NCAA Finals rematch with the rival Bearcats. But disaster struck when Lucas suffered a severe leg injury in the semifinal match with Wake Forest. The hobbled Lucas gamely tried to perform the next night but had to be spelled for much of the contest by promising, though inexperienced, sophomore Gary Bradds. Without their workhorse at full strength, the Big Ten champs were again no match for the national champion Bearcats. Cincinnati won for a second straight season — this time even more convincingly to the tune of 71-59. Thus Jerry Lucas bowed out in most uncharacteristic fashion with only the sixth loss of his collegiate career, yet his second in the prestigious year-ending championship game.

John Havlicek grabs a rebound in front of Ohio State teammate Jerry Lucas while another Buckeye star, Larry Siegfried, far left, keeps an eye on the action. The trio formed the nucleus of a team that won a national championship in 1960 and played for the national title the following two years. (Ohio State University photo)

Cazzie Russell (Michigan)

Only Cazzie Russell can seriously challenge Jerry Lucas' entrenched position as the greatest player in Big Ten history. Had Russell been blessed with a better collection of teammates, he might garner more support for the honor of all-time best than he does. When it comes to mere statistical comparisons, Russell seems to overwhelm Lucas in all but rebounding and field-goal accuracy. Lucas logged 1,990 points, a 24.3 three-year average, a .624 field-goal percentage, a .777 free-throw shooting mark and 1,411 rebounds. Russell boasts 2,164 points, a 27.1 average, a .505 field-goal percentage and .828 free-throw accuracy, and 676 rebounds. But Lucas (who played with Havlicek, Siegfried, Roberts and Nowell) owned a national championship and three Final Four visits. Russell (who played with Bill Buntin, Oliver Darden, Larry Tregoning and George Pomey) lost a national title shot against UCLA in his one NCAA Finals, visited the Final Four a second time to be nipped in the semifinals by Duke, and lost as a senior in the regional finals to national runner-up Kentucky. In reality, there wasn't a whole lot separating them beyond their teammates.

Cazzie Russell owned one the most unusual and memorable first names (and thus one of the most colorful nicknames — "Jazzy Cazzie") found in the collegiate hoops record book. He also owned such special talent that his unique name was assured of being repeated in that record book with great regularity. The later pro star with the New York Knicks and Golden State Warriors still stands among the league's top 10 all-time career scorers and was the third of only six Big Ten athletes ever to earn National Player of the Year selection. He is to date Michigan's only three-time basketball All-American and started his career with a bang by establishing a new school single-season mark of 670 points as a sophomore. That record would be eclipsed in each of his two subsequent seasons. As a senior, Russell both broke his single-season standard (with 800 points) and established a touchstone (30.8) for single-season average that has remained unchallenged up to the present. And three of Russell's other high-water marks still remain etched in the Michigan record book as well — career scoring average (27.1), free throws made (486) and free-throw percentage (.828). It may well take another three decades to erase Cazzie Russell's name from that record book altogether.

Rick Mount (Purdue)

Rick Mount was admittedly a one-dimensional player. But that single dimension was spectacular almost beyond belief. For fans who want pure shooting as the stable of their favorite sport, Mount was the unmatched performer for all ages. And since Mount's game was almost exclusively one of firing the ball at the rim — from any angle, distance, position or moment in the game — there isn't a great deal more to Mount's story than the scoring numbers that defined every corner of his memorable career.

Part of the reason for the paucity of ways to describe Mount falls to the nature of the game itself. The are just so many ways to describe or analyze a perfectly launched jump shot, and most of them fall considerably short of the mark. In Mount's case, one is better served by merely parading out the numbers and leaving the imagination to wrestle with reconstructing the ballet-like artistry from which they resulted. The numbers are a litany of raining rainbow shots and rippled nylon nets: 2,323 points in only 72 games, the only career average of more than 30 points per game found in the Big Ten, a still-unmatched 61-point single-game on-

When it came to shooting the basketball, Purdue's Rick Mount was a wizard. His ability was never more evident than on Feb. 28, 1970, when he scored a conference-record 61 points in a game against Iowa. (Purdue University photo)

slaught, the highest-ever season-long Big Ten scoring average (39.4), the only back-to-back individual league averages of more than 35 points per game and a 30.5 average over four games in the 1969 postseason march to the Final Four. And Rick Mount owns one other important distinction outside of the scoring barrages with which he is so thoroughly identified. It was Mount alone among the Purdue greats (not Dischinger or Schellhase or Carroll or the latter-day Big Dog) whose fireworks propelled a Boilermaker team all the way to a cherished seat in the prestigious national championship game. Rick Mount may have been an undisciplined gunner, but he was a gunner who also carried squarely on his shoulders the finest Boilermaker ballclub ever assembled.

Earvin "Magic" Johnson (Michigan State)

Never has an athlete had a more appropriate nickname than Earvin Johnson. There is no other way to capture Johnson's collegiate and professional performances and his rare brand of athletic gifts than to invoke his now-famous moniker. Johnson was from first to last a performer of pure magic.

Today, the magic of Earvin Johnson's short-lived Michigan State career is nearly obscured by the supernova of his Hall of Fame NBA sojourn. If one remembers Johnson in a Spartan uniform then it is likely to be a memory of a single national championship game in Salt Lake City featuring another Midwest phenom named Larry Bird. Yet for all its brevity, Magic Johnson's two-year tenure with Jud Heathcote's Spartans does not quite boil down to a single showcase contest. The road to the Final Four on which Johnson led the Spartans was one that had more than a few highlights and adventures along the way.

Johnson was only the second leading rebounder and scorer on the 1979 MSU national champion club; the top slot fell to teammate Greg "Special K" Kelser. But Johnson was indisputably the glue and the fuel that held the unit together and launched it on a championship path. Anticipating the versatility he would display in huge quantities as a pro mega-star, Johnson averaged close to a triple-double (17.8 points, 8.0 rebounds, 9.5 assists) throughout eight NCAA postseason games in his two collegiate campaigns. The freshman tourney performance would pull the Spartans as far as a narrow Mideast Regional championship loss to Kentucky (52-49); the sophomore outing would provide enough foundation around Kelser's lofty scoring to spell five straight pressure-packed victories and a national title. Even after the MSU blitzing of Bird and his Indiana State team in the 1979 championship game, surely no one yet knew quite how much magic there actually was in Johnson's high-flying cage act. But for those who had been watching in East Lansing for two seasons, it was not hard to figure out that the basketball world had not really seen anything yet.

Calbert Cheaney (Indiana)

Calbert Cheaney owns the distinction of being the greatest point scorer in Big Ten history. But Cheaney was more than just a free-wheeling shooter or a free-lance one-on-one player. His point totals were a matter or longevity and not of stratospheric per-game averages and he received an added boost in the point-making arena from the lengthened schedules of the early 1990s. The AP, Wooden and Naismith Player of the Year in 1993 was, however, as versatile an offensive machine as ever seen in Bloomington, specializing in three-pointers

Two of the all-time great basketball players in the Big Ten square off as Ohio State's Gary Bradds, left, tries to stop Michigan's Cazzie Russell from driving to the basket. (University of Michigan photo)

(all-time Hoosier leader), maintaining an uncanny eye for the basket despite his long-range bombing (second at IU in career field-goal percentage), and proving a paragon of scoring consistency (65 career games with 20-plus points). The rare consistency of Cheaney's offensive production was best demonstrated by his string of 41 straight games in double figures and 58 double-figure outings in his final 59 times in the IU lineup. In the end it was perhaps the most telling hallmark of Calbert Cheaney's brilliant IU sojourn that the highest point producer in league history would never win a conference scoring crown, would average less that 20 points per game for his four-year stay, and would never post a single 40-point game. Calbert Cheaney did it in relentless waves and not in bulky bunches.

All-Time Big Ten Second Team

Gary Bradds (Ohio State)

Gary Bradds was the basketball equivalent of Haley's Comet. He appeared as a slight glimmer in the background during his sophomore season and was hardly noticed in the shadow of All-Americans Jerry Lucas and John Havlicek. That was until a devastating injury to Lucas in the year's penultimate game suddenly put Bradds in the limelight during the 1962 NCAA Finals. An emergency substitute for the felled Lucas, the spindly sophomore battled gamely (5-for-7 shooting and a team-high 15 points) yet could not prevent a second straight bitter NCAA loss to the Cincinnati Bearcats. When Lucas and Havlicek departed for the pros, the lanky center who had averaged but 4.4 points per game his first season literally exploded unannounced upon the collegiate basketball scene. First his scoring numbers zoomed to 28.0 in 1963, then to over 30 points per game in 1964. He was national player of the year his senior season, OSU's third in four years. Few in fact have ever enjoyed a season more spectacular than the one with which Gary Bradds concluded his OSU career.

And then suddenly the brightest star in the heavens dimmed once more. Bradds suffered through a short-lived and most unproductive pro career. He hardly distinguished himself in 45 games spread over two seasons with the NBA Baltimore Bullets. Next the OSU All-American escaped to the fledgling ABA but fared little better with Oakland, Washington, Carolina and Texas. The numbers for a six-year pro sojourn were less than impressive (254 games, 3,106 points, 12.2 points per game). The legend was forgotten everywhere but in Columbus. It was not just basketball skills that would prove fleeting for one-time superstar Gary Bradds, however. Life itself was a brief burst and then silence. By age 40, Gary Bradds had prematurely succumbed to cancer in July 1983, an untimely death which cut short a promising career as an elementary school principal in Bowerville, Ohio.

Don Schlundt (Indiana)

Don Schlundt was a basketball player well ahead of his time. As great as he was, perhaps a decade later he would have been even greater. Here was a rail-thin 6-foot-9 center who moved like a point guard, shot from a variety of angles and with both hands, outmaneuvered all inside defenders, and used his blade-like elbows with merciless efficiency to cut his path to the basket. Once Schlundt arrived on the IU scene in 1951-52, the era of the lumbering immobile center (á la George Mikan or Bob Kurland) was over and the era of the mobile

Don Schlundt became Indiana's first nationally recognized star after leading the Hoosiers to the national title in 1953 and averaging more than 25 points per game over his three-year playing career. (Indiana University photo)

postman as vital cog in a non-stop fast-breaking offense (á la Bill Russell and the Boston Celtics) was at hand. Schlundt pioneered the prototype in the Big Ten with great efficiency. Behind his three years of high scoring (25.4, 24.3, 26.0) the Hoosiers under Branch McCracken ran to a pair of league championships and an NCAA crown. But Don Schlundt's IU career ended with something of a huge disappointment. Stripped of his backcourt running mate, Bob "Slick" Leonard, the senior captain was surrounded with little in the way of supporting cast. Schlundt's final season resulted in his third-straight individual conference scoring crown, but IU fell to 8-14 overall and limped home with an embarrassing ninth-place league finish.

John Havlicek (Ohio State)

The greatest "sixth man" of NBA history was also the greatest understudy ever to lace up high-tops in the collegiate game. Havlicek played smack in the shadow of Jerry Lucas and together, they were the most unbeatable combo in Big Ten history (78-6, three league titles, one NCAA crown, three Final Fours). Despite his role as "second banana," the player called "Hondo" was nonetheless a recognized franchise player from the start and was twice tabbed All-Big Ten and once as a first-team All-American. His outstanding play in the first and third of his three national title games won Havlicek a spot on the NCAA all-tourney team.

But if Hondo Havlicek never quite emerged from Lucas' shadow in his college days, he soon enough dwarfed his teammate's considerable stature when the two reached the professional game. Havlicek would first enjoy a near-miss tryout with the NFL Cleveland Browns (despite not playing football in college) and then settle on a career with Red Auerbach's Celtics which brought eventual accolades as one of the sport's all-time immortals. Havlicek's reputation was that of the greatest bench player and greatest hustler in all of pro cage history. The Naismith Hall of Famer would one day own eight NBA championship rings, stand sixth all time in career scoring (26,395 points), fourth in career games played (1,270), fourth in career minutes (46,471) and fifth in career field goals (10,513). No other Big Ten alumnus ever posted pro cage numbers even close to this.

Scott May (Indiana)

It is hard to think of a better player in Indiana history than Scott May. Calbert Cheaney had more raw skill, Steve Alford was a better shooter, and Isiah Thomas was a magician with the basketball. But May did it all and was a proven winner to boot. While Kent Benson anchored the inside for the 1976 Hoosier national champions, May provided the emotional leadership, the clutch offense and rebounding assistance that solidified one of the best NCAA title teams ever. May was national player of the year for Coach Bob Knight's best-ever club and earned first-team All-American selections in both his junior and season seasons. While it was May's outstanding tournament play that keyed the 1976 championship drive, it was an injury to the Hoosier star (broken arm) that stalled a similar run in 1975 and left Knight's charges a single game short (a two-point loss to Kentucky in the regional finals) of reaching the Final Four. Although Scott May was back in the lineup for the regional showdown with the Wildcats (92-90), the layoff caused by his injury had left him rusty and ineffective and capable of only two points in a losing cause. It was the only loss May and his Hoosiers would suffer during the final two seasons for the greatest forward in Indiana basketball history.

Scott May was also a Hoosier standout who went on to represent school and conference with pride at the higher level of professional play. The second overall selection of the Chicago Bulls in 1976, May strung together a half-dozen creditable, if not stellar, NBA campaigns, collecting 1,050 points (14.6 points per game) in his rookie season and averaging double figures during two later campaigns as well. By almost any standard of choice — Naismith Player of the Year, Olympic team starter, NCAA All-Decade Tournament Team member for the '70s or NBA regular — Scott May shares the limelight alongside Cheaney and Thomas as the best trio ever bred in Knight's stable of championship thoroughbreds.

Terry Dischinger (Purdue)

Dischinger ("Dish" to Purdue faithful) was a phenomenon the likes of which may never again be seen in college basketball. For starters, he may well have been the greatest pure offensive player in league history. If his point totals fell a whisker's length short of Rick Mount's, his total offensive game was a quantum leap better than that of the Lebanon hotshot. The inherent superiority of Dischinger's game over Mount's was proven beyond any shadow of a doubt when the two Boilers graduated to the subtler challenges of the professional ranks.

Dischinger is remembered by the basketball world at large as an NBA Rookie of the Year in 1962-63 and as a starting member — with "Big O" Oscar Robertson, Jerry West, Jerry Lucas and Walt Bellamy — of the greatest amateur Olympic Team squad of all time. Dish enjoyed an outstanding rookie season as a pro and posted one of the highest rookie scoring marks (25.5 points per game) ever. But the Purdue stalwart's considerable pro career (nine seasons, 9,000 points) pales beside his collegiate accomplishments. The unanimous two-time first-team All-American never played in an NCAA or NIT tournament game nor won a Big Ten championship (Lucas and Havlicek saw to that); and despite averaging more than 30 points per game his senior season and 28 as a junior, Dischinger never led the nation in scoring. He did, however, match the feat of Don Schlundt as a three-time Big Ten scoring champion. The final individual crown was earned by an eyelash over IU's Jimmy Rayl and is surrounded by a unique personal story. On the eve of the season's closing contest at Michigan, Dischinger received a heart-warming telegram from 1960 Olympic buddies Lucas and Havlicek in Columbus. "Don't worry about Rayl," was the message. With the Buckeyes holding the IU forward below his season's average, the door was wide open for Dischinger to close out his career as one of the last three-time league scoring leaders (only Mount has done it since) as well as one of the highest three-year point producers in conference annals.

All-Time Big Ten Honorable Mention

Mychal Thompson (Minnesota)

Nothing in the history of Minnesota basketball comes close to the four-year act staged by Bahamas-born Mychal Thompson. Not Kevin McHale, Lou Hudson, Trent Tucker, Archie Clark or a boat load of other Golden Gophers who also found highly successful careers in the pros. Open the Minnesota basketball media guide or record book and it reads like a Mychal Thompson curriculum vitae. All the following entries are joined with the name of the greatest big man in Gopher history: career marks for points (1,992), field goals (823), field-goal percentage (.568) and rebounds (956); season records for points (647), scoring average (25.9) and field goals (265); plus the individual single-game record for blocked shots (12). One can add to the numbers a unanimous first-team All-American selection in 1978, a second-team All-American accolade a season earlier and a No.1 overall selection (Portland Trail Blazers) in the 1978 NBA college draft.

Mychal Thompson is one of many fine NBA players from the University of Minnesota. (University of Minnesota photo)

But while Thompson's star glittered brightly in the basketball heavens of the Minnesota northlands, it remained something of a dimmer orb in much of the rest of the nation, at least until NBA glory made the Gopher giant a much more recognizable figure. This was due largely to Thompson's complete absence from the media circus of postseason play. He should have been there in 1977 when as a junior he combined forces with freshman Kevin McHale and senior Ray Williams to trigger a brilliant 24-3 campaign (15-3 in the Big Ten) that all went for naught when a series of NCAA rules violations resulted in a forfeited schedule and a seat on the postseason sidelines. It was an unfortunate break which cost thousands of tournament fans a glimpse of a superb shooting and rebounding post player already on a crash course toward certain NBA stardom.

Jim Jackson (Ohio State)

Jim Jackson, like Magic Johnson a decade earlier, was on the verge of superstardom when he folded up his college career prematurely in 1992 and headed for the NBA. A three-year starter who led the school to three NCAA tourney appearances and two Big Ten titles, Jackson did much to restore a brief period of glory to the recently troubled OSU basketball program. Before departing as a fourth overall draft choice of the Dallas Mavericks, the 6-6 guard/forward strung together a list of personal triumphs that would stamp greatness on any career: Big Ten Freshman of the Year (1990), two-time Big Ten Player of the Year (1991-1992), UPI college Player of the Year as a junior (1992); 1,785 career points (fifth in Buckeye history); three-time team leader in scoring, rebounding leader his final season, and a ranking in the school's all-time top 10 in several other important offensive and defensive categories (assists, steals, three-point field goals).

For all his triumphs at the collegiate level, however, Jackson was just beginning to show his prowess, a prowess that was further delayed by a lengthy contractual dispute and holdout which launched his NBA career. In his third season at Dallas, Jackson suddenly emerged as one of the league's leading scorers and one of its brightest offensive stars. Some already are making comparisons with another slow-starting collegian named Michael Jordan. Air Jordan may be a stretch, yet Jim Jackson may yet prove one of the two or three greatest pro players ever to emerge from the venerable Big Ten conference.

Glenn Robinson (Purdue)

For one glorious season college basketball's "Big Dog" was America's most celebrated undergraduate player. But once his ear heard the ringing of NBA coins Purdue's beloved All-American seemingly overnight was transformed into a somewhat tarnished Big Hog. Not that one can easily dismiss $100 million in cold cash (Robinson's original contract demand) for the merely altruistic glory of college athletics, but there is perhaps something still to be said for the rare joys of college sport. Robinson's mega-bucks, in all likelihood, would have been there whether he chose to be an NBA No. 1 pick in 1994 (he was tabbed No. 1 by the Milwaukee Bucks) or whether he opted to wait for Draft Day 1995. What got lost along the way, of course, was a shot at a once-in-a-lifetime national championship for Purdue and its boosters, personal accolades for Robinson as perhaps the greatest collegiate scorer ever, and a ton of school and Big Ten milestones that might have stood unchallenged for years to come.

As it was, Robinson left Purdue with unfulfilled expectations, few thumb prints on the league record book, lingering doubts about how truly great he was (or might have been), and a legion of disappointed Purdue fans left only to dream of what might have been. What is indisputable, of course, is that Robinson enjoyed one of the finest seasons in Big Ten and NCAA history. The Big Dog was only the 15th NCAA player ever to score 1,000 points in a season, the first to log a 30-point average for Big Ten games in 20 years, the first in that same time frame to pace the circuit in both scoring and rebounding, and the first-ever Purdue player to log 1,000 career points, 500 rebounds, 100 steals, 100 assists and 50 blocked shots. But for all those gaudy numbers and with only one huge season to his credit, Robinson's name is nowhere to be found on the lists of the top Big Ten or Purdue career scorers and rebounders. His contributions at Purdue included no national titles and no Final Four trips. Robinson earned some impressive honors in that amazing 1994 season, but they were largely his alone.

Joe Barry Carroll (Purdue)

Joe Barry Carroll was built in the mode of an unfortunately all-too-familiar basketball type. He followed in the footsteps of Walter Dukes, Darrall Imhoff, Ralph Sampson, Stanley Roberts and Benoit Benjamin. He was a gifted 7-foot center whose bark was far worse than his bite; a can't-miss franchise player built on the model of a five-story building — but softer.

This is not to suggest that Carroll was not one of the finest centers ever to grace a Big Ten campus or that his hefty accomplishments during a four-year stay at West Lafayette were not considerable. Here was a unanimous first team All-American (1980); a leading scorer and rebounder for a Purdue team that reached the Final Four for only the second time ever and won a national third-place consolation game; a member of the All-NCAA Tournament Team; a 2,000-point career scorer who stands second on the all-time Boilermaker list, sandwiched between Rick Mount and Dave Schellhase; a member of the career 1,000-rebound club; and a No. 1 overall choice in the 1980 NBA draft. But there was always the lingering feeling that Carroll, like Sampson, was soft, that he should have done more, dominated more thoroughly, been more like Wilt Chamberlain or Bill Russell than Henry Finkel or Shawn Bradley. And if the feeling was unfair and uncharitable it was nonetheless at least partially justified when the towering player whose draft rights cost the Golden State Warriors Kevin McHale turned out in the pro ranks to be more of a journeyman redwood than a franchise oak.

Gary Grant (Michigan)

Gary Grant was a proficient scorer who keyed one of the finest teams in Michigan history. But it wasn't scoring that was Grant's true forte and the source of his lasting reputation on the Big Ten scene. Before his four-year career ended, the quick-fingered and quick-footed guard was jealous owner of all the Michigan school records (career, season and single game) for steals and assists. In fact, Grant was the first-ever Big Ten player to score 1,000 points, hand out 600 assists and collect 200 career steals. This from a player who for all his defensive exploits also ranks third in Michigan career scoring.

Grant's impact at Michigan was immediate. As 1985 Big Ten Freshman of the Year, the 6-3 guard out of Canton, Ohio, led his Wolverine teammates to a 26-4 record and a Big Ten championship. For an encore, Grant led the Wolverines back to the Big Ten winner's circle his sophomore year, earned consensus All-American honors as a senior along with winning UPI and AP Big Ten Player of the Year honors, and won back-to-back All-Big Ten honors for 1987 and 1988. But while personal numbers soared for Bill Frieder's backcourt ace during his two final two seasons — his scoring averages leaped from 12.9 and 12.2 to 22.4 and 21.1 — team fortunes actually slid while he was team captain. Grant had entered the scene at Ann Arbor as a team championship sparkplug and left as an individual superstar. In either role, he was one of the most exciting performers ever to wear Michigan's maize and blue uniform.

Dave Schellhase (Purdue)

First there was Dischinger, then Schellhase and finally Rick Mount. The '60s was the decade that unleashed incredible scorers. It was the decade which opened with Wilt Chamberlain amassing a 50 points per game average and defying imagination with an NBA 100-point game. It was also a decade which closed with a human point-making machine named Pete Maravich averaging more than 40 points per contest in the shortened college game for three seasons running. On the collegiate scene there was no more fertile ground for the prototype of the point-per-minute man than West Lafayette. Terry Dischinger came within an arm's length (1,979) of being the league's first 2,000-point man in only a three-year career. Several seasons later, Rick Mount wore out scoreboards in the Big Ten almost as regularly as Maravich was assaulting them at LSU, and in between, a 6-4 gunner for the Boilermakers actually passed the 2,000-point barrier in just three campaigns (with 2,074), accomplishing something neither Dischinger nor Mount could lay claim too. Dave Schellhase became the Big 10's only national scoring champion between Murray Weir (1948) and Glenn Robinson (1994).

There were several interesting footnotes to Schellhase's top-ranking NCAA scoring performance of 1966 (32.54 points per game). First, it came by one of the narrowest margins ever, four one-thousandths of a point over Idaho State's Dave Wagon (32.50). Second, Schellhase actually paced the nation in scoring but still finished only second in the Big Ten. The rare paradox came about when Michigan All-American Cazzie Russell outpointed his Purdue rival by 15 points in conference games alone. With non-conference games taken into the mix, however, Russell trailed Dave Schellhase by nearly two points per contest (30.8 to 32.5). There was one further irony as well. Despite Schellhase's scoring. the Boilermakers finished dead last in the circuit for the only time in the past 32 years.

Steve Alford (Indiana)

The Hoosiers have had less then their share of mega-stars, especially under the reign of Bob Knight. But Steve Alford comes about as close as anyone to that distinction. Before Calbert Cheaney it was the deadly shooting Alford who climbed atop the school's all-time scoring list (2,438 points) and fell but a point short of overtaking Michigan's Mike McGee for the all-time league leadership as well. Alford's game was shooting and in addition to his lofty overall scoring totals (22.5 and 22.0 his junior and senior seasons, respectively) he earned special distinction as a three-point specialist (still holding the school record with 107 in 1987) and free-throw artist (leading the nation with a .913 average in 1984). It was in the NCAA tournament that Alford was always at his best, averaging 21.3 points per game in 10 NCAA contests (1984, 1986, 1987) in which his Hoosiers posted an 8-2 winning mark. As a pro, (a second-round selection of the Dallas Mavericks) Alford was unfortunately another of the large collection of Knight's alumni to prove a complete bust. He averaged just 4.4 points per game and started in just three games in a bench-riding four-year career with Dallas and Golden State.

His true talent may now be in teaching the game rather than playing it professionally, however. With his professional playing career apparently over, tiny Manchester College in north-central Indiana turned to the former Hoosier star to reverse the school's pathetic basketball fortunes. In his first full season, Alford led the Spartans to their first winning season since 1975-76, a conference tournament championship and a berth in NCAA Division III postseason play. Despite a lackluster NBA playing career, in looking at his Big Ten days alone and now at his apparent success as a college coach, Alford will always be near the top of almost any all-star list.

Rickey Green (Michigan)

Rickey Green was the very model of the perfect two-way backcourt ace, 1960s style. His brief Michigan career was filled with a truckload of honors and a carload of stellar performances. Arriving in 1975 after two productive junior college All-American seasons at Vincennes (Ind.), Green posted consistent scoring averages of 19.9 and 19.5 over his two varsity campaigns, was the leading scorer on the 1976 NCAA runner-up team, earned first-team All-American honors with the 1977 Big Ten champions and scored more points than any other Michigan player who performed for only two seasons. Green was also runner-up to UCLA's Marques Johnson for selection as the 1977 Collegiate Player of the Year.

But it was not as a scorer that Rickey Green was most effective and most valuable. As a relentless pressing defender, Green literally terrorized opponents (especially opposing point guards), time and again making crucial steals and launching the famed Michigan fast-breaking offense that usually found long-legged center Phil Hubbard on the receiving end. Green's collegiate act was just a preview of loftier things to come. One of the quickest athletes to set foot on the hardwood, Green had an outstanding 14-year NBA career (mostly with the Utah Jazz) that included such milestones as 90 percent free-throw shooting in 1988, more than 4,000 career assists, 1,350 career steals, 45 points in one game, 20 assists in another, and the 1984 NBA steals championship.

Robin Freeman (Ohio State)

Robin Freeman could fill the bucket and take it to the hole with the best of them. Ohio State stands second only to Purdue when it comes to production of high-scoring court stars, and Freeman owns his place of prominence right next to Dennis Hopson, Bill Hosket, Gary Bradds, and Jimmy Jackson. Freeman was one of the smallest of Big Ten stars but his diminutive stature was measured in inches, not heart or statistics or star quality.

This 5-11 guard from the mid-1950s was the first Buckeye to include the new-fangled jump shot as the primary weapon of his offensive bag of tricks and perhaps none has ever used it more effectively since. Freeman's legend began with a sensational junior season in which he played in just 13 contests because of assorted health problems. But a 31.5 points per game average in his abbreviated campaign was good enough to outscore his teammates and most of the other shooters around the country as well, and bring him consensus All-American honors. A season later, a healthy Freeman continued his scoring onslaught (32.9), pacing the Buckeyes to a 16-6 mark and becoming the school's first repeat All-American and the league's first repeat 30 points per game man. In the decades that have followed, only Hopson and Gary Bradds have scored more points in a single season at OSU, but Freeman's 28-point career average is still best in school annals. Those who saw him play still consider Robin Freeman the most exciting Buckeye of them all.

Glen Rice (Michigan)

Of all the huge stars in Michigan cage history few have performed consistently better than 1989 NCAA tournament MVP Glen Rice. A part-time player as a freshman (7.0 points per game), Rice slowly matured into an offensive machine who captured league scoring titles his junior (22.9) and senior (24.8) seasons, climbed to first (now second behind Indiana's Calbert Cheaney) on the Big Ten all-time scoring list, surpassed Mike McGee as Michigan's leading career scorer (2,442), and finished his career as leading scorer and rebounder on a crack 1989 Michigan NCAA champion. A mobile 6-7 forward/guard capable of playing inside or out, Rice still reigns as the league's single-season three-point field-goal pacesetter (55 in 1989) and also holds records at Michigan for career games played (134), career three-pointers (135), single-season points (949), and single-season field goals (363). In the summer of 1989, Rice became the NBA's fourth overall draft pick when selected by the expansion Miami Heat. Five seasons later he ranks as that club's all-time scoring leader.

But it was in the dramatic 1989 charge to the national championship under replacement coach Steve Fisher where Rice enjoyed his finest hour. In the two decades from 1975 to 1994 only one player was able to score more than 25 points in each of the two games at a single Final Four (it had last been done by UCLA's Richard Washington). Rice was that player and his championship point production included a record 27 three-point buckets and a record 184 total points in six tournament games. The steady hand of Steve Fisher may well have contributed a much-needed emotional lift for the disoriented Wolverines in the wake of Bill Frieder's sudden departure on the eve of championship play. But it was Rice who provided the bulk of the firepower that was the true key to Michigan's first-ever national title.

Indiana's Calbert Cheaney was the highest-scoring player in Big Ten history. (Indiana University photo)

Murray Wier (Iowa)

Murray Wier is perhaps the best kept secret of Big Ten cage history. He is the stuff of barroom trivia and little more. When the NCAA began to recognize national scoring champions after 1948 it was Wier who walked off with the first honor. Never again would a national scoring leader have so few points (399) or average so little (21.0 points per game), but it was a scoring title nonetheless and one of only three (the others belong to Purdue's Dave Schellhase, 1966; and Glenn Robinson, 1994) ever packed away by Big Ten gunners. To the further delight of trivia buffs, at less than 6 feet tall, Wier was the shortest NCAA scoring champ.

Unable to stand comparison with today's towering, high-flying aerial specialists, Murray Wier was nonetheless one of the finest ballhandling and shooting talents ever produced in Hawkeye land. His averages of 15.1 and 21.0 his final two seasons were approximately a third of his team's total output; Iowa averaged 56.9 points per game for the 1948 season when Wier ripped the nets for his 21 points per game average. His first-team All-American status was also the first accorded to a Hawkeye player. Murray Wier was indeed a throwback to an earlier age of cage play when two-handed set shots, slow-moving, deliberate offensive patterns, and earthbound dribbling tactics were the full order of the day. But in that ancient post-World War II age of men named Mikan (DePaul), Kurland (Oklahoma A&M), Ferrin (Utah), and Cousy (Holy Cross), Iowa's Murray Wier, even at 5-9, was a true giant of the game.

Chris Webber (Michigan)

One unfortunate moment of infamy will perhaps always capsulize the unfilled collegiate promise of the most precocious among Michigan's stable of "Fab Five" phenoms. With the final precious seconds ticking away in the 1993 NCAA title game and North Carolina nursing a slim 73-71 lead, Michigan's touted sophomore center was trapped with the ball along the sideline by two pressing Tar Heel defenders. In a crucial loss of concentration which will likely haunt Wolverine faithful for eons, the consensus All-American desperately called for a time-out which Michigan no longer had. In a single lapse of court presence the game was lost, as was the national title and ultimately the Fab Five dream of championship success.

It's an unfortunate image to permanently brand an otherwise stellar collegiate career. But the moment is perhaps made all the bigger by Webber's own subsequent actions — his early departure from Michigan a few months later to join the pro ranks, his contractual disputes with the Golden State Warriors on the heels of his 1994 NBA Rookie of the Year season, and his complaints about respected coach Don Nelson which forced an early-season 1994 trade to the Washington Bullets.

But for all his later misjudgments and tarnished image, Webber was for two seasons a marvelous player for one of the most talented Michigan teams in decades. He was the leading scorer and rebounder on two NCAA runner-up teams in just two seasons of play, remains but one of a tiny handful of players to end each of his undergraduate campaigns in the final tournament game, appeared in a dozen NCAA contests and led his team to victory in all but the two most important of these showdowns. Finally, he was the first player taken in the NBA draft (by Orlando, who immediately traded him to Golden State), thus joining the select club of Walt Bellamy, Kent Benson, Mychal Thompson, Magic Johnson, Joe Barry Carroll (and now Glenn Robinson) among Big Ten stalwarts who can boast that ultimate honor.

John Wooden (Purdue)

Few fans today know anything of John Wooden the basketball player. The aura surrounding a marvelous coach has all but obliterated the record of one of the sport's earliest on-court playing legends. Yet the stature of Wooden the player was only by degree lesser than the stature of Wooden the coach; no other basketball great owns two seats in the Naismith Hall of Fame — one as a Purdue All-American (elected in 1960) and the other as a UCLA dynasty coach (tabbed in 1972).

As a Purdue All-American (1930-32), Wooden was the legs under Piggy Lambert's revolutionary fast-breaking style of play. As a backcourt ace, he was known primarily for his hustle and daring defensive play; Wooden soon earned the nickname of "India Rubber Man" for his suicidal dives on the court in pursuit of loose balls. His scoring totals, while modest by today's standards, were

Long before John Wooden earned the title "Wizard of Westwood" he was a three-time All-American as a player at Purdue. (Purdue University photo)

enough to set a new Western Conference offensive record (154 points in league games, 12.2 average) during his senior season. It was during his senior season that the Wooden-led Boilermakers captured their second conference title during his three-year varsity career and earned a Helms Foundation national championship.

There was no lucrative pro career awaiting John Wooden when he left undergraduate days in the early '30s. The sport was still in its primitive barnstorming days, and although Wooden was a part-time player for several winters in the semipro NBL, organized pro circuits were still two decades away. Nevertheless, the basketball world had certainly not heard the last of Purdue's first bona fide cage star. Modern-day fans need constant reminders, however, that Wooden would have deserved a treasured place in basketball's hallowed halls had he never coached a single game as the renowned Wizard of Westwood four decades down the road.

Kent Benson (Indiana)

It is hard to think of a greater riches to rags story than that surrounding the star center of the national champion 1976 Indiana Hoosiers. The championship year of '76 was truly Benson's banner year and a year like few other Big Ten cage heroes have ever known. The junior pacesetter on the undefeated Hoosier "dream team" was dubbed the outstanding player of the Final Four weekend, earned unanimous first-team All-American honors, led his club in both rebounding and scoring, and stretched his two-year NCAA tourney record to 7-1 (19.6 points, 10.9 rebounds per game). For an encore, Benson capped his career with a senior season filled with similar achievement — consensus first-team All-American, leading IU scorer (19.8) and rebounder (fourth straight year), and No. 1 NBA draft selection by the Milwaukee Bucks. NBA stardom appeared certain for the greatest Hoosier big man since Walt Bellamy.

But it never happened at the pro level for Benson. In fact, no first overall pick of the NBA draft has ever proven a larger disappointment. With his confidence eroded by a rookie-season fight with the Lakers' Kareem Abdul-Jabbar, Benson floundered for two seasons in Milwaukee (7.7 points per game as a rookie) and then for nine more in Detroit, Utah and Cleveland. His career scoring average in the end was under double figures (9.1), his rebounding barely proficient enough to earn his salary (8.7 per game in his best season of 1982). Kent Benson had apparently left his once dominant game back in Bloomington, the place where he also left a slew of memories surrounding some of the best moments in Hoosier cage history.

Isiah Thomas (Indiana)

Isiah Thomas was Bob Knight's problem child; but what a marvelous problem child to have on board. Behind Thomas's brilliant display in the NCAA title game of 1981 (23 points and several clutch second-half steals) the Hoosiers claimed the most dramatic and unexpected of their three national titles under Knight. Two brilliant seasons at Indiana University were not exceptionally happy times, however, for the Chicago product who earned All-Big Ten plaudits as a freshman and consensus All-American honors for his sophomore and final season. Thomas and Knight clashed repeatedly and the flashy point guard never could adjust to what he considered impolite and dehumanizing behavior toward players by his fiery mentor. Knight once grabbed Thomas by the jersey to administer admonishment before national TV cameras during a 1979 Pan American Games contest.

Despite flammable moments with Knight and poor early-season play by the 1980-81 Hoosiers, the sophomore team captain rallied his IU squad all the way to the memorable national championship victory over North Carolina in Philadelphia's famed Spectrum arena. The upset title victory and NCAA tournament MVP performance marked the swan song of Thomas' brief collegiate career. As a first-round and second overall (after fellow Chicagoan Mark Aguirre) hardship draft choice of the Detroit Pistons in the 1981 NBA player lottery, Thomas entered the pros as a much-heralded but slightly undersized 20-year-old rookie in the fall of 1981. But skeptics were quickly answered as Thomas's impact on the NBA was immediate and lasting. A decade-and-a-half later, the short-term IU great would stand behind only Havlicek and Magic Johnson as the most distinguished NBA Big Ten alumnus.

Roster of the Big Ten's 25 Greatest Players

Player (School)	Years	Games	Points	PPG	All-American
		First Team			
Jerry Lucas (Ohio State)	3 (1960-62)	82	1,990	24.3	**1960-61*-62***
Cazzie Russell (Michigan)	3 (1964-66)	80	2,164	27.1	1965-66*
Rick Mount (Purdue)	3 (1968-70)	72	2,323	**32.2**	1969-70
Earvin Johnson (MSU)	2 (1978-79)	62	1,059	17.1	1979
Calbert Cheaney (Indiana)	4 (1990-93)	132	**2,613**	19.8	1993*
		Second Team			
Gary Bradds (Ohio State)	3 (1962-64)	74	1,530	20.7	1964*
Don Schlundt (Indiana)	4 (1952-55)	94	2,192	23.3	1954
John Havlicek (Ohio State)	3 (1960-62)	84	1,223	14.6	1962
Scott May (Indiana)	3 (1973-76)	90	1,593	17.7	1975-76*
Terry Dischinger (Purdue)	3 (1960-62)	70	1,979	28.3	1961-62
		Honorable Mention			
Mychal Thompson (Minn)	4 (1975-78)	96	1,992	20.8	1978
Jim Jackson (Ohio State)	3 (1990-92)	93	1,785	19.2	1991-92
Glenn Robinson (Purdue)	2 (1993-94)	62	1,706	27.5	1994*
Joe Barry Carroll (Purdue)	4 (1977-80)	123	2,175	17.7	1980
Gary Grant (Michigan)	4 (1985-88)	129	2,222	17.2	1988
Dave Schellhase (Purdue)	3 (1964-66)	72	2,074	28.8	1965-66
Steve Alford (Indiana)	4 (1984-87)	125	2,438	19.5	1986-87
Rickey Green (Michigan)	2 (1976-77)	60	1,184	19.7	1977
Robin Freeman (Ohio State)	3 (1954-56)	57	1,597	28.0	1955-56
Glen Rice (Michigan)	4 (1986-89)	**134**	2,442	18.2	1989
Murray Wier (Iowa)	4 (1945-48)	72	958	13.3	1948
Chris Webber (Michigan)	2 (1992-93)	70	1,218	17.4	1993
John Wooden (Purdue)	3 (1930-32)	48	475	9.9	1930-31-32
Kent Benson (Indiana)	4 (1974-77)	114	1,740	15.3	1976-77
Isiah Thomas (Indiana)	2 (1988-91)	63	968	15.4	1981

* = National Player of the Year

Chapter 14
GREAT TEAMS
AND MEMORABLE MOMENTS

The great stars and memorable coaches of the Big Ten conference have enriched beyond measure each decade of college basketball's first century. Names like Lucas, Russell, Mount, Knight, Lambert, Meanwell and Magic Johnson remain forever part of the lasting fabric of the collegiate sport.

But when it comes to legend and lore of Big Ten seasons past, there have also been lesser-known names and less heroic figures who etched their reputations and images boldly on the pages of basketball's unfolding saga. Wherever hoop fanatics gather to celebrate seasons past, they talk not only of the nearly invincible combo of Lucas and Havlicek, the mano-a-mano duel of Magic and Larry, Keith Smart's miracle shot and the night Rick Mount burned up the scoreboard light bulbs; they also conjure dusty images of a Cinderella Wisconsin Badger five rising from the league cellar and shocking Washington State for an improbable national title, Slick Leonard's ice-water NCAA shooting eye, the patriotic "Whiz Kids" of Illinois, the original "Fab Five" of Iowa, the gala night Lew Alcindor and Rick Mount christened Mackey Arena, and still another night in Mackey when Mount collected 61 points and still couldn't rescue his Purdue team from losing both a game and a Big Ten crown.

Each Big Ten fan undoubtedly harbors his own special memories of some of the league's most unmatchable teams, unforgettable games and special magical moments. Those landmarks of conference history which follow here are little more than a sampler of the grandest mileposts of Big Ten action. But they are huge mileposts nonetheless and recalling them underscores the excitement which has made Big Ten basketball — indeed collegiate basketball — the heartland's No. 1 sporting crown jewel.

Birth of the Hurryin' Hoosiers (1940 NCAA Finals)

At first it was the National Invitation Tournament and not the NCAA postseason party that was hoopdom's true showcase. Launched in 1938, just one season before the NCAA got off the ground and a mere year before James Naismith's death, the NIT boasted the initial backing of Madison Square Garden (i.e., New York City) promoters and press and thus commanded serious attention from most of the nation's sporting public. NIT title games throughout the '40s provided some of the classic matchups of collegiate basketball's first great boom era. Mikan performed there, as did Bob Kurland of Oklahoma A&M, Whizzer White of Colorado, Arnie Ferrin of Utah, and most of the nation's other hoop heroes of the immediate post-World War II sporting heyday.

The NCAA tourney debuted less auspiciously. The idea of the tourney's original backers (Midwest representatives among the National Association of Collegiate Basketball Coaches, who felt a true national tournament should be sponsored by a college organization and not New York arena promoters) was to match qualified regional opponents from Eastern and Western sectors of the country. But NCAA contests for several seasons would have to be played after the close of the NIT matchups in order not to be lost to the media attention lavished on the Madison Square Garden event.

In the very first NCAA title matchup it would fittingly be a Western Conference school — Ohio State — that would carry the Midwest banner. Much of the credit for unveiling a new national tourney falls to former Wisconsin player and later Ohio State coach Harold Olsen, whose Buckeyes rewarded his administrative efforts by reaching the "finals" of the new eight-team event. The first NCAA title game would of course be played far from the glitter of college basketball's Mecca in New York. It was instead staged on Northwestern University's campus in Evanston, Ill., and thus had a thoroughly Western Conference air about it. For all the advantages of a "home-court" venue, however, in the end the Western Conference boosters had to lick their wounds as the Buckeyes fell 46-33 to a strong Oregon team noted for its lineup of tall players (6-foot-8 center Slim Wintermute and a pair of 6-4 forwards) and disciplined ball-control game.

If the Western Conference had been an integral part of the very first NCAA postseason affair, the conference would maintain a stranglehold on the event for the next two seasons. In both 1940 and 1941 it would again be Western Conference teams that would climb into the finals and succeed in bringing home a cherished tourney title. First Indiana turned the trick for Branch McCracken in only his second season as Everett Dean's replacement in Bloomington. Then it was Wisconsin's turn to pull an upset as stunning as any in the tourney's subsequent long history. Of course the NCAA version of a "national championship" did not yet ring with today's level of prestige. It was the NIT — featuring matchups like DePaul against St. John's and Temple against Colorado — that was still undisputed king of the hill.

The Indiana team that brought the first taste of NCAA prestige to the nation's oldest conference was truly a team nurtured on pioneering firsts. For starters, the Hoosiers featured a remarkably novel style of play in McCracken's run-and-gun free-lancing version of the offensive game. Second, they launched the very first title run for a school that would one day lay sole claim to NCAA titles in four different decades. And thirdly, they launched a long-standing tradition of tournament success for the conference that was already informally being called the Big Ten. Over the coming decades the league would earn more success in tourney play than any other — most Final Four appearances (33), most title game appearances (18), most tournament appearances overall (121). And it all started with McCracken's team in 1940.

The term "Hurryin' Hoosiers" was born with McCracken's 1940 NCAA title outfit. Although fast-break basketball had been around for several years and had even found roots in the teams of Lambert at Purdue in the early '30s, none had previously exploited it any more thoroughly than this McCracken-coached Indiana team. It was a team without much height — center Bill Menke was 6-5 but sprinted around the floor like a much shorter man — and also one drilled to avoid dribbling and to handle the basketball as though it were a "hot potato" or a sizzling lump of coal. Exploiting constant exhausting motion, court-length passes, and a preference for layups over set shots, the "Hurryin' Hoosiers" battered both Springfield College (48-24) and Duquesne (39-30) on the way to their title fray with highly rated Kansas. The cautious and probing play of the Jayhawks was simply overrun by a balanced Hoosier onslaught that featured Marv Huffman (12 points), Jay McCreary (12) and Curly Armstrong (10). While Kansas waited for perfect shots and rarely found them, the Hoosiers threw up the ball at every opportunity en route to the 60-point night that would stand for a dozen years as an unmatched record tournament total.

Kansas newspapers would later call this blitzing Indiana team a "tornado" in the wake of the one-sided championship game. "That tornado was us," boasted IU guard Marv Huffman, "and we just blew them out of the stadium!" A team that was second in the Big Ten that year had indeed blown through the postseason field and was soon headed back to America's heartland with a huge prize. With their glamorous high-scoring presence, McCracken's men accomplished something else as well — the future popularity of the postseason tournament itself.

Once Upon a Time They Were Badgers (1941 NCAA Finals)

By the time the fledgling NCAA tournament was showing signs of gaining momentum on the eve of World War II, the glory years of Wisconsin cage play were already a distant memory. During the second decade of the century a British-born coach named Doc Meanwell (he held an actual medical degree) put both Wisconsin and the Western Conference on the map with his revolutionary style of controlled offensive play. Meanwell's famed "Wisconsin System", which featured rapid, short passes, plus constant crisscrossing and screen setting, transformed the rough and tumble physical game inherited from Naismith into a sport of grace and finesse. But Meanwell's last title team — one featuring Bud Foster as its floor general — had come way back in 1929. The intervening span of the '30s had been largely a wasteland in Madison, with Foster returning as Meanwell's replacement and earning another league title during his debut year in 1935, but then enduring a series of losing seasons the remainder of the decade.

The 1940s opened for the Badger hoop program with little sign of an imminent upgrade. In the season when Branch McCracken's Hoosiers hurried to victory in the second-ever NCAA playoff, Bud Foster's lackluster outfit brought up the conference rear with a ninth-place finish and 5-15 overall debit sheet. But this low point in school cage history soon served as a launching pad for the greatest Badger team of all. With lanky 6-4 center Gene Englund providing senior leadership and a pair of talented sophomores named Johnny Kotz (6-3 forward) and Fred Rehm (6-2 guard) offering reinforcements, it appeared that Foster had the troops capable of executing his own modified version of Meanwell's timeworn ball-control system. It was no longer a universally popular system, as IU's fast-breaking champs of a year earlier had already demonstrated. And until Foster's charges perfected it, there would be some very rough spots in the early going. Wisconsin looked like the clumsy Badgers of old when they failed to make a single second-half basket in the conference opener against Minnesota and suffered one of the most embarrassing defeats in years.

But Foster's message of on-court discipline and his dogged loyalty to Meanwell's precision passing game would soon bear startling dividends. The ball-control tactics received a sudden boost when the Badgers visited Bloomington and came away with a morale-lifting 38-30 victory over the defending NCAA title team. So inspired was Foster's young team after shocking the Hoosiers that Wisconsin rolled on to a clean slate of conference victories following their opening-game shellacking at the hands of Minnesota. Thus it was Foster and his deliberate set-pattern game and not McCracken and his racehorse Hoosiers who would carry the league's 1941 postseason banner. The infant NCAA playoff party was still an eight-team affair and the Badgers were joined for the festivities by Dartmouth, Pittsburgh and North Carolina from the East, and Washington State, Creighton, Arkansas and Wyoming representing the West.

The toughest hurdle proved to be Ivy League entrant Dartmouth in the opener. The Badgers enjoyed an apparently huge advantage in the early rounds since NCAA organizers decided to increase the coffers by holding opening and semifinal Eastern action in the Badgers' 13,000-seat arena, one of the largest in the nation. But the homecourt almost provided no bonus as Foster's Badgers needed a furious second-half rally to overcome Dartmouth, 51-50. Against Pittsburgh in the regional final, the Badgers again trailed at intermission. A tough 36-30 victory, however, catapulted a Big Ten team into the Finals for the third straight year. On the horizon for the surprising Wisconsin upstarts loomed one final challenge composed of Washington State, massive 6-8 center Paul Lindeman and the Cougars' own version of Indiana's fast-paced attack.

The championship clash of styles provided a seesaw battle which left the outcome in doubt almost to the end. Wisconsin planned a defensive strategy in which Englund shut off the Cougars' inside game involving Lindeman and outscored his rival pivot man 13-3. Kotz matched Englund's point production up front for the Badgers and provided key buckets in the crucial closing moments. The victory would belong to Wisconsin, 39-34, and the championship MVP medallion to Kotz. It was the greatest rags-to-riches story ever to surround a team which called the Big Ten Conference home, but it was a rare moment in the winner's circle for Wisconsin. The Badgers have captured just one lonely Big Ten trophy in all the subsequent seasons since.

Strange Saga of the Illini "Whiz Kids" (1942-1943)

The three-year domination of the NCAA tourney by the Western Conference ended during the heart of the war years. But this was not for lack of a great Western Conference team. That next memorable team emerged on the campus of Illinois University and was man-for-man the equal of its two league predecessors and then some. Unfortunately for proud Illini boosters, this best Illinois team ever to dribble and rebound became the mere stuff of trivia questions and pointless nostalgic "what might have beens."

The team that Doug Mills put on the floor for the first time in 1942 seemed bound for certain glory. For one thing, it was a team that started Andy Phillip, a now-forgotten Hall of Famer who carved out a huge piece of Big Ten history in the years immediately before Wier, Rehfeldt, Ragelis, Schlundt, Freeman and the other formidable stars of the late '40s and early '50s. Later elected by the Associated Press to the all-time All-American team, the 6-2 forward from Granite City, Ill., set Western Conference milestones for points in a season (255 in 1943

Illinois' "Whiz Kids" finished the 1943 season unbeaten in the Big Ten and 17-1 overall but didn't get the chance to vie for a national title. After the final regular-season game, all five starters left school to serve in World War II. From left are Andy Phillip, Ken Menke, Art Mathisen, Jack Smiley and Gene Vance. (University of Illinois photo)

which made him the league's first 20 points per game scorer), points in a single game (40) and field goals in a single game (16). The future BAA and NBA player was surrounded by Ken Menke, Art Mathisen, Jack Smiley and Gene Vance. Together they lost two conference games in two years, road losses to Iowa and Indiana in 1942 that failed to block the first of back-to-back Big Ten championships.

Bumped immediately from the 1942 NCAA tourney by Kentucky (46-44), the team, already known as Mills' "Whiz Kids", earned a first-year reputation for rolling up unprecedented scores, registering 63 points against Northwestern and cracking the 50-point barrier four other times in 1942 league play. The following season the "Whiz Kid" youngsters appeared even more potent. The season opened with a 69-27 embarrassing of Nebraska followed by four straight 60-point games early in conference play. At season's end, the Illini steamroller crushed Northwestern 86-44 and Chicago 92-25. So dominant was this Illinois team that four of the five starters (Menke was the only exception) comprised the all-conference team; only Northwestern's Otto Graham gathered enough votes to prevent a "Whiz Kids" sweep of the All-Big Ten first team.

But if this Illini wonder team toyed regularly with Big Ten rivals it never got the chance to flex its muscle in postseason play a second time. Sentimental favorites in the Midwest to earn still another NCAA trophy for the heartland league, the Illinois players found little motivation to attend the first NCAA title bout to be staged in the basketball Mecca of New York City. There was a world war going on and patriotism seemed a far more urgent call. On the very day of the season-closing rout of Chicago the team disbanded and the five starters who had played together so well as a unit departed campus for military duty. In December of 1946 four of the five would return to finish out their careers on the Illinois hardwood in Mills' last season as head coach. Despite a late-season rally that brought eight wins in 10 games, a slow conference start that winter by the out-of-condition GIs doomed this final edition of the once-invincible "Whiz Kids" to a second-place tie.

Ugliest NCAA Finals Ever (March 18, 1953, Indiana vs. Kansas)

Bob Leonard's March 1953 clutch free throw allowed Indiana to post a thrilling NCAA title win over Kansas in a fight-marred championship contest which highlighted the Don Schlundt years at Indiana. The bitterly fought struggle had come down to the final minute in a 68-all deadlock with Indiana holding the ball and working for a final shot. Kansas defender Dean Kelley, whose drive to the hoop knotted the contest seconds earlier, bumped Leonard and sent the Indiana guard to the charity stripe with 27 ticks remaining. Leonard flirted with disaster by missing the first free toss; he then recovered to bury the second and provide a slim margin of apparent victory. A final off-balance shot failed to connect for the Jayhawks, Leonard's toss held up, and Indiana once more sat squarely atop the entire amateur basketball world.

Leonard's clutch shot not only closed the door on a second Indiana national title but punctuated a season of great personal satisfactions for Branch McCracken's Hoosiers. McCracken had continued producing first-rate ballclubs on the heels of his first juggernaut, the point-happy 1940 national championship contingent which had been the first IU team to post 20 victories. Over his 11 previous seasons his teams had been second-place bridesmaids seven times but he had never had a conference winner. His run-and-gun style of offense was still intact season after season but he always lacked the big man needed for the proper execution of his racehorse game plan. One stellar Indiana-bred pivot man, Clyde Lovellette out of Terre Haute, was lost in the recruiting wars to Kansas. An adequate alternative to Lovellette was not found until Don Schlundt finally arrived in 1951. It was only now with Schlundt in his second season that the long-coveted league crown had finally been won and a measure of revenge simultaneously extracted against the Jayhawks, the team that had earlier pilfered Lovellette (who closed his Kansas career the previous spring).

If the final game of the 1953 season will always be remembered as somewhat "ugly" on account of its sloppy style of aggressive play and its numerous fourth-quarter technical fouls, it was nonetheless a game that certainly never lacked for rare thrills. Exactly 13 seasons had passed since the same two teams met on the same floor (in Kansas City) with the same NCAA title at stake. That first time had been a Hoosier cakewalk but this time the issue would be far harder to decide. A first half full of momentum swings found the Hoosiers falling behind 39-33 with Schlundt assigned to the bench in foul trouble before a Hoosier rally knotted the affair at 41 by intermission. The final quarter (the game was then played in four periods, not two) came down to a series of squabbles involving both benches plus a heated dispute over the number of fouls charged to Kansas' high scorer B.H. Born (who eventually did foul out, but only after a break from the official scorer). Schlundt, Leonard and Charles Kraak all drew costly technical fouls for the Hoosiers, fouls which permitted the Jayhawks to remain close at the charity stripe until almost the final buzzer.

This set the stage for Leonard's last-second heroics. Schlundt led the way with 30 points. Kraak balanced a costly late-game technical (allowing Kansas to deadlock the contest) with 17 points, but Leonard stood out as the unlikely hero on the strength of his 12th and final point of the night, a point which proved as vital as any found across the decades of Indiana hoop mayhem.

Iowa's "Fab Five" Meet the Unbeatable Dons (March 24, 1956)

"Fabulous Five" is a colorful designation that seems naturally suited to any well-balanced, star-studded cage "dream team." It has a perfect ring for headline writers and a bold grandeur consistent with a sport that features flamboyant personal styles and showy one-on-one moves. And it is a label that has therefore popped up more than once through the decades. The first Fabulous Five of note was the University of Kentucky outfit (Alex Groza, Ralph Beard, Wah Wah Jones, Cliff Barker and Dick Barnstable) that earned Adolph Rupp his greatest claim to fame, as well as claiming back-to-back NCAA titles in '48 and '49 and a 1948 Olympic crown. Smack on the heels of that great Wildcat club of the late 1940s came another Midwest all-star five that seemed to wear the title equally as well.

Like Kentucky's unit and the wartime Illini Whiz Kids, the Iowa "Fabulous Five" of the mid-50s was anything but a one-year wonder. The lineup of Bill Logan, Carl Cain, Bill Seaburg, Sharm Scheuerman and Bill Schoof already had one season under its belt when it piled Iowa's first-ever NCAA appearance on top of an outright conference title (at 11-3) in the spring of 1954. With the 6-7 Logan in pivot and leading the way with a 15.9 scoring average the point-happy Hawkeyes of Coach Bucky O'Connor became the first Iowa club to nudge the 80-point plateau with a season-long 79.7 points per game scoring mark. In the postseason wars they got by Penn State and Marquette to earn a trip into the Final Four in the school's very first crack at postseason play.

A year later the same talented Hawkeye quintet was back on the scene stronger than ever. With Cain as a first-team All-American and Logan again leading the scoring (17.7) and rebounding (10.2) parade, O'Connor's balanced outfit rode a 13-game conference winning streak to a second consecutive league title and another postseason berth. Again, the Hawks emerged as a regional champion with a surprise victory over Kentucky and thus a berth in the final weekend of festivities to be held on familiar Big Ten turf in Evanston, Ill.

Yet for all their achievements over the span of two seasons, this greatest of all Iowa teams is best remembered for a single losing effort in the limelight of the 1956 NCAA title game. Iowa was not the only repeat member of the Final Four in March 1956; also on board was a defending champion San Francisco team featuring Bill Russell and Hal Perry that had manhandled Tom Gola and LaSalle a season earlier. (K.C. Jones had also played for USF in the regular season but had used up his eligibility by tournament time.) The invincible Dons had stretched their two-season unbeaten skein to 55 and were proud owners of a 28-0 mark by the time they lined up opposite the Iowa Fab Five for another season's finale. Iowa could do little

Although Michigan's Fab Five (below) of, from left, Ray Jackson, Chris Webber, Juwan Howard, Jalen Rose and Jimmy King was greatly hyped, it wasn't the first group to earn the nickname. Above is Iowa's version of the Fab Five which earned fame in 1955 and 1956.

more than keep the game respectably close before falling 83-71 under Russell's one-man offensive and defensive show. The gangly giant, who would earn a reputation in Boston as a defender only, would here show plenty of scoring punch as he pounded the Hawkeyes for 26 points. In the end, the original Big Ten "Fab Five" was destined to stand for posterity as the "other team" that fell by the wayside in the face of a cyclone from the West to be known to history as Bill Russell's San Francisco Dons.

Jerry Lucas and the Greatest Team Ever Invented (1960-1962)

The Celtics tower above the rest of the NBA story like a single Everest. When it comes to major-league baseball, the Yankees demand the largest chapter. In pro hockey, the story always comes back to the Montreal Canadiens. Even college football and basketball — where dynasties are largely prevented by fixed player tenures — still there is Notre Dame looming above the pigskin world while roundball has the Wooden-led UCLA Bruins. When the tale turns to the Big Ten, the story has always been one of parity. Indiana, Michigan, Ohio State, Michigan State and Purdue have shared the modern era on top of the heap. But if ever there was a dynasty candidate, it would have to be Ohio State in the early 1960s.

This was truly a team for all ages. For starters, no previous college starting five had ever graduated into the pro ranks en toto as did the contingent of Lucas, Havlicek, Nowell, Roberts and Siegfried from Ohio State. All five had been high school centers. But when blended together they became the greatest unit college basketball had ever seen. No team before this Ohio State group had ever led the nation in offensive output and won a national title as well. But it was the spectacular won-lost record and the ability to march through an entire schedule into championship showdowns three straight seasons that was in the end the true hallmark of this greatest of Big Ten wonder teams.

The greatest season for Lucas and company was the first. Kentucky and Utah provided early-season losses, but once the sophomore-studded club (Joe Roberts was a senior and Larry Siegfried a junior) reached its stride in conference play, it would lose only at Indiana the rest of the way. By postseason, this was not only the best team in OSU annals but the best in conference annals as well. And it may have been the most dominant team of collegiate basketball history, a worthy rival for the best clubs fielded by John Wooden's dynasty Bruins. The team which trailed Oscar Robertson's Cincinnati Bearcats and California's Golden Bears (with All-American center Darrall Imhoff) in the national polls entering the NCAA fray would improve with each outing and battered Western Kentucky and Georgia Tech to reach the exclusive Final Four. The top-ranked Bears and Bearcats then locked horns in one semifinal in which the defending national champs from California eliminated Oscar from the tournament for the second year in a row. OSU in the meantime toyed with New York University 76-54 as Lucas and Siegfried each logged 19 points. The Finals would thus pit the nation's leader in offense (Ohio State at 90.4 points per game) against the national pacesetter in defense (California yielded but 49.5 points per game), and this time the old sports adage about the superiority of defense would fly out the window. The Buckeyes were superb at both ends of the court and simply overwhelmed the California defenders by hitting 16 of 19 first-half shots while holding the Bears to 30 percent shooting in the same stanza. With Lucas shackling Imhoff inside, the Buckeyes rolled to the title by a comfortable 20-point margin.

The next two years fell short of repeat glory by only a single game each. The fatal irony was that this single game in each case happened to be the most important contest of the year; each time it happened to be against the downstate rival Cincinnati Bearcats who were now without Oscar Robertson but even better on balance; and each time it ruined a season that was by all other measures superior to the title campaign of Lucas' sophomore year. It was indeed a very bitter pill to swallow for Buckeye supporters at the tail end of so much winning.

It should also be noted that in both of their championship game losses over the course of the next two seasons, the Buckeyes were done in each time by a twist of fate more than by their own flaws or any true superiority of the rival Bearcats. The 1961 Finals brought one of the rare classics of NCAA history, a thrilling overtime match in which a clutch game-tying bucket from reserve junior Bob Knight was eventually nullified by superb team defensive play on the part of the Bearcats as they pulled away for good during the extra session. Cincinnati won on exceptional team play from a lineup of Paul Hogue, Tom Thacker and Tony Yates, but it was Lucas who was, for the second time, the tournament MVP.

If a rare upset had felled the Buckeyes in 1961 it would be an even more fateful injury that would do them in during one final try at recapturing the championship glories of 1960. The 27-0 record that the '61 club carried into the tourney Finals was nearly replicated by the 26-1 mark of Lucas' senior season. The Bearcats (28-2) would be back as well, primed to prove that the first showdown had been anything but a fluke when it had fallen in their favor. But the second shootout between the bitter state rivals would lose something of its glamour even before the final night tipoff when Lucas was felled by a debilitating knee injury in the semifinal contest, tipping the balance hopelessly in Cincinnati's favor. Gary Bradds would perform nobly as Lucas' replacement in the final match but it would not be enough to prevent a Bearcat runaway and a final rare black mark on the OSU dynasty string. The loss in the tournament of 1962 was indeed a rare disappointing moment for Coach Fred Taylor's three-season OSU dream team. But in the end this had been the greatest conference glory run of all time — a three-year visit to the Final Four not replicated before or since.

Mount Sets the Nets on Fire (February 28, 1970, Purdue vs. Iowa)

Mackey Arena has been home to many thrilling moments during the cage sport's past quarter century. Since its opening Dec. 2, 1967, the Boilermakers' arena has staged thrilling conference shootouts, showcase intersectional matchups, and a string of NIT and NCAA early-round postseason games. Yet for a brief while it appeared as though no game witnessed on the Purdue campus would quite equal the dramatic shootout staged on the building's gala opening night. The Mackey Arena lid lifter was truly a game for all ages. Defending national champion UCLA ,with Lew Alcindor in the lineup and local legend of yesteryear John Wooden at the helm, came to town for the prime time occasion. The hometown club boasted the Hoosier State's greatest shooting legend in sophomore Rick Mount and one of the school's finest floor generals ever in Billy Keller. Mount would pour home 28 points while Alcindor would gather in 19 rebounds as the top-ranked Bruins squeezed out a thrilling 73-71 victory that set high standards for future Mackey play. Veteran Purdue fans must have exited that inaugural contest convinced it would be a long time indeed before the same level of excitement could be matched in the new Purdue facility.

But it wasn't long at all before a spectacular night of rare shooting by two gun-crazy Big Ten clubs all but obliterated the memories of Alcindor vs. Mount. It was in late February of 1970 that the Mount-led Boilermakers squared off with an Iowa club they trailed by a scant two games in the tightly contested Big Ten race. Purdue had only lost once on its home floor since the inaugural UCLA game three seasons earlier and a 31st consecutive West Lafayette victory was essential to any postseason plans. Mount took things into his own hands as the game unfolded and soared to the 32-point level in the first half alone. Nonetheless the black and gold trailed the Hawkeyes 49-47 at the break.

This was a night that Mount was in a rare zone — even for him — and the exceptional sharpshooter continued to pour in vital points at a record pace. Mount's shooting soon neared the boiling point as did the heated contest itself and the emotions of the home crowd, which twice littered the floor with debris in response to unpopular foul calls. Soon Mount passed Dave Schellhase's single-game conference mark of 57. His final points came at the buzzer and numbered 60 and 61. But even this scoring onslaught by The Rocket failed to shake the Hawkeyes who somehow held on for a breathtaking 108-107 victory.

What has been nearly lost in the glare of Mount's record-breaking 61-point performance is what the opposing Hawkeyes also accomplished that night. Iowa also rattled the record books behind the prolific duo of "Downtown" Freddie Brown and John Johnson. This Iowa team was the highest-scoring in conference history (102.9 points per game) and had reached the century mark for the eighth time (of 12) during the season. And Iowa took home something else of importance that night as well — the last outright Big Ten title to date in the school's own proud cage history.

All-Big Ten NCAA Final (March 29, 1976, Indiana vs. Michigan)

When the ballots are cast for the greatest club of Big Ten history, the polling (carried out anywhere perhaps but in Bloomington) would likely have to give the nod to Lucas, Havlicek and mates. But Bob Knight's first great NCAA title team of Scott May, Kent Benson, Bob Wilkerson, Ted Abernethy and Quinn Buckner has to run a very close second. This is the team that came within a whisker of something the Buckeyes with Lucas never achieved — two straight unblemished seasons. In conference play, IU's 36-0 record over this two-year span is the most impressive multi-season run in conference history.

The crowning achievement for IU's best team came with a bicentennial NCAA title match in the nation's most historic city of Philadelphia. And it was altogether fitting that this crowning moment for the most successful (if not man-for-man the "greatest") conference ballclub would come in a matchup with none other than a venerable conference rival. When Knight's Hoosiers squared off with Johnny Orr's Wolverines for the national title, it was the first and only time that the nation's showcase collegiate game would be an exclusive Big Ten party.

The game itself was anything but a nail biter. The Michigan team that had clawed its way to a second-place conference finish in the shadow of the Hoosiers and then snuck by Wichita State, Notre Dame and Missouri to reach the Final Four was a solid unit built around a pair of stars in center Phil Hubbard and guard Rickey Green. But Hubbard and Green were not Cazzie Russell and Bill Buntin, and a backup starting cast of Wayman Britt, John Robinson and Steve Grote had already proven insufficient to handle the Hoosiers in two regular-season meetings.

Indiana would again leave no doubt about its conference superiority once the supercharged Hoosiers warmed to the task at hand. For a brief while it looked like the Wolverines might be up to the challenge. With Green leading the famed Michigan fast break, the underdogs raced to a 35-29 halftime margin. Further clouding the first-half picture for the Hoosiers was the injury loss of starter Bobby Wilkerson who had been knocked out of action by an accidental but devastating elbow from Michigan forward Britt.

Down the stretch, however, Knight's team easily won the war of attrition. With the Hoosiers answering the second half bell by scoring on nearly every possession, the deficit was quickly translated into a lead which quickly expanded from 39-37 to 73-59. Green and the Wolverine offense had run out of gas and it was all over but the mop-up operations. With the eventual 86-68 margin, the inspired Hoosiers would not only own the school's third NCAA crown and Knight's first (as a coach), but they would own as well an important slice of history as only the seventh club ever to complete both the regular season and NCAA postseason schedules with an undefeated tally sheet.

Magic and Larry Show (March 26, 1979, MSU vs. Indiana State)

Basketball writer Joe Gergen has suggested that perhaps a bronzed monument would be in order somewhere inside the Salt Lake City Special Events Center on the campus of the University of Utah. The purpose would be to mark the precise site where a first oncourt meeting took place — under the heightened drama of a national championship clash — between the two greatest rivals of basketball's modern television era. The head-to-head cage rivalry between Larry Bird and Magic Johnson that was launched in Salt Lake City on March 26, 1979, would prove to have all the stature and built-in drama of the game's most titanic clashes — Mikan vs. Bob Kurland, Wilt vs. Russell or Oscar vs. Jerry West. In terms of media focus, of course, Magic vs. Bird would eventually dwarf all such earlier legendary confrontations.

Indeed, far more was launched with that memorable clash between Bird and Magic than a budding NBA rivalry alone. The Michigan State-Indiana State showdown which closed the 1979 season would stand as the single game that more than any other secured a permanent spot for the Final Four in the national consciousness, smack alongside the Super Bowl and the venerable World Series. With Bird and Magic arrived the full dizzying heights of the phenomenon today known as March Madness.

The two most charismatic college hoop stars to come along in years had seemingly been on a collision course all season. The stage had been perfectly set for the dramatic meeting by the pair of outstanding semifinal performances turned in by the exceptional pair. Johnson had blitzed Pennsylvania with 29 points (a dozen above his average) in a laughably easy 101-67 rout that would have been sleep-inducing except for Magic's riveting display of pinpoint passes to prolific teammate Greg Kelser. Bird's own 35-point performance had been even more vital to assuring victory for Indiana State in a tense 76-74 victory over DePaul. But Bird's performance was also dotted with an awesome display of dynamite passing that almost stretched the credulity of those watching.

As one of the most hyped curtain-call games of NCAA history — the first to fully benefit from basketball's new-found television popularity — the original Magic and Larry Show didn't

When Magic Johnson, right, and Larry Bird (33) squared off in the 1979 NCAA champion-ship game, it not only was a memorable moment for the Big Ten but launched a new era of popularity for college basketball. (Michigan State University photo)

disappoint in the slightest. The game was a thing of joy, despite the relative one-sidedness of the contest and Bird's surprising ineffectiveness in the final game of his otherwise spectacular collegiate career. The Spartans played their matchup zone defense to perfection against Bird and never let the ISU one-man gang get very far out of the starting blocks. With Bird pressing his game in an attempt to carry the Sycamores as he had done in the past, things only seemed to go from bad to worse for the remarkable Hoosier sharpshooter. By halftime Bird had connected on only four of 11 shots and his team trailed by nine. In the second stanza the talented Spartan defense turned up the pressure even further. While Bird was contained at one end of the floor, Sycamore attempts to harness Johnson at the other end backfired. With Johnson double-teamed, MSU guard Terry Donnelly was left open for four long jumpers on feeds from Magic which blew the game wide open in the early stages of the second half.

Magic easily won the first showdown on each and every important count. The final team score read 75-64 in favor of the Big Ten champions. Bird would persist long enough at his shooting game to register 19 points but would connect on only seven of 21 missiles. Johnson would own the tourney MVP award as well as a national championship with a brilliant performance that included 24 points, eight-for-15 field-goal shooting, seven rebounds and a slew of vital assists. Bird, for his part, would snatch a game-high 13 rebounds and defend well against MSU scoring ace Greg Kelser. But the victory for Magic was so convincing for the Big Ten star that Bird would spend the next decade trying to catch up.

The Glory Run of Isiah's 1981 Indiana Hoosiers

Bob Knight's second roller-coaster trip to an NCAA title game was hardly the smooth-paced joyride he experienced the first time around. Knight's invincible 1976 champs hardly broke a sweat in amassing their unblemished 32-game perfect ledger. But this time, five years later, the club struggled uncharacteristically in the early going, standing at 2-2 after a pair of close losses to Kentucky and Notre Dame, and finishing the month of December with an unbecoming 7-5 mark. Knight and his star sophomore guard Isiah Thomas seemed bent on providing a watered-down hoops version of Charlie Finley's bickering Oakland A's. And despite winning a Big Ten crown, the nine losses carried into the tournament was hardly reflective of the kind of team Knight boasted in the bicentennial year. The combo of Thomas, Ray Tolbert (the only senior), Randy Wittman, Landon Turner and Ted Kitchel, however, was clicking on all cylinders down the stretch run as the Hoosiers pulled out the Big Ten title on the season's final day and then dismantled two respectable teams (Maryland, 99-64, and LSU, 67-49) on the way to the Final Four.

Once IU reached the title round with North Carolina, the road would certainly not get any smoother. For this was the year the NCAA title game was almost never played. As the Hoosiers and Tar Heels (along with their legions of fans) focused on roundball and a classic matchup in Philadelphia's Spectrum between mastermind coaches Knight and Dean Smith, the remainder of the nation stood near panic and thought little of something as trivial as basketball drama. The afternoon of the scheduled title affair, President Ronald Reagan had been wounded by an assassin's bullets which had also felled the President's press secretary, a Secret Service officer and a DC policeman. The tournament committee was pressed with a decision about whether or not to go ahead with the contest. NBC also had to make an 11th-hour call about whether or not to beam the game into the nation's living rooms. Only when an announcement was released that the President's surgery had been successful and that the chief executive was out of serious danger did the threatened show go on as scheduled.

Ultimately the show from Philadelphia did reach the airwaves as a prime-time attraction. Once launched, it was quickly transformed into little more than a personal stage for Thomas, the talented Hoosier point guard who was both Knight's biggest weapon and sometimes his biggest headache. Thomas all season long had reportedly been nearly as large a thorn in Knight's side as had the opposition forces. Few doubted that this was the backcourt prodigy's final collegiate game before opting for an NBA career and escape from Knight's stifling control of his creative game. And that game was never more creative than on the night that the nation's bragging rights were at stake. Thomas' well-timed steals and deft playmaking assists at the start of the second half propelled the Hoosiers to a sudden 10-point spread. Thomas would pour in 10 points early in the stretch run, finish with 19 of his 23 in the second half, and turn the game around with four clutch steals just after the intermission. The heady result for Hoosier fans was a surprisingly easy 63-50 victory that crowned Isiah's swan song performance with a tournament MVP trophy as well as an NCAA championship ring. It was indeed a most stylish show and one timed perfectly to entertain a national audience on a night of high national anxiety.

Biggest Surprise of All — Michigan's 1989 Champion Wolverines

There have been some huge surprises through the years in NCAA tournament play. In recent seasons fans had been shocked by a 1986 Louisville team led by a freshman named Pervis Ellison which upset Duke's powerhouse in the finals despite a seven-loss regular season. A season earlier brought an even greater eye-opener with the poor-cousin Big East Conference landing three teams in the Final Four and a 19-10 regular-season Villanova ballclub taking home the big prize. But the biggest surprise of all — 1980s style at least — was the one provided by the 1989 Michigan Wolverines. No title-bound team ever entered the postseason fray with a head coach yet to earn his first victory — or for that matter to coach his first game.

Such were the unprecedented circumstances that surrounded one of the most unusual championship clubs in Big Ten and NCAA history. The story of Michigan's "Shock the World Boys" is now familiar to cage fanatics everywhere. This was not an untalented Michigan team nor one that didn't possess the tools to make a serious championship run. The club offensive leader, Glen Rice, enjoyed a stellar senior season which featured a 25.6 scoring average and second-team consensus All-American honors. A 24-7 pre-tourney record included a third-place Big Ten finish and a string of high-scoring victories before a season-ending loss to Illinois. Four potent juniors — Loy Vaught, Rumeal Robinson, Mike Griffin and Terry Mills — and a strong bench supplemented Rice. A favorable draw in the Southeast Regional offered bright prospects for a Michigan challenge at the Final Four.

Then chaos struck just two days before the opening of the tournament. Coach Bill Frieder publicly announced plans to depart the program at season's end for a plush contract with the Arizona State University. Stunned and disappointed, the Michigan Athletic Department fired

Michigan's 1989 team under Steve Fisher was the Big Ten's most recent and most surpris-ing national champion. (University of Michigan photo)

Frieder and named longtime assistant Steve Fisher to fill the void. Against this backdrop, most teams would have packed it in for the campaign and merely gone through the motions in the tournament opener; others might have pressed so hard in the first game as to self-destruct. The gutsy Wolverines did neither.

Out of the gate, the team now led by the largely unknown Fisher first climbed the hurdle of a determined and upset-minded Xavier team by a narrow 92-87 margin. A second near-upset was brushed aside when South Alabama was held at bay, 91-82. Things really heated up for the Wolverines and their still-reeling followers at that point. North Carolina had dispatched Michigan from the NCAA postseason the previous two years, but the emotionally charged Wolverines made a charm of the third encounter with a thrilling 92-87 triumph over the Tar Heels. The corner had now been turned and the championship wagon gaining speed as it swung down the backside of the mountain. Virginia fell helplessly 102-65 during the most one-sided game in Michigan's tournament history. New coach Steve Fisher, staring at the Final Four, was suddenly a celebrity as the only coach in history to enter the final round having never lost a collegiate game.

Clearly on a roll, Michigan was handed a break with a semifinal matchup against confer-ence rival Illinois, a team that had already beaten them twice in the regular season. Riding the odds that seemed to hang in their favor, Fisher's charges hung on for a narrow victory sealed by sub Sean Higgins' dramatic buzzer-beating final shot. The final plateau had been reached and the reward would be one of the most exciting and well-played championship games ever witnessed by the nation's legions of college basketball fanatics.

It was a classic matchup from the start which featured Michigan's high-scoring offense keyed by Rice versus the durable defense of the Seton Hall Pirates, surprise survivors from the

Big East Conference who featured a gunner of their own in John Morton. Rice and Morton didn't disappoint, the Pirates' ace canning 35 while Rice poured in 31 in a flaming individual duel that left fans breathless. Michigan held the halftime lead by five (37-32), but Seton Hall turned up its famed defense in the second stanza and forced a 71-71 tie to send the game into overtime. In the first overtime session in a championship game since 1963, the two juggernauts remained deadlocked down to the final seconds. It would be guard Rumeal Robinson who would complete Michigan's Cinderella championship dream when he canned two pressure-packed free throws with three seconds remaining. And it would be Glen Rice whose tournament-record 184 points would earn individual MVP honors. But it had been a total team victory if there had ever been one. Against huge odds, the team left without a head coach only hours before the opening of the tournament miraculously pulled together under huge pressures and provided one of the most surprising stretch runs ever to grace March Madness.

The Rise and Fall of Michigan's Modern-Era Fab Five

The '90s have so far been anything but disappointing when it comes to thrilling chapters in the Big Ten chronicle. First Calbert Cheaney and more recently Shawn Respert have chased down the league's mark for all-time scoring; Glenn Robinson set new standards for single season greatness; Bob Knight, Gene Keady and Lou Henson have climbed over impressive milestones in career coaching victories; and Indiana and Purdue have each added another length to the their wide lead in conference championships. But the single dominating story of the 10th decade of league play has to be the three-year roller-coaster ride of the most talented single group of recruits ever simultaneously to arrive on the collegiate hoop scene. The story of '90s Big Ten basketball to date — no matter how you slice it — has been largely the story of Michigan's "Fab Five" lineup of Chris Webber, Juwan Howard, Jalen Rose, Jimmy King and Ray Jackson. It was from the start a team rich in unlimited potential, yet cursed with impossible expectations. And it was a team that over the next several years didn't fail to reward the expectations of boosters and nay-sayers alike.

Basketball pundits across the nation were unanimous in the opinion at the outset of the 1991-92 season that the starting freshman unit recruited by Coach Steve Fisher would instantly vault Michigan back near the top of the Big Ten pecking order. For one thing, this talented group was also supported by a stellar cast of second stringers — 7-footer Eric Riley (soon an NBAer with the Houston Rockets), James Voskuil and Rob Pelinka. But the realistic view was that it would take at least a year of seasoning before any freshman five could compete at the highest level. It soon proved to be a view that shortchanged Fisher's coaching genius and the awesome talents of the five phenoms — especially Webber. The team's leading rebounder and No. 2 scorer (behind Jalen Rose), Webber keyed a 25-9 season and a surprise romp through NCAA tourney competition that brought a near miracle — an all-frosh ballclub holding a cherished spot in the prestigious Final Four. The final two giant steps into the national championship came for the talented Michigan youngsters with a regional championship victory over league rival Ohio State, followed by a second-half comeback that eliminated another Cinderella club, Cincinnati, in the national semifinals match. The 75-71 conquering of Ohio State with All-American Jim Jackson was especially sweet since the Buckeyes twice pasted the Wolverines during the regular season. In the end, the miracle would dissipate in the 11th hour for the charmed freshmen, however, as Fisher's team was ultimately overwhelmed 71-51 in the NCAA title shootout by a far more seasoned Duke team, punctuating a bitter-sweet end to perhaps the most surprising and exciting season in Wolverine history.

It had been, of course, only a start for the young miracle team. When the following campaign opened, Michigan boosters expected further great things from their now-seasoned Fab Five and were about to get them. This team looked like the best bet for a Final Four repeat since the Lucas-Havlicek club and they wouldn't disappoint. While the conference title would again escape the powerhouse club, the team would nonetheless finish with a 26-4 regular-season ledger, a No. 5 ranking in the national polls, and high odds in their favor as a No. 1 seed in the NCAA West Regional. A thrilling overtime tussle with UCLA almost derailed the championship charge, as did a second extra-session game with Kentucky in the national semifinal. Webber's 27 points and Jalen Rose's clutch last-second free throws, however, were enough to assure a second straight crack at the national title. Yet again it would be an opportunity squandered in the face of a veteran and unflappable ACC ballclub. This time it was North Carolina which staved off a late Wolverine rally and salvaged victory when Webber suffered a costly mental lapse in the game's closing seconds. Any hopes for victory collapsed for the Maize and Blue when Webber, his team trailing 73-71, called for a time-out that Michigan no longer had. The resulting technical foul and loss of possession with a half-minute left sealed a 77-71 victory for the Tar Heels.

Chris Webber's crucial misjudgment had sealed a second season for the Fab Five. A few weeks later Webber would make a more carefully reasoned judgment that would prematurely close the door on the Fab Five era altogether after but two seasons and two painful near misses with NCAA immortality. Webber had opted after two years of play to leave Michigan for the NBA draft and put NCAA and Big Ten championship dreams behind for himself and his team-mates as well. A reduced "Fab Five" squad with Rose and Howard doing the bulk of the heavy scoring did well a season later, finishing second in conference play and fighting all the way to the Midwest Regional title game before bowing to eventual national champion Arkansas, 76-68. But this was the true swan song for a team that was doomed for all its glory never to reach full potential. Rose and Howard also now opted for early entry into the NBA player lottery, leaving King and Jackson alone to finish the senior season for the once sterling quintet.

For Michigan fans, the Fab Five adventure had fallen a step short of expected glory and contained nearly as much heartache as hoopla. Yet for Big Ten fans everywhere, the Michigan wonder team of the early '90s had simply written but one more in a lengthy tome of stirring chapters which comprise perhaps the greatest college basketball story ever told.

III

Big Ten Trivia Quiz

Trivia Questions

1. Name the schools (and the years) that have had undefeated seasons in Big Ten league play. Hint: It has happened exactly one dozen times.

2. Who is the only player in conference history to have been named *Chicago Tribune* Big Ten Most Valuable Player for three seasons?

3. What is the only team (school and year) to complete an undefeated schedule in Big Ten play and not win the conference title outright?

4. Who were the first and last players to be named *Chicago Tribune* Big Ten Most Valuable Player two seasons in a row?

5. Six Big Ten players have been NCAA Division I Players-of-the-Year. But only one has been named twice. Who are the six winners and the only two-time winner?

6. Name the four Big Ten All-Americans elected to the Naismith Basketball Hall of Fame for their playing (not coaching) achievements.

7. What pro football hall of famer was a consensus All-American in basketball for Northwestern University in 1944?

8. Five times since 1975, Big Ten coaches have been selected as National Collegiate Basketball Coach-of-the-Year. Name the coaches and the years.

9. Four famous Big Ten coaches with more than 100 career victories hold lifetime winning percentages above the .700 plateau. Who are the four? Hint: Two are currently active Big Ten coaches.

10. Who were the two most productive single-season individual scorers in Big Ten history? Hint: One for total points and the other for scoring average.

11. Who is the only player in Big Ten history to score more than 1,000 points in conference games during his first two seasons?

12. This player holds the career record for blocked shots for one Big Ten school, but also holds the distinction of leading the conference in blocks for yet another school as well. Name the player and the two different teams he played for.

13. What Northwestern University player was a conference statistical leader during the 1990s? Name the player, the year and the category in which he led the conference.

14. What was the greatest rebounding team in Big Ten history? Name the school and the season.

15. Who was the first Big Ten player to average more than 30 points per game in two consecutive seasons during league competition?

16. What Big Ten basketball all-star put his pro basketball career on hold long enough to try out as a wide receiver for the NFL Cleveland Browns before launching his Hall of Fame NBA career?

17. Who holds the distinction of coaching a Big Ten team and leading the conference in scoring during the very same season? Hint: It happened in the very early seasons of the informally organized Western Conference, forerunner to the Big Ten.

18. Which Big Ten school (excluding newcomer Penn State) has had the **fewest** consensus first-team All-Americans in its history?

19. Has any Big Ten school ever boasted two first-team consensus All-Americans in the same season? If so, which school or schools, which season or seasons, and which players?

20. Who was the first player to average more than 20 points per game for a full season in Big Ten play? Name the player, school and year.

21. Who was the first player to average more than 30 points per game for a full season in Big Ten play? Name the player, school and year.

22. Name the NCAA season scoring champions who have hailed from the Big Ten conference. Give the schools and years. Hint: There have only been three since the NCAA began keeping records in the 1947-48 season.

23. Has a Big Ten player ever led the nation in rebounding? If so, what player or players and what year or years?

24. Who is the only Big Ten player to rank in the top 25 all-time NCAA leaders in career assists? Hint: It is **not** Magic Johnson.

25. Which Big Ten campus hosted the first-ever NCAA basketball finals back in 1939, the year that Oregon was crowned as the sport's first national champion?

26. Who were the first two Big Ten players named "Most Outstanding Player" of the NCAA tournament?

27. Indiana heads the pack with five NCAA tournament championships. But what Big Ten school has been the NCAA runner-up the most times?

28. Only one player has ever led the conference in field-goal percentage for three straight seasons and only one other has done so two years in a row. Name these repeat champions.

29. What Big Ten championship basketball coach also played in the National Football League?

30. Who owns the record for the highest rebound average for a season in Big Ten play? Name the player, school and year.

31. Which conference team has won the most conference games? And which has the best overall conference won-lost percentage?

32. Which Big Ten players have won both an NCAA championship and an NBA title? Hint: There are six players.

33. What coach has the most consecutive Big Ten championships (including co-championships)? Name the coach, the school and the years of the streak.

34. Which player from which Big Ten School currently holds the NCAA single-season free-throw percentage record?

35. Who was the last player to pace the conference in free-throw shooting accuracy twice and in which seasons?

36. Who is the most recent Big Ten player to play on an NBA championship team? Name the player, NBA team and year.

Purdue's Terry Dischinger shares a distinction with Indiana's Walt Bellamy and Ohio State's Jerry Lucas. (Purdue University photo)

Purdue's Glenn Robinson didn't stay in college long enough to rewrite many Purdue or collegiate records, but there is one two-year scoring distinction that is Robinson's alone. (Penn State University photo)

37. Only three Big Ten players have ever gone on to stardom as NBA Rookie-of-the-Year. Who were they? Hint: Ironically, they entered the NBA in three consecutive years and the first two were rookies with the same NBA team (although the team had changed its name from one season to the next).

38. Only one man has enjoyed national championship victories as both a Big Ten player and coach. Name him.

39. Which current longtime NBA coach led his Big Ten team in scoring for three consecutive seasons? Name the player and his school.

40. Who was the last Big Ten individual scoring champ to average less than 20 points per game. What year did he do it?

41. In 1994, Glenn Robinson became only the 15th player in NCAA history to score 1,000 points (all games) in a single season. Who was the first Big Ten player to reach this milestone? Can you name the non-Big Ten players who have done it?

42. Which Big Ten team has had the most MVPs in the NCAA Final Four? How many, which players and what years?

43. Penn State has only been in the Big Ten wars for two seasons, yet the Nittany Lions already boast one league individual statistical champion. Who is he and in what category did he pace the conference?

44. He smacked 382 major-league home runs and was National League Rookie-of-the-Year in 1960. But before that he was an All-American basketball player in the Big Ten and still holds two Madison Square Garden Holiday Festival Tournament rebounding records. Who is he and what Big Ten team did he play for?

45. What Big Ten player was a back-to-back NCAA Final Four MVP?

46. Name the only Purdue player with at least 1,000 points, 500 rebounds, 100 steals, 100 assists and 50 blocked shots during his career.

47. What four players each led the Big Ten Conference in individual scoring for three consecutive seasons?

48. What school was the first to repeat as conference champion, with four straight titles between 1907 and 1910?

49. When the award was first instituted in 1984, who was selected by Big Ten radio broadcasters as the first Big Ten Defensive Player of the Year?

50. What pair of brothers have each reigned as Big Ten individual scoring champions? Name them and their school(s).

51. Who are the only three three-time consensus All-American players in Big Ten basketball history? Hint: They played for Purdue, Ohio State and Northwestern.

52. Name the Big Ten players who had their uniforms retired as NBA players.

Trivia Answers

1. Chicago (1909, 12-0), Wisconsin (1912, 12-0), Purdue (1912, 10-0), Wisconsin (1914, 12-0), Illinois (1915, 12-0), Minnesota (1919, 10-0), Purdue (1930, 10-0), Illinois (1943, 12-0), Ohio State (1961, 14-0), Iowa (1970, 14-0), Indiana (1975, 18-0), Indiana (1976, 18-0).

2. Jerry Lucas of Ohio State, in 1960, 1961 and 1962.

3. Purdue finished 10-0 in 1912, yet still trailing 12-0 Wisconsin for the league's best record.

4. First was Archie Dees of Indiana in 1957 and 1958. Most recent was Jim Jackson of Ohio State in 1991 and 1992.

5. Jerry Lucas, Ohio State (1961 and 1962); Gary Bradds, Ohio State (1964); Cazzie Russell, Michigan (1966); Scott May, Indiana (1976); Calbert Cheaney, Indiana (1993) and Glenn Robinson, Purdue (1994).

6. Andy Phillip, Illinois (All-American, 1942-1943); Branch McCracken, Indiana (All-American, 1930); Jerry Lucas (All-American, 1960-1961-1962); and John Wooden, Purdue (All-American, 1930-1931-1932). John Havlicek of Ohio State was elected to the Naismith Hall of Fame for his NBA playing achievements but he was never a consensus All-American.

7. Forward Otto Graham later earned fame as a quarterback with the Cleveland Browns and as one of the NFL's all-time great passers.

8. Bob Knight, Indiana (1975, 1976); Gene Keady Purdue (1984, 1990); and Tom Davis, Iowa (1987).

9. Bob Knight, Indiana (640-223, .742); Walter Meanwell, Wisconsin (246-99, .712); Ward "Piggy" Lambert, Purdue (371-152, .709); and Steve Fisher, Michigan (123-45, .730).

10. Terry Furlow of Michigan State and Rick Mount of Purdue. Furlow scored 588 points and averaged 32.7 points in 18 conference contests in 1976, a record which still stands. Mount, however, holds the record for scoring average, with a 39.4 mark during 14 games in 1970.

11. Glenn Robinson of Purdue.

12. Brad Sellers is the career leader in blocks for Wisconsin, recording 120 in 1982 and 1983. After transferring to Ohio State, Sellers also led the conference in blocks for the Buckeyes in 1985.

13. Pat Baldwin of Northwestern was the individual leader in steals in 1991 (52 steals for a 2.89 per-game average).

14. Led by Jumpin' Johnny Green with a 16.6 rebounds per game individual average, the 1959 Michigan State team averaged an incredible 63.7 per game with 892 caroms during league play.

15. Ohio State All-American center Gary Bradds, who averaged 30.9 in 1963 and 33.9 the following season.

16. John Havlicek of Ohio State, never an All-American as a collegian but eventually a Hall of Famer with the Boston Celtics.

17. Emmett Angell of Wisconsin in the 1905-06 inaugural season of the conference.

18. Michigan State, with only one. He, of course, was Earvin "Magic" Johnson, selected for the 1978-79 season. Iowa (Murray Wier in 1948 and Chuck Darling in 1952) and Wisconsin (Gene Englund in 1941 and John Kotz in 1942) have each had only two.

Northwestern's Otto Graham was an All-American in 1944 but later became better known for his ability in another sport. (Northwestern University photo)

19. It has happened twice, first with Purdue in 1930 (Charles "Stretch" Murphy and John Wooden), and then with Indiana in 1976 (Scott May and Kent Benson)

20. Andy Phillip, Illinois all-star forward, posted a 21.3 average in 12 conference games in 1943.

21. Robin Freeman of Ohio State averaged 32.5 during 14 games in 1956.

22. Murray Wier (Iowa, 1948, 21.0 ppg.); Dave Schellhause (Purdue, 1966, 32.5 ppg.); and Glenn Robinson (Purdue, 1994, 30.3 ppg.).

23. Jerry Lucas (Ohio State) in both 1961 and 1962.

24. Bruce Douglas of Illinois (1983-1986), whose 765 career assists rank him 21st on the career NCAA list.

25. Evanston, Illinois, home of Northwestern University.

26. Marvin Huffman of Indiana (1940) and John Kotz of Wisconsin (1941), as the Hoosiers and Badgers won the second and third NCAA crowns on the heels of Oregon's pioneering 1939 championship.

27. Michigan has lost in the Finals a remarkable four times (1965 to UCLA, 1976 to Indiana, 1992 to Duke, 1993 to North Carolina). Ohio State has lost the title game three times (1939 to Oregon, and 1961 and 1962, both to Cincinnati).

28. The three-time pacesetter is Jerry Lucas of Ohio State (1960-1962). Lucas was followed by his teammate Gary Bradds for the 1963 and 1964 seasons, meaning Ohio State kept a tight grip on this category for five straight years.

29. Gene Keady, coach of four (1984, 1987, 1988, 1994) Big Ten champion Purdue teams, was a successful collegiate (Kansas State) and NFL (Pittsburgh Steelers) football player.

30. Horace Walker of Michigan State averaged 18.3 rebounds per game in 1960, the second season complete rebound statistics were recorded.

31. Purdue enters the 1994-95 season as the leader in victories with 706, one better than Illinois. But Indiana still holds the best winning percentage at .595 (704-479).

32. **Jerry Lucas** (Ohio State, 1960 and New York Knicks, 1973); **John Havlicek** (Ohio State, 1960 and Boston Celtics, 1963, 1964, 1965, 1966, 1968, 1969, 1974, 1976); **Larry Siegfried** (Ohio State, 1960 and Boston Celtics, 1964, 1965, 1966, 1968, 1969), **Quinn**

Buckner (Indiana, 1976 and Boston Celtics, 1984), **Magic Johnson** (Michigan State, 1979 and Los Angeles Lakers, 1980, 1982, 1985, 1987, 1988), and **Isiah Thomas** (Indiana, 1981 and Detroit Pistons, 1989, 1990).

33. Fred Taylor, Ohio State University, five straight (1960-1964).

34. Craig Collins, Penn State University, who shot 95.9 for the 1984-85 full season.

35. Ted Kitchel of Indiana in 1982 and 1983. The league's only other back-to-back winner in this individual category was Purdue's Billy Keller in 1968 and 1969.

36. Chris Jent of Ohio State was a late-season roster addition of the 1994 NBA champion Houston Rockets.

37. Walt Bellamy, Indiana (NBA rookie in 1962 with Chicago Packers), Terry Dischinger, Purdue (NBA rookie in 1963 with Chicago Zephyrs), and Jerry Lucas, Ohio State (NBA rookie in 1963 with Cincinnati Royals).

38. Bob Knight, playing member of the 1960 NCAA champion Ohio State Buckeyes and coach of Indiana NCAA champions in 1976, 1981 and 1987.

39. Don Nelson, Golden State Warriors, who paced the Iowa Hawkeyes in scoring in 1960, 1961 and 1962.

40. Northwestern's Ray Ragelis, who paced the circuit with a 14-game 19.8 points per game average in 1951.

41. Glenn Robinson was the first from the Big Ten. Others have been Frank Selvy, Furman (1954); Oscar Robertson, Cincinnati (1960); Billy McGill, Utah (1962); Pete Maravich, LSU (1968-1969-1970); Elvin Hayes,

Iowa's Don Nelson became a Hall of Fame player with the Celtics and later a successful NBA coach. He also made his mark in Iowa's scoring records. (University of Iowa photo)

Houston (1968); Austin Carr, Notre Dame (1970-1971); Rich Fuqua, Oral Roberts (1972); Dwight Lamar, Southwestern Louisiana (1972); Freeman Williams, Portland State (1977); Otis Birdsong, Houston (1977); Hersey Hawkins, Bradley (1988); Hank Gathers, Loyola-California (1989); Bo Kimble, Loyola-California (1990); and Kevin Bradshaw, U.S. International (1991).

42. Indiana with four: Marvin Huffman (1940), Kent Benson (1976), Isiah Thomas (1981) and Keith Smart (1987).

43. John Amaechi, who paced the conference in blocked shots with 50 during the 1992-93 season.

44. Frank Howard of Ohio State spent the bulk of his better-known baseball career with the Los Angeles Dodgers and Washington Senators.

45. Ohio State's Jerry Lucas in 1960 and 1961.

46. Glenn Robinson, of course.

47. John Schommer, Chicago (1907-1908-1909), Don Schlundt, Indiana (1953-1954-1955), Terry Dischinger, Purdue (1960-1961-1962), and Rick Mount, Purdue (1968-1969-1970).

48. The University of Chicago Maroons, with outright titles in 1909 (the first undefeated season in league history) and 1910, and ties in 1907 (with Minnesota and Wisconsin) and 1908 (with Wisconsin).

49. Ricky Hall, Purdue University guard.

50. Jay Vincent (1980 and 1981) and Sam Vincent (1985), both of Michigan State.

51. John Wooden, Purdue (1930-1931-1932); Jerry Lucas, Ohio State (1960-1961-1962); and Joe Reiff, Northwestern (1931-1932-1933).

52. There are eight. Lou Hudson (Minnesota, No. 23 retired by Atlanta Hawks), John Havlicek (Ohio State, No. 17 retired by Boston Celtics), Don Nelson (Iowa, No. 19 retired by Boston Celtics), Kevin McHale (Minnesota, No. 32 retired by Boston Celtics), Rudy Tomjanovich (Michigan, No. 45 retired by Houston Rockets), George McGinnis (Indiana, No. 30 retired by Indiana Pacers), Dick VanArsdale (Indiana, No. 5 retired by Phoenix Suns), Fred Brown (Iowa, No. 32 retired by Seattle SuperSonics),

IV

Big Ten Records and Statistical Summary

BIG TEN STATISTICAL SUMMARY AND RECORDS

All-Time Big Ten Standings

School (Year Started in Big Ten)	Won	Lost	Pct.	Years	Games	Titles
Indiana (1905)	704	479	.595	87(a)	1,183	19
Purdue (1905)	706	505	.580	89	1,211	19
Illinois (1905)	705	523	.574	89	1,228	12
Ohio State (1912)	600	540	.530	82	1,140	15
Michigan (1917)	583	509	.530	77	1,092	12
Iowa (1908)	573	562	.505	82(b)	1,135	8
Michigan State (1950)	344	356	.490	43	700	6
Minnesota (1905)*	582	637	.480	87	1,219	8
Wisconsin (1905)	548	679	.447	89	1,227	14
Chicago (1905)	168	296	.362	40(c)	464	6
Northwestern (1908)	394	784	.330	86	1,178	2
Penn State (1993)	8	28	.220	2	36	0

Above standings include conference records only. Key: * = NCAA declared all Minnesota games forfeited for 1977 season; (a) = Indiana missed 1907 and 1908 seasons; (b) = Iowa missed 1930 season; (c) = Chicago missed 1945 season and dropped out of conference after 1946 season.

Big Ten NCAA Tournament Winners

1940	Indiana (Indiana 60, Kansas 42)
1941	Wisconsin (Wisconsin 39, Washington State 34)
1953	Indiana (Indiana 69, Kansas 68)
1960	Ohio State (Ohio State 75, California 55)
1976	Indiana (Indiana 86, Michigan 68)
1979	Michigan State (Michigan State 74, Indiana State 64)
1981	Indiana (Indiana 63, North Carolina 50)
1987	Indiana (Indiana 74, Syracuse 73)
1989	Michigan (Michigan 80, Seton Hall 79, OT)

Big Ten NIT Winners

1974	Purdue (Purdue 87, Utah 81)
1979	Indiana (Indiana 53, Purdue 52)
1984	Michigan (Michigan 83, Notre Dame 63)
1986	Ohio State (Ohio State 73, Wyoming 63)
1993	Minnesota (Minnesota 62, Georgetown 61)

Danny Jones, left, (1986-90) is Wisconsin's all-time scoring leader with 1,854 points. Above, Deon Thomas ranks as Illinois' top scorer.

Year-by-Year in the Big Ten (Team Achievements and Honors)

Season	Champion (League Record)	2nd Place (League Record)	MVP**	Coach of the Year*
1905-06	Minnesota (6-1)	Wisconsin (6-2)	No Award Given	No Award Given
1906-07	Chicago (6-2, tie)	Minnesota/Wisconsin (6-2)	No Award Given	No Award Given
1907-08	Chicago (7-1, tie)	Wisconsin (7-1)	No Award Given	No Award Given
1908-09	Chicago (12-0)	Purdue (6-4)	No Award Given	No Award Given
1909-10	Chicago (9-3)	Minnesota (7-3)	No Award Given	No Award Given
1910-11	Purdue (8-4, tie)	Minnesota (8-4)	No Award Given	No Award Given
1911-12	Wisconsin (12-0, tie)	Purdue (10-0)	No Award Given	No Award Given
1912-13	Wisconsin (11-1)	Northwestern (7-2)	No Award Given	No Award Given
1913-14	Wisconsin (12-0)	Ohio State (5-1)	No Award Given	No Award Given
1914-15	Illinois (12-0)	Chicago (9-3)	No Award Given	No Award Given
1915-16	Wisconsin (11-1)	Illinois/Northwestern (9-3)	No Award Given	No Award Given
1916-17	Minnesota (10-2, tie)	Illinois (10-2)	No Award Given	No Award Given
1917-18	Wisconsin (9-3)	Minnesota (7-3)	No Award Given	No Award Given
1918-19	Minnesota (10-0)	Chicago (10-2)	No Award Given	No Award Given
1919-20	Chicago (10-2)	Purdue (8-2)	No Award Given	No Award Given
1920-21	Michigan (8-4, tie)	Wisconsin/Purdue (8-4)	No Award Given	No Award Given
1921-22	Purdue (8-1)	Michigan/Wisconsin (8-4)	No Award Given	No Award Given
1922-23	Iowa (11-1, tie)	Wisconsin (11-1)	No Award Given	No Award Given
1923-24	Wisconsin (8-4, tie)	Illinois/Chicago (8-4)	No Award Given	No Award Given
1924-25	Ohio State (11-1)	Indiana/Illinois (8-4)	No Award Given	No Award Given
1925-26	Purdue/Indiana (8-4, tie)	Michigan/Iowa (8-4)	No Award Given	No Award Given
1926-27	Michigan (10-2)	Indiana/Purdue (9-3)	No Award Given	No Award Given
1927-28	Indiana (10-2, tie)	Purdue (10-2)	No Award Given	No Award Given
1928-29	Wisconsin (10-2, tie)	Michigan (10-2)	No Award Given	No Award Given
1929-30	Purdue (10-0)	Wisconsin (8-2)	No Award Given	No Award Given
1930-31	Northwestern (11-1)	Three Teams Tied (8-4)	No Award Given	No Award Given
1931-32	Purdue (11-1)	Minnesota/Northwestern (9-3)	No Award Given	No Award Given
1932-33	Ohio State (10-2, tie)	Northwestern (10-2)	No Award Given	No Award Given
1933-34	Purdue (10-2)	Wisconsin/Northwestern (8-4)	No Award Given	No Award Given
1934-35	Purdue (9-3, tie)	Illinois/Wisconsin (9-3)	No Award Given	No Award Given
1935-36	Indiana (11-1, tie)	Purdue (11-1)	No Award Given	No Award Given
1936-37	Minnesota (10-2, tie)	Illinois (10-2)	No Award Given	No Award Given
1937-38	Purdue (10-2)	Minnesota (9-3)	No Award Given	No Award Given
1938-39	Ohio State (10-2)	Indiana (9-3)	No Award Given	No Award Given
1939-40	Purdue (10-2)	Indiana (9-3)	No Award Given	No Award Given
1940-41	Wisconsin (11-1)	Indiana (10-2)	No Award Given	No Award Given
1941-42	Illinois (13-2)	Three Teams Tied (10-5)	No Award Given	No Award Given
1942-43	Illinois (12-0)	Indiana (11-2)	No Award Given	No Award Given
1943-44	Ohio State (10-2)	Iowa/Wisconsin (9-3)	No Award Given	No Award Given
1944-45	Iowa (11-1)	Ohio State (10-2)	No Award Given	No Award Given
1945-46	Ohio State (10-2)	Indiana (9-3)	Max Morris (NW)	No Award Given
1946-47	Wisconsin (9-3)	Illinois/Indiana (8-4)	Glen Selbo (Wis.)	No Award Given
1947-48	Michigan (10-2)	Iowa (8-4)	Murray Wier (Iowa)	No Award Given
1948-49	Illinois (10-2)	Minnesota (9-3)	Dwight Eddleman (Ill.)	No Award Given
1949-50	Ohio State (11-1)	Wisconsin (9-3)	Don Rehfeldt (Wis.)	No Award Given
1950-51	Illinois (13-1)	Indiana (12-2)	Don Sunderlage (Ill.)	No Award Given
1951-52	Illinois (12-2)	Iowa (11-3)	Chuck Darling (Iowa)	No Award Given
1952-53	Indiana (17-1)	Illinois (14-4)	Don Schlundt (Ind.)	No Award Given
1953-54	Indiana (12-2)	Iowa (11-3)	John "Red" Kerr (Ill.)	No Award Given
1954-55	Iowa (11-3)	Illinois/Minnesota (10-4)	Chuck Mencel (Minn.)	No Award Given
1955-56	Iowa (13-1)	Illinois (11-3)	Robin Freeman (OSU)	No Award Given

1956-57	Indiana (10-4, tie)	Michigan State (10-4)	Archie Dees (Ind.)	No Award Given
1957-58	Indiana (10-4)	Michigan State/Purdue (9-5)	Archie Dees (Ind.)	No Award Given
1958-59	Michigan State (12-2)	Three Teams Tied (8-6)	John Green (MSU)	No Award Given
1959-60	Ohio State (13-1)	Indiana (11-3)	Jerry Lucas (OSU)	No Award Given
1960-61	Ohio State (14-0)	Iowa/Purdue (10-4)	Jerry Lucas (OSU)	No Award Given
1961-62	Ohio State (13-1)	Wisconsin (10-4)	Jerry Lucas (OSU)	No Award Given
1962-63	Ohio State (11-3, tie)	Illinois (11-3)	Gary Bradds (OSU)	No Award Given
1963-64	Michigan (11-3, tie)	Ohio State (11-3)	Gary Bradds (OSU)	No Award Given
1964-65	Michigan (13-1)	Minnesota (11-3)	Cazzie Russell (Mich.)	No Award Given
1965-66	Michigan (11-3)	Michigan State (10-4)	Cazzie Russell (Mich.)	No Award Given
1966-67	Indiana (10-4, tie)	Michigan State (10-4)	Jim Dawson (Ill.)	No Award Given
1967-68	Ohio State (10-4, tie)	Iowa (10-4)	Sam Williams (Iowa)	No Award Given
1968-69	Purdue (13-1)	Illinois/Ohio State (9-5)	Rick Mount (Purdue)	No Award Given
1969-70	Iowa (14-0)	Purdue (11-3)	Rick Mount (Purdue)	No Award Given
1970-71	Ohio State (13-1)	Michigan (12-2)	Jim Cleamons (OSU)	No Award Given
1971-72	Minnesota (11-3)	Ohio State (10-4)	Jim Brewer (Minn.)	No Award Given
1972-73	Indiana (11-3)	Minnesota (10-4)	Steve Downing (Ind.)	Bob Knight (Ind.)
1973-74	Indiana (12-2, tie)	Michigan (12-2)	Campy Russell (Mich.)	Johnny Orr (Mich.)
1974-75	Indiana (18-0)	Michigan (12-6)	Scott May (Ind.)	Bob Knight (Ind.)
1975-76	Indiana (18-0)	Michigan (14-4)	Scott May (Ind.)	Bob Knight (Ind.)
1976-77	Michigan (16-2)	Purdue (14-4)	Kent Benson (Ind.)	Johnny Orr (Mich.)
1977-78	Michigan State (15-3)	Indiana/Minnesota (12-6)	Mychal Thompson (Minn)	Jud Heathcote (MSU)
1978-79	Michigan State (13-5, tie)	Purdue/Iowa (13-5)	Magic Johnson (MSU)	Lute Olson (Iowa)
1979-80	Indiana (13-5)	Ohio State (12-6)	Mike Woodson (Ind.)	Bob Knight (Ind.)
1980-81	Indiana (14-4)	Iowa (13-5)	Ray Tolbert (Ind.)	Bob Knight (Ind.)
1981-82	Minnesota (14-4)	Three Teams Tied (12-6)	Clark Kellogg (OSU)	Jim Dutcher (Minn.)
1982-83	Indiana (13-5)	Four Teams Tied (11-7)	Randy Wittman (Ind.)	Eldon Miller (OSU)
1983-84	Illinois (15-3, tie)	Purdue (15-3)	Jim Rowinski (Purdue)	Gene Keady (Purdue)
1984-85	Michigan (16-2)	Illinois (12-6)	Roy Tarpley (Mich.)	Bill Frieder (Mich.)
1985-86	Michigan (14-4)	Indiana (13-5)	Scott Skiles (MSU)	Jud Heathcote (MSU)
1986-87	Indiana (15-3, tie)	Purdue (15-3)	Steve Alford (Ind.)	Tom Davis (Iowa)
1987-88	Purdue (16-2)	Michigan (13-5)	Gary Grant (Mich.)	Gene Keady (Purdue)
1988-89	Indiana (15-3)	Illinois (14-4)	Glen Rice (Mich.)	Bob Knight (Ind.)
1989-90	Michigan State (15-3)	Purdue (13-5)	Steve Smith (MSU)	Gene Keady (Purdue)
1990-91	Ohio State (15-3, tie)	Indiana (15-3)	Jim Jackson (OSU)	Randy Ayers (OSU)
1991-92	Ohio State (15-3)	Indiana (14-4)	Jim Jackson (OSU)	Randy Ayers (OSU)
1992-93	Indiana (17-1)	Michigan (15-3)	Calbert Cheaney (Ind.)	Lou Henson (Ill.)
1993-94	Purdue (14-4)	Michigan (13-5)	Glenn Robinson (Purdue)	Gene Keady (Purdue)

** = *Chicago Tribune* Big Ten Most Valuable Player; * = Selected by media and coaches (after 1987) and media only (after 1992)

Year-by-Year in the Big Ten (Individual Achievements)

Season	Scoring Leader	Rebounds Leader	Assists Leader
1905-06	Emmett Angell, Wis. (96)*	Records Not Kept	Records Not Kept
1906-07	John Schommer, Chicago (95)	Records Not Kept	Records Not Kept
1907-08	John Schommer, Chicago (105)	Records Not Kept	Records Not Kept
1908-09	John Schommer, Chicago (104)	Records Not Kept	Records Not Kept
1909-10	David Charters, Pur. (112)	Records Not Kept	Records Not Kept
1910-11	Frank Lawler, Minn. (143)	Records Not Kept	Records Not Kept
1911-12	Otto Stangel, Wis. (177)	Records Not Kept	Records Not Kept
1912-13	Homer Dahringer, Ill. (125)	Records Not Kept	Records Not Kept
1913-14	Harold Whittle, NW (109)	Records Not Kept	Records Not Kept
1914-15	George Levis, Wis. (140)	Records Not Kept	Records Not Kept

1915-16	Henry Brockenbraugh, Pur. (119)	Records Not Kept	Records Not Kept
1916-17	Harold Gillen, Minn. (126)	Records Not Kept	Records Not Kept
1917-18	Earl Anderson, Ill. (162)	Records Not Kept	Records Not Kept
1918-19	Paul Gorgas, Chicago (106)	Records Not Kept	Records Not Kept
1919-20	Charles Garney, Ill. (188)	Records Not Kept	Records Not Kept
1920-21	Don White, Pur. (154)	Records Not Kept	Records Not Kept
1921-22	Charles Garney, Ill. (172)	Records Not Kept	Records Not Kept
1922-23	Jack Funk, Iowa (143)	Records Not Kept	Records Not Kept
1923-24	George Spradling, Pur. (128)	Records Not Kept	Records Not Kept
1924-25	John Miner, OSU (133)	Records Not Kept	Records Not Kept
1925-26	Arthur Beckner, Ind. (108)	Records Not Kept	Records Not Kept
1926-27	Wilbur Cummins, Pur. (128)	Records Not Kept	Records Not Kept
1927-28	Bennie Oosterbaan, Mich. (129)	Records Not Kept	Records Not Kept
1928-29	Charles Murphy, Pur. (145)	Records Not Kept	Records Not Kept
1929-30	Branch McCracken, Ind. (147)	Records Not Kept	Records Not Kept
1930-31	Joe Reif, NW (120)	Records Not Kept	Records Not Kept
1931-32	John Wooden, Pur. (154)	Records Not Kept	Records Not Kept
1932-33	Joe Reif, NW (168)	Records Not Kept	Records Not Kept
1933-34	Norm Cottom, Pur. (119)	Records Not Kept	Records Not Kept
1934-35	Bill Haarlow, Chicago (156)	Records Not Kept	Records Not Kept
1935-36	Bob Kessler, Pur. (160)	Records Not Kept	Records Not Kept
1936-37	Jewell Young, Pur. (172)	Records Not Kept	Records Not Kept
1937-38	Jewell Young, Pur. (184)	Records Not Kept	Records Not Kept
1938-39	Jimmy Hull, OSU (14.1)	Records Not Kept	Records Not Kept
1939-40	Bill Hapac, Ill. (13.7)	Records Not Kept	Records Not Kept
1940-41	Joe Stampf, Chicago (13.8)	Records Not Kept	Records Not Kept
1941-42	John Kotz, Wis. (17.3)	Records Not Kept	Records Not Kept
1942-43	Andy Phillip, Ill. (21.3)	Records Not Kept	Records Not Kept
1943-44	Dick Ives, Iowa (17.3)	Records Not Kept	Records Not Kept
1944-45	Max Morris, NW (15.8)	Records Not Kept	Records Not Kept
1945-46	Max Morris, NW (16.5)	Records Not Kept	Records Not Kept
1946-47	Bob Cook, Wis. (15.6)	Records Not Kept	Records Not Kept
1947-48	Murray Wier, Iowa (22.7)	Records Not Kept	Records Not Kept
1948-49	Don Rehfeldt, Wis. (19.1)	Records Not Kept	Records Not Kept
1949-50	Don Rehfeldt, Wis. (22.1)	Records Not Kept	Records Not Kept
1950-51	Ray Ragelis, NW (19.8)	Records Not Kept	Records Not Kept
1951-52	Charles Darling, Iowa (26.0)	Records Not Kept	Records Not Kept
1952-53	Don Schlundt, Ind. (25.5)	Records Not Kept	Records Not Kept
1953-54	Don Schlundt, Ind. (27.1)	Records Not Kept	Records Not Kept
1954-55	Don Schlundt, Ind. (26.4)	Records Not Kept	Records Not Kept
1955-56	Robin Freeman, OSU (32.5)	Records Not Kept	Records Not Kept
1956-57	Archie Dees, Ind. (25.4)	Records Not Kept	Records Not Kept
1957-58	Archie Dees, Ind. (25.9)	Records Not Kept	Records Not Kept
1958-59	M.C. Burton, Mich. (22.6)	M. C. Burton, Mich. (17.8)	Records Not Kept
1959-60	Terry Dischinger, Pur. (27.4)	Horace Walker, MSU (18.3)	Records Not Kept
1960-61	Terry Dischinger, Pur. (28.3)	Walt Bellamy, Ind. (17.6)	Records Not Kept
1961-62	Terry Dischinger, Pur. (32.8)	Jerry Lucas, OSU (18.1)	Records Not Kept
1962-63	Gary Bradds, OSU (30.9)	Bill Buntin, Mich. (15.4)	Records Not Kept
1963-64	Gary Bradds, OSU (33.9)	Gary Bradds, OSU (13.9)	Records Not Kept
1964-65	Dave Schellhase, Pur. (27.9)	Skip Thoren, Ill. (14.4)	Records Not Kept
1965-66	Cazzie Russell, Mich. (33.2)	Jim Pitts, NW (15.2)	Records Not Kept
1966-67	Tom Kondla, Minn. (28.3)	Bill Hosket, OSU (13.8)	Records Not Kept
1967-68	Rick Mount, Pur. (29.7)	Joe Franklin, Wis. (13.9)	Records Not Kept

Kevin Kunnert (1970-73) launched a career as an NBA journeyman after becoming Iowa's all-time leading rebounder. (University of Iowa photo)

1968-69	Rick Mount, Pur. (35.2)	Rudy Tomjanovich, Mich. (12.8)	Records Not Kept
1969-70	Rick Mount, Pur. (39.4)	Rudy Tomjanovich, Mich. (16.2)	Records Not Kept
1970-71	George McGinnis, Ind. (29.9)	George McGinnis, Ind. (14.9)	Records Not Kept
1971-72	Mike Robinson, MSU (27.2)	Kevin Kunnert, Iowa (15.9)	Records Not Kept
1972-73	Mike Robinson, MSU (26.7)	Kevin Kunnert, Iowa (14.5)	Records Not Kept
1973-74	Campy Russell, Mich. (24.0)	Lindsay Hairston, MSU (14.2)	Records Not Kept
1974-75	Terry Furlow, MSU (21.4)	Lindsay Hairston, MSU (11.3)	Bruce Parkinson, Pur. (7.2)
1975-76	Terry Furlow, MSU (32.7)	Mychal Thompson, Minn. (12.3)	Cal Wulfsberg, Iowa (7.7)
1976-77	Mychal Thompson, Minn. (22.8)	Bruce King, Iowa (12.9)	Ray Williams, Minn. (6.6)
1977-78	Mychal Thompson, Minn. (22.7)	Mychal Thompson, Minn. (11.6)	Magic Johnson, MSU (6.8)
1978-79	Joe Barry Carroll, Pur. (23.8)	Herb Williams, OSU (10.5)	Magic Johnson, MSU (7.4)
1979-80	Jay Vincent, MSU (22.1)	Joe Barry Carroll, Pur. (9.4)	Kelvin Ransey, OSU (6.3)
1980-81	Jay Vincent, MSU (24.1)	Clark Kellogg, OSU (11.8)	Brian Walker, Pur. (6.7)
1981-82	Keith Edmonson, Pur. (20.6)	Clark Kellogg, OSU (11.0)	Derek Harper, Ill. (5.6)
1982-83	Randy Breuer, Minn. (20.9)	Kevin Willis, MSU (10.2)	Bruce Douglas, Ill. (5.7)
1983-84	Vacated (Cory Blackwell, Wis.)	Vacated (Cory Blackwell, Wis.)	Bruce Douglas, Ill. (5.6)
1984-85	Sam Vincent, MSU (23.7)	Roy Tarpley, Mich. (9.9)	Steve Reid, Pur. (5.8)
1985-86	Scott Skiles, MSU (29.1)	Brad Sellers, OSU (11.5)	Bruce Douglas, Ill. (6.2)
1986-87	Dennis Hopson, OSU (28.3)	Ken Norman, Ill. (9.6)	Tony Wysinger, Ill. (6.1)
1987-88	Glen Rice, Mich. (22.9)	Richard Coffey, Minn. (8.9)	Gary Grant, Mich. (6.5)
1988-89	Glen Rice, Mich. (24.8)	Ed Horton, Iowa (10.9)	B.J. Armstrong, Iowa (5.7)
1989-90	Kendall Gill, Ill. (20.4)	Loy Vaught, Mich. (10.7)	Tony Jones, Pur. (5.9)
1990-91	Steve Smith, MSU (23.2)	Chuckie White, Pur. (8.6)	Mark Montgomery, MSU (5.7)
1991-92	Jim Jackson, OSU (22.0)	Chris Webber, Mich. (9.8)	Mark Montgomery, MSU (6.2)
1992-93	Glenn Robinson, Pur. (25.5)	Chris Webber, Mich. (9.7)	Tracy Webster, Wis. (6.3)
1993-94	Glenn Robinson, Pur. (30.3)	Glenn Robinson, Pur. (10.1)	Mont Glasper, Iowa (5.2)

(* Scoring leaders determined by total points until 1938, and by scoring average after the 1939 season)

Bob Weiss, a member of Penn State's 1,000-point club, became an NBA backcourt regular and coach. (Penn State University photo)

Top Dozen Big Ten Career Scorers (All Games)

2,613	Calbert Cheaney (Indiana, 1990-93)
2,442	Glen Rice (Michigan, 1986-89)
2,439	Mike McGee (Michigan, 1978-81)
2,438	Steve Alford (Indiana, 1984-87)
2,323	Rick Mount (Purdue, 1968-70)
2,263	Steve Smith (Michigan State, 1988-91)
2,222	Gary Grant (Michigan, 1985-88)
2,192	Don Schlundt (Indiana, 1952-55)
2,175	Joe Barry Carroll (Purdue, 1977-80)
2,164	Cazzie Russell (Michigan, 1964-66)
2,145	Scott Skiles (Michigan State, 1983-86)
2,116	Roy Marble (Iowa, 1986-89)

Top Dozen Big Ten Career Scorers (Conference Games)

1,503	Mike McGee (Michigan, 1978-81)
1,477	Mychal Thompson (Minnesota, 1975-78)
1,461	Rick Mount (Purdue, 1968-70)
1,451	Don Schlundt (Indiana, 1952-55)
1,406	Calbert Cheaney (Indiana, 1990-93)
1,361	Steve Alford (Indiana, 1984-87)
1,358	Scott Skiles (Michigan State, 1983-86)
1,279	Mike Woodson (Indiana, 1977-80)
1,266	Glen Rice (Michigan, 1986-89)
1,248	Terry Dischinger (Purdue, 1960-62)
1,247	Herb Williams (Ohio State, 1978-81)
1,237	Gary Grant (Michigan, 1985-88)

Top Dozen Big Ten Coaches (All Games, Minimum 10 Years in Big Ten)*

Bob Knight (Indiana, 1972-Present)	640-223, .742 (23 years)
Walter Meanwell (Wisconsin, 1912-17, 1921-34)	246-99, .712 (20 years)
Ward "Piggy" Lambert (Purdue, 1917, 1919-45)	371-152, .709 (28 years)
Doug Mills (Illinois, 1937-47)	151-66, .696 (11 years)
Gene Keady (Purdue, 1981-Present)	335-154 .690 (14 years)
Harry Combes (Illinois, 1948-67)	316-150, .678 (20 years)
Branch McCracken (Indiana, 1935-43, 1947-65)	364-174, .677 (24 years)
Lou Henson (Illinois, 1976-Present)	626-306, .672 (19 years)
Burke M. Herman (Penn State, 1916-17, 1920-32)	148-74, .667 (15 years)
L.J. Cooke (Minnesota, 1897-1924)	238-122, .660 (27 years)
Fred Taylor (Ohio State, 1959-76)	297-158, .653 (18 years)
Johnny Orr (Michigan, 1969-80)	209-111, .653 (12 years)

*Coaches ranked by overall winning percentage (200 or more wins)

Top Dozen Big Ten Coaches (Conference Games)

Wins	Coach (School, Years)
293	Bob Knight (Indiana, 1972-Present)
228	Ward "Piggy" Lambert (Purdue, 1917, 1919-45)
210	Branch McCracken (Indiana, 1935-43, 1947-65)
197	Lou Henson (Illinois, 1976-Present)
174	Harry Combes (Illinois, 1948-67)
168	Jud Heathcote (Michigan State, 1976-Present)
161	Gene Keady (Purdue, 1981-Present)
158	Fred Taylor (Ohio State, 1959-76)

158 .... Walter Meanwell (Wisconsin, 1912-17, 1921-34)
154 .... Harold Olsen (Ohio State, 1923-46)
143 .... Harold "Bud" Foster (Wisconsin, 1935-59)
138 .... Arthur Lonborg (Northwestern, 1928-1950)

Individual Big Ten Career Records

Points Scored (Conference) .... Mike McGee, Michigan (1,503, 1977-81)
Points Scored (All Games) .... Calbert Cheaney, Indiana (2,613, 1989-93)
Rebounds (All Games) .... Jerry Lucas, Ohio State (1,411, 1959-62)
Assists (All Games) .... Bruce Douglas, Illinois (765, 1982-86)
Steals (All Games) .... Bruce Douglas, Illinois (324, 1982-86)
Blocked Shots (All Games) .... Acie Earl, Iowa (365, 1989-93)

Individual Big Ten Single-Season Records

Points Scored (Conference) .... Terry Furlow, Michigan State (558, 1976)
Points Scored (All Games) .... Glenn Robinson, Purdue (1,030, 1994)
Points Per Game (Conference) .... Rick Mount, Purdue (39.4, 1970)
Field-Goal Percentage (Conference) .... Stephen Scheffler, Purdue (.767, 1990)
3-Point Field Goals (Conference) .... Glen Rice, Michigan (55, 1989)
Free-Throw Percentage (Conference) .... Steve Alford, Indiana (.935, 1985)
Rebounds (Conference) .... Horace Walker, Michigan State (256, 1960)
Rebounds (All Games) .... Jerry Lucas, Ohio State (499, 1962)
Assists (Conference) .... Cal Wulfsberg, Iowa (138, 1976)
Assists (All Games) .... Magic Johnson, Michigan State (269, 1979)
Steals (Conference) .... Melvin Newbern, Minnesota (62, 1989)
Steals (All Games) .... Melvin Newbern, Minnesota (101, 1989)
Blocked Shots (Conference) ....Acie Earl, Iowa (71, 1992)
Blocked Shots (All Games) .... Jim Pitts, Northwestern (123, 1966)

Individual Big Ten Single-Game Records

Points Scored (Conference) .... Rick Mount, Purdue (61, vs. Iowa, 2-28-70)
Points Scored (All Games) .... Rick Mount, Purdue (61, vs. Iowa, 2-28-70)
Field Goals Made (Conference) .... Rick Mount, Purdue (27, 2-28-70)
3-Point Field Goals (Conference)............................ Shawn Respert, Michigan State
(9 vs. Indiana, 1-11-95)
Free Throws Made (Conference) .... Greg Graham, Indiana (26, 2-21-93)
Rebounds (Conference) .... Walt Bellamy, Indiana (33, 3-11-61)
Assists (Conference) .... Bruce Parkinson, Purdue (18, 3-8-75)
Steals (Conference) .... Michael Finley, Wisconsin (10, 2-13-93)
Blocked Shots (Conference) .... Mychal Thompson, Minnesota (12, 1-27-76)

Big Ten Players Named NCAA (Division I) Player of the Year

1961 .... Jerry Lucas, Center, Ohio State
1962 .... Jerry Lucas, Center, Ohio State
1964 .... Gary Bradds, Center, Ohio State
1966 .... Cazzie Russell, Guard, Michigan
1976 .... Scott May, Forward, Indiana
1993 .... Calbert Cheaney, Guard, Indiana
1994 .... Glenn Robinson, Forward, Purdue

Big Ten Defensive Players of the Year

1984 .... Ricky Hall, Guard, Purdue
1985 .... Bruce Douglas, Guard, Illinois
1986 .... Bruce Douglas, Guard, Illinois
1987 .... Gary Grant, Guard, Michigan
1988 .... Gary Grant, Guard, Michigan
1989 .... Steve Bardo, Guard, Illinois
1990 .... Ken Redfield, Forward, Michigan State
1991 .... Not Awarded
1992 .... Acie Earl, Center, Iowa
1993 .... Greg Graham, Guard, Indiana
1994 .... Patrick Baldwin, Guard, Northwestern

Big Ten Freshmen of the Year

1986 .... Gary Grant, Guard, Michigan
1987 .... Dean Garrett, Center, Indiana
1988 .... Jay Edwards, Guard, Indiana
1989 .... Eric Anderson, Center, Indiana
1990 .... Jim Jackson, Guard, Ohio State
1991 .... Damon Bailey, Guard, Indiana
1992 .... Chris Webber, Forward, Michigan
1993 .... Greg Simpson, Guard, Ohio State
1994 .... Jess Settles, Forward, Iowa